SHERLOCK
CHRONICLES

SHERLOCK
CHRONICLES

STEVE TRIBE

DESIGNED BY RICHARD ATKINSON

1 2 3 4 5 6 7 8 9 10

BBC Books, an imprint of Ebury Publishing
20 Vauxhall Bridge Road,
London SW1V 2SA

BBC Books is part of the Penguin Random House
group of companies whose addresses can be found
at global.penguinrandomhouse.com

Text copyright © Steve Tribe 2014
Foreword © Mark Gatiss 2014

This book is published to accompany the television series entitled *Sherlock*
first broadcast on BBC One in 2010. *Sherlock* is a Hartswood Films
production for BBC Cymru Wales, co-produced with Masterpiece.

Executive Producers: Beryl Vertue, Mark Gatiss and Steven Moffat
Executive Producer for the BBC: Bethan Jones
Executive Producer for masterpiece: Rebecca Eaton
Series Producer: Sue Vertue

First published by BBC Books in 2014

www.eburypublishing.co.uk

A CIP catalogue record for this book is available from the British Library

ISBN 978 1 849 90762 0

Commissioning Editor: Albert DePetrillo
Project Editors: Steve Tribe & Kate Fox
Design: Richard Atkinson
Production: Phil Spencer

Colour origination by Altaimage, London.
Printed and bound in Germany by Mohn Media GmbH

Penguin Random House is committed to a sustainable
future for our business, our readers and our planet. This book
is made from Forest Stewardship Council® certified paper.

CONTENTS

FOREWORD

BY MARK GATISS

wo men, sitting in a train carriage, rattling through the countryside. Each wears an expression of introspection as they wrestle with a deep and profound problem. Should they risk having another disappointing bacon sandwich?

This was myself and Steven Moffat, what now seems like half a lifetime ago, on a train from Cardiff to London. It was here, dear reader, that a conversation which had ranged in a desultory, spasmodic fashion from *Doctor Who* to James Bond to the causes of the change in the obliquity of the ecliptic (I may have misremembered that) came round at last to the question of... Sherlock Holmes. It turned out that, among many other shared enthusiasms, we both loved the Great Detective and his loyal Boswell. Loved him in all his myriad manifestations. The rarely seen Douglas Wilmer and Peter Cushing episodes; Cushing again in the wonderful Hammer version of *Hound of the Baskervilles*, the great Jeremy Brett in the era-defining Granada series – all twitching nerves and Edwardian brio; even dear old Roger Moore in *Sherlock Holmes in New York*. But the two versions which rose head and shoulders above the others for us were Billy Wilder and I.A.L. Diamond's gorgeously bittersweet *The Private Life of Sherlock Holmes* and the giddily enjoyable Basil Rathbone / Nigel Bruce series of films from the 1930s and 1940s. On paper, the two versions could hardly have less in common. One, a love letter to Holmes from a Viennese master film-maker to the character he'd loved since childhood, the other, a series of cheap, B-movie pot-boilers made by clever film executives with an eye on the main chance. But, curiously, somewhere in there lay for us the spirit – the heart – of Sherlock Holmes and Dr Watson. It was a desire to get closer to Sir Arthur Conan Doyle's original thinking, to restore the idea of two radically different young men becoming unlikely friends in even more unlikely adventures that inspired us both.

In this book, you'll find lots of details about the process which led us to devise *Sherlock* and take the Baker Street boys into the twenty-first century. Of how exciting and punishing and wonderful it's been to make a series which has inspired the attention, loyalty and love of a vast worldwide audience and made superstars of its leads. It is a tale of risk, of loyalty, of danger, of hair dye, big coats and romance. It's a tale of cheekiness and fun, of cold Welsh winters and warm Welsh welcomes, of Aunt Sallys and big dogs and falling off buildings. But most of all, it's the story of a team of dedicated professionals all of whom have come to love Sherlock and John as much as Steven and I ever did. And it's to the entire *Sherlock* team that this lovely book is dedicated. For all of us, it's been a life-changing experience.

And to this day, we do all our best thinking on trains.

Mark Gatiss
September 2014

1

THE ADVENTURE OF THE LEGENDARY DETECTIVE

                          SHERLOCK
              Well dressed, quite expensive clothes –

Whoosh! Now zooming down to Steven's jacket.

                          SHERLOCK
              – but not City suits. They've been in Cardiff on business
              but not *for* a business. I'm guessing something in the media,
              going by the frankly alarming shade of pink.

Whoosh! Out to a wide shot of Mark.

                          SHERLOCK
              Their haircuts and the way they hold themselves say success –
              they're at the top of their game, they're on the verge of being
              able to realise just about any idea they come up with –
              but their conversation as they sit on the train –

Flashback: Mark and Steven talking animatedly.

                          SHERLOCK
              – says enthusiasm, creativity... *fanboys*. So – media professionals.
              What is there in Cardiff? Finance? Industry? No – a BBC drama
              village. Television. Obvious!

*Whoosh! To Mark's hand, gripping on to a well-thumbed paperback. We don't
see the full cover, but can just glimpse the words 'Study in'.*

                          SHERLOCK
              There's no argument, no disagreement, just eagerness – it's an
              ideas conversation. That says they're talking about a shared
              appreciation. What's behind that enthusiasm? A boyhood hero?
              Adventure stories? Investigation? Puzzles? Then there's that
              paperback –

Flashback. Whoosh! On frozen Mark's hand, zooming right on his book.

                          SHERLOCK
              A novel. A bit battered, been in the same pocket as keys and coins.
              The man in front of me wouldn't treat a book like this, so it's been
              read lots of times – he's had this book for years, decades. Something
              they've both loved since childhood, then. And they want to bring it
              back. Next bit's easy – you know it already. The phone call.

Flashback: Steven calling a contact on his phone. Snatches of conversation:
**'Hi Sue ... Kids OK? ... Oh, is he? ... Yes, pretty good, everyone likes
the statues, just need a blinking name for them ... No, I'm on my way back
with Mark now ... Yeah, listen, we've had an idea ...'**

SHERLOCK

Now Sue, who's Sue? He's asked about the kids - family, then.
Could be a friend, a sister, no - his first question was about
the kids, so they're *his* children. So Sue's his wife. But he's
telling her about the work he's been doing in Cardiff, she
knows who Mark is, and he's gone straight to her with their new
idea. The power connection. She's not just his wife, she's a
colleague, another professional. Agent? Editor? Producer? Let's
assume producer, because he's going to her to get things moving.
So, what's their big new idea?

Flashback: super-close on back cover of Mark's book. We whoosh down to –
'*... **legendary detective. A potent mix of murder, suspense, cryptic**
clues, red herrings and revenge. It introduces us to the world-famous
character of ...'*

SHERLOCK

'World-famous character'. Clearly an iconic figure, a name
recognised by millions. Someone they want to bring back to life,
put them back on screen, modernised, updated... Doctor Who?
Robin Hood? Merlin? Jekyll? No, it's a 'legendary detective'.
Someone incredibly clever, perceptive... and *popular* – not a
character stuck in any one time, no, a detective who can be
taken out of their original time and reworked for a contemporary
audience. And they're confident it could work, so it's been done
before – a famous fictional detective who can function in
any era, any setting, any medium. So – Miss Marple it is. There
you go, you see? You were right. The police don't consult
amateurs.

A DYNAMIC SUPERHERO

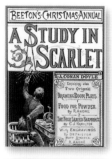

'**M**ark Gatiss and I were talking about our mutual love of Sherlock Holmes,' says Steven Moffat, co-creator of *Sherlock*, 'and we just thought wouldn't it be fun to do it again, to update it to now.'

'We were talking about how much we loved these heretical, incredibly exciting and fun Sherlock Holmes films which had been modernised in the 1940s,' confirms Mark, 'and I said it was odd that in the very first Doyle story Dr Watson is invalided home from war service in Afghanistan – a war which has been happening again, the same unwinnable war. That was a sort of light-bulb moment: we just thought *of course* it should be modernised. And we nodded and drank our tea, and had this conversation another twenty times,

always saying someone was going to do that.'

'And we were going to be cross!' continues Steven. '"It should have been us!" And I mentioned it to Sue, as one of many things, and she grabbed hold of it.'

Sue Vertue has been a television producer since 1991, when she helmed nine episodes of *Mr Bean*. She went on to produce or executive produce series and one-offs including *Hospital*, *Gimme Gimme Gimme*, and *The Vicar of Dibley*, as well as 1999's Comic Relief, featuring a *Doctor Who* special, and *Coupling*, both written by Steven. She is also Steven's wife.

'It was interesting because she'd never shown the slightest interest in Sherlock Holmes before. But she kept on about it, and made us tell her all about Sherlock Holmes. At lunch in Monte Carlo. We were there for another reason; we don't just lunch in Monte Carlo for the hell of it.'

'Another reason' was an industry awards ceremony the three were attending. By this point, their television careers were well established. Mark's mid-1990s success as co-writer and performer with *The League of Gentlemen* had continued with roles in a couple of dozen films and series and a number of high-profile writing credits, *Randall & Hopkirk (Deceased)*, *Crooked House* and *Agatha Christie's Poirot* among them. Steven had first made his mark with *Press Gang* in 1989, which was followed by *Joking Apart*, *Chalk*, *Jekyll* and

The Adventures of Tintin. They also shared a love of *Doctor Who* and were among the first contributors to the show when Russell T Davies revived it in 2005. With that sort of TV pedigree, they might have pitched *Sherlock* to any of countless TV companies, but it took Sue's interest in the concept to really set the ball rolling.

'I still have the napkin from that Monte Carlo restaurant,' remembers Sue. 'While they talked, I was using it to jot down my questions – Who are these characters? What do they call each other? Where do they live? Is John married? And then they sat and told me all about Sherlock Holmes...'

ELEMENTARY

Sherlock Holmes, consulting detective, made his debut in 1887 in *Beeton's Christmas Annual* in *A Study in Scarlet* by Arthur Conan Doyle, a Scottish physician and writer. Over the next forty years, Conan Doyle wrote another three Holmes novels, as well as fifty-six short stories, the bulk of which were published in *The Strand Magazine*. The character and his adventures soon became a massive hit.

'It's hard to state just how big a hit they were; they were enormous,' Steven says. 'People were obsessed with Sherlock Holmes and behaved as if he was real. And Doyle encouraged the idea that these were true stories, by having Holmes – in one of the great master strokes of fiction – negatively review the stories in which he appeared. The fact that these stories are appearing in *The Strand* is referenced in the stories themselves. Everybody knows it's a fiction but everyone joyously plays along and likes to imagine that if they just popped to this entirely fictitious address...'

Doyle's stories were indeed such a success that the building society then occupying the site that might have been 221B Baker Street actually employed

The original Sherlock Holmes stories in *The Strand Magazine* (far left), and the latest editions published by BBC Books (above)

Steven Moffat, Sue Vertue and Mark Gatiss (left)

Steven and Mark during their legendary lunch at the Criterion (top left)

somebody to reply to all the letters written to Sherlock Holmes. The writer himself, meanwhile, experienced the nineteenth-century equivalent of a Twitter storm, when he attempted to kill Holmes off in 1893. 'He was attacked in the street by an irate woman with an umbrella,' Mark notes, 'and young men of fashion took to wearing black crepe in their hats in mourning!'

Sherlock Holmes rapidly eclipsed his recent forerunners in the popular imagination. 'There are certain antecedents,' Mark acknowledges. 'Edgar Allan Poe had a character who appeared in a couple of his stories, principally "Murders in the Rue Morgue", and who is a sort of prototype of Sherlock Holmes – C. Auguste Dupin. Doyle explicitly refers to him; it's almost as if he needs to acknowledge there is a certain amount of influence there, but then he gets his own character to slag him off!'

Sherlock Holmes rose and lit his pipe. 'No doubt you think that you are **complimenting** me in comparing me to **Dupin**,' he observed. 'Now, in my opinion, Dupin was a very **inferior fellow.** That trick of his of breaking in on his friends' **thoughts** with an apropos remark after a quarter of an hour's silence is really very **showy** and **superficial**. He had some analytical genius, no doubt; but he was by no means such a **phenomenon** as Poe appeared to imagine.'

Sherlock's Baker Street sets include a nod to Poe – a picture of the writer in the detective's bedroom – but Mark points out that Dupin is rarely remembered now, largely because Doyle went much further: 'He took those ideas and ran with them based on his own experiences with Joseph Bell. Bell had this astonishing ability to diagnose what was wrong with his patients just by watching them walk into the room.' Arthur Conan Doyle often cited surgeon Joseph Bell as his prime inspiration in the creation of Sherlock Holmes. Bell was indeed involved in a number of police investigations in Edinburgh, although he once told Doyle, 'You are yourself Sherlock Holmes and well you know it.'

Mark thinks of Doyle as 'a wonderful personality; he has an embraceable quality about life. He was a doctor, a soldier, a whaler, a spiritualist... He was a big fella, a big burly Scotsman, and he looked solidly Watsonian, but had the mind of Sherlock Holmes. It's clear that a lot of the most original, spectacular deductions in the stories are drawn from that, while Bell must have had a very narrow field. He would have known his patients, the workers of that area of Scotland, and what might happen to their thumbs if they worked in, say, the timber yard, so he was able to draw on all that. Doyle's genius was to extrapolate from that and imagine how a detective might work.'

Steven goes further: 'What's interesting about the genre that Doyle creates is that he has a claim to have invented the television series, in a strange way. He identified a gap in the market for a magazine like *The Strand*, because there were short stories and there were serialised novels, and you couldn't dive in in the middle of a book, so he thought of combining the two as the single adventures of the same character. You then have the accumulation of a novel and the accumulated readership of a novel, but you don't have to get every instalment – you can start anywhere and go in any order. Essentially, he invented the TV series when he did that, and he's the first person to have created novels that were serialised short stories, a continuing narrative of brand new, standalone stories involving the same character.'

SIDNEY PAGET
1893

A GREAT GAME

As Sherlock Holmes's success took hold in Britain and America, Arthur Conan Doyle was quite open about how much he disliked and resented his creation – or at least affected to dislike and resent him. He claimed to regard Holmes as an inconsequential part of his literary output, hoping to be remembered more for his historical and romantic fiction, his poetry, his histories, even an operetta. He was also a well-known and fervent campaigner against miscarriages of justice and was involved in various international political causes. The famous consulting detective obscured all that and so, in 1893, Doyle made a bold move. 'Thank God I've killed the brute!' he exclaimed on completing 'The Final Problem', the short story in which Holmes plunges to his apparent death at the Reichenbach Falls.

'Doyle did declare, repeatedly, that he had killed Holmes off, definitively, and there was no chance of bringing him back,' says Steven. 'I don't believe a word he says, because he kills him off-stage; he doesn't have Holmes dying in Watson's arms, as surely he must, he doesn't do any of that. He knows what it means when the body isn't recovered from a body of water where it would float! So he knew perfectly well that he was leaving the door open to Sherlock Holmes's return, but he wanted to do other things for a while. Those original runs in *The Strand* were an enormous hit, and he became sick of it – I'd imagine that was probably true, because he must have been writing one a month.'

'I don't think he was being disingenuous,' Mark agrees. 'As the years went by, he had a lot more interesting experiences as a person, as a writer and a knight and a war correspondent and all these things, and I feel he mellowed towards Holmes.'

'He does actually say he discovered in practice it didn't really get in the way of anything,' Steven points out. 'It's not a great big lie; it's just the writer in him – the storyteller in him – knows how good it is, and he can't let go of it. I sometimes think that he doesn't like how much he likes it, but he loves writing these things, because there is so much exuberance and so much humour in Sherlock Holmes. Maybe he's just feeling, as an earnest young man, that he shouldn't be loving this quite as much – he should be a serious proper writer – not realising that

he's created the single biggest character in fiction.'

So Sherlock Holmes returned, after an eight-year absence, in a new adventure set some time before his death. Serialised from August 1901, *The Hound of the Baskervilles* was a worldwide bestseller, and, as Mark notes, 'the reason it's still the most famous story is because of the impact it made in 1902. As a result of it, the Americans offer him what is now, an incalculable amount of money to write some new stories, and he sort of holds out for a bit. Then they offer him

Sidney Paget's *Strand Magazine* illustration for the climax to 'The Final Problem' in 1893 (far left)

Sherlock Holmes returns to hunt the Hound of the Baskervilles... (below)

SMOKING

SP

Sidney Paget's depiction of Holmes (top) was supposedly based on his brother Walter (above). Illustrations by Paget and Frederic Dorr Steele (above) influenced screen portrayals of Sherlock Holmes (right).

something like £6,000 per story, which was unbelievable in 1903, and eventually he just telegraphs back: "Very well." And then he comes back on absolute top form.'

'And everyone takes him at face value on this,' says Steven, 'despite the fact he is a professional liar (or, as we know them, writers). He claims he doesn't really like Sherlock Holmes, and yet he writes them for the rest of his life.'

PRIVATE EYE

The story goes that *The Strand* magazine, embarking on their serialisation of the stories subsequently collected as *The Adventures of Sherlock Holmes*, intended to commission illustrations from the artist Walter Stanley Paget. The editors then mistakenly sent their invitation to his older brother,

Sidney Edward Paget. Although another brother (Henry Marriott Paget) later denied it was the case, it's widely believed that Sidney based his depiction of Holmes on Walter – 'a way of paying his brother back for stealing his job', suggests Mark. 'When you look at a photograph of Walter Paget, it is essentially a photograph of Sherlock Holmes. Walter was a very handsome man, and quite a lot of Holmes's appeal is probably to do with the fact that he's quite a dashing figure.'

'Without the Walter Paget model,' agrees Steven, 'there is no Basil Rathbone or Jeremy Brett or Benedict Cumberbatch playing that part, because we take it as read now that Sherlock Holmes has to be handsome.'

The Adventures were also serialised in the American magazine *Collier's Weekly*, with illustrations by Frederic Dorr Steele. 'Holmes definitely looks a bit older,' notes Mark, 'which again contributes to our ideas of how he should be. He's a bit more solid, quite grey at the sides, and he has these amazing coats and silhouettes and the hats. So there's an evolving impression of Sherlock Holmes, from the very first time he's described in *A Study in Scarlet*.'

In **height** he was rather over **six feet**, and so excessively lean that he seemed to be considerably taller. His eyes were **sharp** and **piercing** … and his thin, hawk-like nose gave his whole expression an air of **alertness** and **decision.** His chin, too, had the prominence and squareness which mark the man of **determination.**

On first publication, *A Study in Scarlet* was illustrated by Doyle's father, Charles Altamont Doyle, who offered the world what Steven calls 'the first continuity error in Sherlock Holmes': he gave the detective a beard. The Paget illustrations dispensed with the facial hair, but introduced another impression of Holmes 'quite contrary to what Doyle thought he should be like, and then he gets a deerstalker, never referenced in the story except as a travelling cap. That becomes the image of Sherlock Holmes very, very early on.'

The next additions to the classic Holmes image came about during the eight-year hiatus before *The Hound of the Baskervilles*. Holmes returned, but this time in the theatre, initially played by an

American actor, William Gillette. 'Again a handsome man,' says Steven, 'very much in the mould of what we expect Sherlock Holmes to look like. He has the deerstalker, and he has the Meerschaum pipe, which makes its first appearance.' Gillette, who wrote the script for the play, was also responsible for a certain phrase that's famously nowhere to be found in Doyle's stories:

> Oh, this is **elementary,** my dear fellow.

'And then Doyle,' Steven observes, 'never one to ignore a cash cow, realises it's time for Sherlock Holmes to make his return. He's just been a huge hit in the theatre, he's coining it in, so there's *The*

Hound of the Baskervilles. He relents and admits he didn't really kill off Sherlock Holmes.'

The Gillette stage play was remade as a silent film in 1916, not quite the first Holmes movie and, of course, not the last – in fact, there were dozens of screen adaptations between 1900 and 1939. March 1939 then saw the launch of what grew into a 14-film series when Basil Rathbone and Nigel Bruce starred as Holmes and Watson in *The Hound of the Baskervilles.* The first film, Steven points out, 'far from being the first updated Sherlock Holmes, is the first *period* Sherlock Holmes. That's the very first time that Hollywood makes a Holmes film set in the Victorian era. But this novelty lasts for two films, and then they switch studios, go to Universal, the budgets shrink and they make these short, fast-paced potboilers set in the modern day.'

'The general feeling is that they're not quite right,' adds Mark. 'But we got very excited about how fantastically *heretical* they were – and therefore much more like Doyle – in their joie de vivre.'

Mark and Steven agree that one of the biggest influences on their *Sherlock* is a film made by Billy Wilder and Izzy Diamond in 1970: *The Private Life of Sherlock Holmes*, with Robert Stephens as Holmes and Colin Blakely as Watson. 'Although it's extremely funny,' Mark declares, 'it's tinged throughout with melancholy, which I think also hangs over our series. It wasn't a hit, and the received wisdom was it was a noble failure. But it never left either of us, because it's unbelievably well written. It has this rather beautiful little structure of a mini case about a ballerina who asks Holmes to father her child. And he, to get out of it, claims to be gay, and Watson is appalled! Then there's this other elaborate case about a female spy and the Loch Ness monster... We've taken so many elements of that film. Obviously, we've played the gay joke as well, quite

William Gillette's stage production (top left) and its 1916 movie version (bottom left); Rathbone and Bruce (left); Robert Stephens and Colin Blakely (above) in *The Private Life of Sherlock Holmes* by Billy Wilder and Izzy Diamond (bottom)

cheerfully. Wilder and Diamond also develop the character of Sherlock's brother, Mycroft: instead of just being a great name and a great idea, he is turned into this much more powerful, much more dangerous character who, basically, *is* the British government. They make the relationship between the brothers much more abrasive, and also hint that the Diogenes Club is essentially the British Secret Service. We just ran with all that because it's gorgeous.

'It's not a detective story at all; it's a movie about a detective. That's a very big difference, and it's what we always say about *Sherlock* – it's not a detective series, it's a series about a detective. It's about his life and the things that happen to him, his relationships with people. So we can't just do the story of the week on *Sherlock*. We have to explore what this meant to Sherlock, what it meant to John – how has this changed everything for them?'

THE FULL MONTE

'So we sat in Monte Carlo and told Sue all about Sherlock Holmes,' remembers Steven. 'Which was odd because at that point we didn't actually have a series, we didn't have that many ideas about what we were going to do, all we had was Doyle, the original series and who all the characters were.'

'Although it's a model we have since followed,' Mark points out. 'In the process of talking about it, we got so excited, the ideas started to tumble out, looking for modern equivalents... If Sherlock's going to be in his early thirties again, he can't smoke a pipe, that'd be ridiculous – so what could that be? So Doyle's three-pipe problem became our three-patch problem. It was a sort of heresy to attempt to update them, but the more we thought about it the more we realised that the later Conan Doyle stories were being published in the 1920s, and the first films were done as if Holmes

and Watson were still around. They were very much current and not set in some misty past. Somehow, along the way, the essential characters had become literally lost in the fog of multiple adaptations and the trappings of the Victorian period. But the characters have lasted because the friendship between Holmes and Watson was so fantastic.'

'And part of the appeal of the original set of stories in *The Strand* was that they were embracing the contemporary,' adds Steven. 'They had dates on them – "This took place on 4th September 1882" – they would actually tell you when they took place, and it would be really recently. Characters coming into Sherlock Holmes's study would refer to the fact they'd read Watson's stories. So they couldn't have felt more contemporary to their audience. There isn't a huge amount of period detail clotting up those stories because he didn't need to put that in – everyone knew what Victorian London was like because everyone was living in it. Over the years, that element of Sherlock Holmes has been lost.'

Steven and Mark fleshed out their ideas with Sue over a second lunch – this time at the Criterion restaurant

Robert Stephens and Colin Blakely explore the Diogenes Club in *The Private Life of Sherlock Holmes* (top left)

Benedict Cumberbatch ponders a three-patch problem (below left)

Baker Street.
Come at once
if convenient.

SH

in London, chosen because it was the scene, in *A Study in Scarlet*, of Dr Watson's meeting with Stamford, who goes on to introduce him to Sherlock Holmes. 'We systematised it a bit more,' says Mark. 'We talked about how Dr Watson's stories could be represented in a modern way, and I said, "Well, it's a blog, isn't it? It must be a blog."'

'And that,' Steven notes, 'was when we started to realise there were certain things that were only *now* right again.' Such as? 'We've reinvented telegrams! After all these years of telephones, we've discovered that all we really want to do is send each other telegrams. We call them texts, but that's how we prefer to communicate. I don't know why, But we'd rather type at each other.'

'At one point, we'd wondered whether we should just pitch Victorian Sherlock Holmes,' Mark reveals, 'but, having understood that he was still relevant, we had the genuine feeling that Sherlock Holmes gets clearer to you when you're thinking of what he'd be like to know in *your* world. A strange young man with an outrageous sense of entitlement, whose older brother is something mysterious in the Civil Service, solving crimes with his adrenalin-junkie mate – all of that is in the original stories. As much as we adore the Victorian versions, they have become museum pieces where people approach them like great edifices, which is the absolute diametric opposite of how Doyle thought of them himself. So we wanted to blow away the Victorian fog, to get back to the fantastic relationship between these two men, and that's what's happened.'

A key element in presenting that relationship was deciding what the characters would call each other. 'It was really quite hard to get past,' admits Steven, 'but getting past it was incredibly important – they were going to have to call each other John and Sherlock. In

Doyle's stories, they're always Holmes and Watson to each other, as would not be untypical in that era, it'd be normal. But if two young men in modern London called each other Holmes and Watson, they'd be public schoolboys, and we didn't want both of them to be. I remember thinking that was really radical. Strangely difficult to imagine "John" in particular. We spent a long time worrying about how they would talk, as if it was going to be a huge issue. And then, when we wrote our episodes, it wasn't, really. It's kind of liberating that they talk like people, today, and he doesn't say "elementary" and all that... Once you just take that away, he talks like he would talk now.'

'I think we'll probably find a way that he does eventually say it,' laughs Mark. 'But again, it's like opening the curtains on the original writing, on the original characterisation. They talked like real people then, but now they've become fusty in our minds. They just talk like friends now.'

Mark suggests that another crucial strategy was to make John Watson the co-lead. 'That was a huge part of the process of working out what we would do. Obviously, the show's called *Sherlock* but, it was vitally important to us to do that. Over the years, a lot of the versions – even some of the very, very good ones – haven't quite known what to do with Watson. When you read the stories, he is narrating them so you are aware of his presence, but as soon as you dramatise it he's a man scribbling in a book... Some versions have tried to turn him into Sherlock Holmes; they try and give him some of his powers, as if it's rubbing off on him. But it was a very important thing for us to make him a much more three-dimensional character.' That approach applies across the board. 'Mrs Hudson, for example, has a life in ours, unlike any other Mrs Hudson. A huge amount is to do with casting Una Stubbs, but she's not just

Recording the pilot episode (bottom)

Basil Rathbone and Nigel Bruce in 1944's *Sherlock Holmes and the Spider Woman* (above)

someone who flits in and out with a cup of tea; she's got a growing and evolving back story, which is great fun to do.'

Steven agrees that many previous versions have had trouble with the Dr Watson character. 'People have regularly ignored him. Nigel Bruce does something brilliant with him, though purists are offended – he makes him into a comedy buffoon, a man who would clearly have difficulty doing his own shoelaces. But it's a wonderful, loveable, hilarious performance and, for the first time, he is on an equal footing with Basil Rathbone; it would be inconceivable and slightly dull to have one without the other. Basil Rathbone is not Sherlock Holmes unless Nigel Bruce is next to him. I would say that Colin Blakely is also a brilliant comic Watson in *The Private Life of Sherlock Holmes*, and again you feel that's a part of

equal size. So what did we do? We did a bit of deducing, I suppose. We were wondering what Watson would have been like. He must have been an adrenalin junkie! He always talks about Sherlock Holmes getting bored between cases, but so does Watson. He's desperate for it as well: the thrill in his heart, the revolver in his coat – he loves it.'

Mark remembers their discussions about 'a modern war veteran, a man who lost his mojo. And next to him we have Sherlock, who is on the verge of becoming a psychopath. They meet each other at exactly the right moment, and they become one unit essentially. So it was all about making the parts of equal size, giving them a hinterland of experience. It's a huge moment in *A Study in Pink* when Mycroft says, "You're not haunted by the war, Dr Watson, you miss it." That explains everything about what John Watson puts up with and why he puts up with it – because in the end it's worth it to him.'

'He's just as addicted,' says Steven. 'He likes to pretend that he's the sane, rational, normal one, but he's as bad as Sherlock in all those respects. He's as keen for adventure as Sherlock, and as irritable when it's absent. I think you always have to remember that, of all the people that Sherlock Holmes ever met, this is the one he chose to rely on. In the judgement of a genius, this is a brilliant man. He's not a brain, but Sherlock doesn't need another brain. He needs the most reliable, competent, dependable human being in the world. At the beginning of the story, John thinks his life is over, he thinks all the adventures are behind him, he's now just going to disappear into dust. So the opening to *A Study in Pink* has John saying, "Nothing ever happens to me", and then we bring the music in. And we know, watching the story, it's just the beginning and what's about to happen is going to dwarf everything that's ever happened.'

Subject: Sherlock
From: Steven Moffat
To: Mark Gatiss
Sent: 8 March 2008

Right, here's some Sherlock nonsense. Finally. Some right woolly bits in here, but I'm still working on those. And we probably need some cutaways of the killer in action earlier in the plot. But it's a start.

Steven

Subject: Sherlock
From: Mark Gatiss
To: Steven Moffat
Sent: 4 June 2008

Hi Steven

Guy Ritchie to direct "funky" modern Sherlock movie! Let's get the scripts in now!

M x

Subject: Re: Sherlock
From: Steven Moffat
To: Mark Gatiss
Sent: 4 June 2008

Agreed!

Am happy with mine, if you are. Why don't we just do half a day on whatever continuity issues we have, and get going!

Steven

Subject: Sherlock commissioned!
From: Sue Vertue
To: Mark Gatiss
Sent: 3 August 2008 11:06

Dear Mark,

Steven, and I (and kids obviously) are on hols in Greece at the moment – well I say that, 3 of us are on holiday and Steven's fretting in the room trying to finish a script!!!

Anyway, we just heard the great news that apparently Jane is keen to pilot the first ep of Sherlock!!! Quite a surprise actually as we were angling for more scripts which I still think we should do anyway.

I don't know much more about it but hoping to get a meeting for when we get back. What I have heard is that she wants it as an hour and delivery in March. The date makes me slightly nervous as we obviously want to make sure we get the absolute best Sherlock and not just one who's not working!

Hopefully this is the first step on the journey to our long, long running series.

Lots of love,
Sue

Subject: Re: Sherlock commissioned!
From: Mark Gatiss
To: Sue Vertue
Sent: 3 August 2008 11:14

Dear Sue –

How wonderful! And how weird! I was just thinking 'when will we hear about Sherlock?' this morning as I got up. Fantastic. Next step?

I've almost finished filming and should know tomorrow about my ghost stories but I have a relatively free Autumn to concentrate on the Great Detective. Thrilling!

Well done all and speak soon.

Love
Mark x

Subject: Sherlock
From: Mark Gatiss
To: Steven Moffat
Sent: 7 September 2008

Hi Steve

Love the new script. Just a couple of thoughts. Phone?

M x

Subject: Re: Sherlock
From: Steven Moffat
To: Mark Gatiss
Sent: 8 September 2008

Points taken, will have another trawl.

Discussing with Sue moving my schedule round a bit round a bit, so I might get a crack at another Sherlock script – do you think you'll be able to do the same. Saying this partly cos – having reread both in the last week – I think this is potentially huge! Mostly cos I just love it.

We should meet up, plan a season, a Hound, a Moriarty, a speckled band, get drunk, punch a policeman.

This is seriously going to be brilliant!

Steven

On 19 December 2008, the BBC issued a press release to announce a forthcoming new drama production:

BBC DRAMA ANNOUNCES SHERLOCK, A NEW CRIME DRAMA FOR BBC ONE

BBC Wales Drama, **BBC One** and **Hartswood Films** announce *Sherlock*, a contemporary remake of the Arthur Conan Doyle classic, starring **Benedict Cumberbatch** (*Starter for Ten*, *Stuart: A Life Backwards*) as the new Sherlock Holmes and **Martin Freeman** (*The Office*, *Hot Fuzz*) as his loyal friend, Doctor John Watson. **Rupert Graves** (*God on Trial*, *Midnight Man*) plays Inspector Lestrade.

The drama is co-created by the amazing partnership of **Steven Moffat** (*Doctor Who*, *Coupling*) and **Mark Gatiss** (*The League of Gentlemen*, *Doctor Who*, *Crooked House*) and produced by **Sue Vertue** (*Coupling*, *The Cup*).

The 1 x 60-minute episode, written by Moffat, will shoot in January 2009 and will be directed by **Coky Giedroyc** (*Virgin Queen*, *Blackpool*, *Oliver Twist*).

Sherlock is a thrilling, funny, fast paced take on the crime drama genre set in present day London. The iconic details from Conan Doyle's original books remain – they live at the same address, have the same names and, somewhere out there in the London of 2009, Moriarty is waiting for them.

Piers Wenger, Head of Drama, BBC Wales, says: "Our Sherlock is a dynamic superhero in a modern world, an arrogant, genius sleuth driven by a desire to prove himself cleverer than the perpetrator and the police, everyone in fact."

Sherlock will be produced by Hartswood Films, continuing their fruitful relationship with the BBC. Past productions include *Coupling*, *Men Behaving Badly*, *Jekyll* and, most recently, *The Cup* for BBC Two.

Steven Moffat says: "Everything that matters about Holmes and Watson is the same, Conan Doyle's original stories were never about frock coats and gas light; they're about brilliant detection, dreadful villains and blood-curdling crimes – and frankly, the hell with the crinoline.

"Other detectives have cases, Sherlock Holmes has adventures and that's what matters."

"Mark and I have been talking about this project for years, on long train rides to Cardiff for *Doctor Who*. Quite honestly we'd still be talking about it if Sue Vertue of Hartswood Films (conveniently, also my wife) hadn't sat us down for lunch and got us to work."

Mark Gatiss says: "The fact that Steven, myself and millions of others are still addicted to Conan Doyle's brilliant stories is testament to their indestructibility. They're as vital, lurid, thrilling and wonderful as they ever were.

"It's a dream come true to be making a new TV series and in Benedict and Martin we have the perfect Holmes and Watson for our time."

Sue Vertue says: "Steven and Mark are such huge fans of the Sherlock Holmes stories that I had a feeling they really would just go on and on talking about it, so I picked the Criterion for our lunch as I knew of its iconic significance in the meeting of Sherlock and Watson and thought it might get the boys' attention!

"It did and what has evolved from that meeting is hugely exciting."

Commissioned by Ben Stephenson, Controller, BBC Drama Commissioning, and Jay Hunt, Controller, BBC One, Sherlock will shoot in Wales and on location in London in January 2009.

Sherlock is executive produced by Beryl Vertue, Mark Gatiss and Steven Moffat.

Behind the scenes on the pilot episode (above)

With their ideas taking shape, Mark, Steven and Sue approached the then Head of Drama at BBC Wales, Julie Gardner. 'We had a very elaborate, hour-long pitch, and Julie said, "Modern Sherlock Holmes? Yes." From the BBC's point of view, it's a bit of a no brainer because it's the most popular character in fiction, and it's not as expensive as period drama. So then we spent an hour just talking to Julie about what we would have said to her! Really, there will never be another meeting like that. The journey to actually create what we did was obviously much more involved, but that was a very, very lovely day.'

Steven believes that was another indication that they had something that was going to be popular. 'The fact that Sue was instantly interested, the fact that Julie Gardner just said yes straight away – it just meant the time had come. I don't know how everybody knew that they wanted a modern Sherlock. This audience didn't build, they all arrived on the first day of transmission. How did they know it was going to be good? That's what a successful show is: it's not just that it's good – it's the right moment. People want this now.'

The 60-minute episode *A Study in Pink* was intended as the first of a run of six episodes. It ended up as a pilot, which was shown to sample audiences. Their feedback was interesting, notes Sue: 'What we found out was that people liked Sherlock and John together. They also thought that we'd made Lestrade and the police a bit stupid, which wasn't the intention at all. And they all wanted to know where Moriarty was! Even people who hadn't read the stories knew there was a Moriarty. None of them seemed to worry that it was modern-day.'

The feedback from the BBC proved even more interesting... A series was promptly commissioned – but a series of three 90-minute episodes. 'They were so happy with it,' Mark recalls, 'that they asked us to change the format!' *Sherlock* was suddenly transformed from a standard television drama series into a mini-series of movies for television with a far greater sense of scale.

The big advantage, in Steven's view, was that the new format allowed the strong central characters and their developing relationship to co-exist with the cases they were working to solve. 'You need enough space for both. And we couldn't just stick in extra bits – we had to rework the story to justify its greater length.'

So, to all intents and purposes, they started again...

Sherlock's 'series bible', prepared by Steven Moffat and Mark Gatiss after the making of the pilot episode to brief incoming writers on the show before the decision to make three 90-minute episodes.

SHERLOCK

'You may marry him, murder him or do anything you like with him.'
Sir Arthur Conan Doyle in response to a request to marry off Holmes in a play

We love Sherlock Homes. The best and wisest man any of us have ever known and the most filmed character in all literature. That's worth saying again. The *most filmed* character in all literature. More than Dracula or Tarzan or Jesus Christ. So, why do it again?

Because, through countless adaptations and interpretations, brilliant, good, bad or indifferent, the essence of these wonderful stories has got a bit lost. Sherlock Holmes and Dr John Watson – the unlikeliest of partnerships and therefore the best. They're chalk and cheese but they adore each other. And the world they inhabit is a world of high adventure, of edge of the seat peril, of shocking villainy.

Our mission, then is to rescue Holmes and Watson from the clutter of Victoriana. Literally, to blow away the fog from these fantastic characters and let them live again. And the simplest and most effective way to do this, is to set them loose in the modern world. Not as Victorians frozen in time but as the characters Conan Doyle created. As relevant, three dimensional and modern as they were when the stories were first published.

So, starting from essentials. Think of them as Sherlock and John, because people don't use surnames like that any more! If it sounds immediately heretical – good! But it's a great way in to reimagining these characters and their stories.

What we've discovered making the pilot is that modern hugely works for us. Cheeky and up-to-the-minute is where this show really sings. And somehow, magically, makes it all the more Sherlock Holmes. Like removing ALL the Victorian trappings really exposes the characters. We want lurid without the trappings of lurid. Once, fog and stormy nights were genuinely scary. Repetition has made them funny. We want the same, gorgeous melodrama of those mad old stories but in a wholly new way. The same end, by different means.

SHERLOCK

All the arrogance of the original, of course and glacial when he wants to be but cheeky and modern and fun. Attractively confident and ALWAYS comfortable in his own skin. He LIKES being Sherlock Holmes. He's weird, yes, but so unrepentant you just sort of accept it. Above all, he is NOT a transplanted Victorian thawed out in 2009. He's a completely modern man at home in his age. Sherlock Holmes as he would be now!

JOHN

Harder to get right but every bit as important. Tougher than he looks. Sensible, alert, competent. Of course he's an idiot next to Sherlock. We all are. But he's the idiot who spots the genius and he has the strength and confidence to admire him, not resent him. A military man to his backbone, brave, resourceful, loves adventure, with no problems taking orders from the right man in the right spot. Putting John into the heart of the story, and allowing him to articulate the absurdity/danger/horror of their various predicaments, brings the stories alive. Doyle's two attempts to do Holmes-without-Watson are plain boring – you need to live the adventure THROUGH John, and to know Sherlock through him too. This is a long-winded way of saying, keep them together as much as you can – John is our man in the show, we can't do without him.

MRS HUDSON

Again, we're ringing the changes here. She's usually portrayed as doddery and vaguely crotchety, but our Mrs Hudson is a warm, maternal figure. She certainly gets cross with her strange lodgers but they're like sons to her and she worries sick when they're out in the big, dangerous world. She's lived a bit too and we want her to have a life beyond housekeeping.

LESTRADE

We like to think that, if Sherlock wasn't around, Inspector Lestrade would have his own show! He's an extremely capable cop who simply knows his limitations. He finds Sherlock exasperating but knows how incredibly useful he can be. 'Mediocrity recognises only itself. Talent recognises genius.' And Lestrade is a talented man.

It's worth bearing in mind, though, that Lestrade won't necessarily be a constant presence. Other policemen and women should come and go through the stories. Some may be very sympathetic to Sherlock's methods, others openly hostile. Characters such as Anderson, Donovan and Miss Hooper are there as potential players: a rep company in Sherlock and John's world.

THE ADVENTURES

The starting point for us was that John Watson is wounded in the Afghan war. It's virtually the same war we have today. Every time we strike modernity with this idea, it comes up trumps. So, for Sherlock's endless records of sensational crime, read access to the internet and constant use of a PDF. For a cocaine habit, read three nicotine patches to help him think. For all those Victorian narks and grasses, read a network of *Big Issue* sellers: Sherlock's eyes and ears on the streets of his city. For Dr Watson's *Strand Magazine* stories, we have John's blog: and it makes Sherlock famous. The parallels are not just fun, they work!

And so, with the stories, the adage is: other detectives have cases, Sherlock has *adventures*. For us, the most faithful adaptations, heretical as it might seem, were the Basil Rathbone / Nigel Bruce films of the 30s and 40s. Because they're faithful to the spirit of Conan Doyle. The breathless, lurid, pacey, thrilling short stories, not careful but dry recreations.

Take a magpie approach. 'The Five Orange Pips' has a sensational idea at its heart, but is rarely adapted. Is there a way of putting the central idea inside a different type of adventure altogether? If we look at the original stories, patterns emerge. Purloined documents, stolen gems, disguise, fraud, past indiscretions, revenge, codes. All these elements go up to make the Sherlock Holmes that we know so use what you like to make a strange and wonderful whole.

Series One

We have a rare opportunity here. Almost every adaptation begins with Holmes and Watson comfortably middle-aged and old friends. We're starting right at the beginning. The first episode brings Sherlock and John together and, in the course of the adventure, the physically and mentally wounded John finds his life made whole by the friendship of the most extraordinary man.

With this freshness in mind, we're thinking of our first season as 'the Ascent of Sherlock Homes'. Each adventure, though as dark and crazy as we like, should reflect this being the best and most uncomplicated time of these young men's lives. Yes, it's terrifying and dangerous but that's what they thrive on! So we want each story to reflect a real sense of the fun of the thing. Building to just a hint of the darker times to come at the end of the series.

Episodes

An achingly fashionable South Bank art gallery. A toy warehouse stiffed with grinning clowns. And a naked man dragged from the Thames, his throat cut from ear to ear. So why does Sherlock think that a newly discovered Vermeer painting is a fake? And who is the terrifying Czech assassin known only as the Limper?

Mysterious ciphers are appearing all over London. Hidden under railway arches, scrawled in filthy Soho alleys. So why is a huge multinational Merchant Bank so concerned? And what does the shiningly respectable corporation have to do with the ancient Tong of the yellow Dragon?

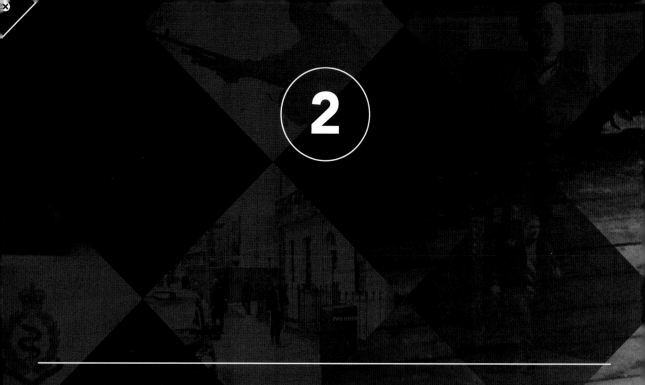

2

BAKER STREET BOYS

Casting the leads, decorating their new home,
and investigating their first case... twice

'HELLO, FREAK'

'We saw exactly one person for Sherlock,' says Steven Moffat, 'and that was Benedict Cumberbatch. Sue and I had seen him in a film called *Atonement*, and she immediately cottoned on to him and said he looked perfect.

'Mark knew him and we discussed it, and we all thought it was a great idea. Benedict then came in and did a reading for us, and at the end of that reading there wasn't really any point in going anywhere else. There wasn't going to be anybody else who looks the part, sounds the part and walks the part to that degree.'

'Benedict's mother said he couldn't be Sherlock because he had the wrong nose,' laughs Sue Vertue. 'At the beginning, I'd had very basic questions for Steven and Mark – who lives where, what was John like, what does Sherlock have to look like... And they said he had to be tall, he had to be thin, and he had to have a big nose. And then we saw Benedict, and we cast him in spite of his not having a big nose! It was very odd, because nobody really knew him – he's done some stunning work, but the public maybe didn't quite know who he was, and he'd never really played a sex symbol. But the first show went out and he was an overnight star.'

'For me, the classics as Sherlock Holmes are Basil Rathbone and Jeremy Brett,' says Benedict Cumberbatch. 'Brett particularly is the benchmark: he's the blueprint for the serialisation of the stories on the small screen. So when I first heard about the project, I was a little bit dubious because I thought those were very hefty profiles to chase away. And then I heard it was an update, and I got equally worried. The minute I read the script, all of those fears completely vanished. Steven and Mark have done an incredible job of bringing Sherlock crashing into the twenty-first century. I didn't grow up reading or knowing every single Sherlock Holmes story, but I was very aware of the character and the genre, and when I read those scripts I could see they'd been written with real reverence.

'I tried very hard not to watch or listen to any other renditions when we started making the first series. I wanted it to be something that I took fresh from the scripts, the director and the other actors. I did revisit them afterwards, which was interesting. I'd watched Jeremy Brett when *The Adventures of Sherlock Holmes* was first on television, and I remember being very impressed with his poise and his elegance, and this incredible, predator-like authority. He had a big physical presence, and you could see this burning intelligence but also this growing madness in his eyes. And I knew what it was about him that I wanted to bring to Sherlock: a man who's very high functioning, and has got there by dint of effort. You do see, as the series progresses, that he actually had a normal childhood – as normal as it could have been until the point where they realised he was slightly different.

'The Paget drawings were interesting and beautiful things in themselves, and

Benedict Timothy Carlton Cumberbatch
Born 19 July 1976, Hammersmith, London

AWARDS

Best TV Detective for *Sherlock* (National Television Awards, 2014)
Hottest Movie Star (Critics' Choice Movie Awards, 2013)
Britannia Awards for **British Artist of the Year** (2013)
Best Actor for *Frankenstein* (Critics' Circle Theatre Awards, 2012)
Best Actor – Miniseries or TV Film for *Sherlock* (Satellite Awards, 2012)
Best Actor for *Sherlock* (Crime Thriller Awards, 2012)
Critics' Choice Television Award for **Best Movie/Miniseries Actor** for *Sherlock* (Television Critics Association awards, 2012)
Best Actor for *Frankenstein* (Laurence Olivier Awards, 2012)

Best Actor for *Frankenstein* (Evening Standard Theatre Awards, 2011)
GQ UK magazine **Actor of the Year** (2011)
Best Actor for *Sherlock* (Crime Thriller Awards, 2010)
Mini-Series – Best Performance by an Actor for *To the Ends of the Earth* (Monte-Carlo Television Festival The Golden Nymphs awards, 2006)
Best Classical Stage Performance for *Hedda Gabler* (Ian Charleson Awards, 2005)
Television Films – Best Performance by an Actor for *Hawking* (2004)

SELECTED FILM ROLES

2014	The Hobbit: The Battle of the Five Armies Smaug
	The Imitation Game Alan Turing
2013	The Fifth Estate Julian Assange
	The Hobbit: The Desolation of Smaug Smaug
	August: Osage County Little Charlie
	12 Years a Slave William Ford
	Star Trek Into Darkness Khan
2012	The Hobbit: An Unexpected Journey Smaug
2011	War Horse Major Stewart
	Wreckers David
	Tinker Tailor Soldier Spy Peter Guillam
2010	The Whistleblower Nick Phillips
	Third Star James
	Four Lions Ed
2009	Creation Joseph Hooker
2008	Burlesque Fairytales Henry Clark
	The Other Boleyn Girl William Carey
2007	Atonement Paul Marshall
2006	Amazing Grace William Pitt
	Starter for Ten Patrick Watts

SELECTED TV ROLES

2012	Parade's End Christopher Tietjens
2010–2014	Sherlock Sherlock Holmes
2010	Van Gogh: Painted with Words Vincent Van Gogh
2009	Small Island Bernard
	The Turning Point Guy Burgess
	Marple: Murder is Easy Luke Fitzwilliam
2008	The Last Enemy Stephen Ezard
2007	Stuart: A Life Backwards Alexander Marsters
2005	Broken News Will Parker
	To the Ends of the Earth Edmund Talbot
	Nathan Barley Robin
2004	Hawking Stephen Hawking
	Dunkirk Lt Jimmy Langley
2003	Fortysomething Rory Slippery
	Spooks Jim North
	Cambridge Spies Edward Hand
	Heartbeat Charles/Toby
2002	Silent Witness Warren Reid
	Tipping the Velvet Freddy
	Fields of Gold Jeremy

SELECTED RADIO ROLES

2013	Neverwhere Angel Islington
	Copenhagen Werner Heisenberg
2011	Tom and Viv T.S. Eliot
2009-2014	Rumpole Young Rumpole
2009	Good Evening Dudley Moore
2008-2014	Cabin Pressure Captain Martin Crieff
2008	Spellbound Dr Murchison
	Chatterton: The Allington Solution Thomas Chatterton
	At War with Wellington Duke of Wellington
	The Last Days of Grace GF
	The Pillow Book Tadanobu
2006	The Possessed Nikolai Stavrogin
2005	The Cocktail Party Peter Quiipe
	Seven Women Tovey

SELECTED STAGE ROLES

2011	Frankenstein
2010	The Children's Monologues gala
	After the Dance
2008	The City
2007	The Arsonists
	Rhinoceros
	Period of Adjustment
2005	Hedda Gabler
2004	The Lady by the Sea
2002	Romeo and Juliet
	As You Like It
	Oh What a Lovely War
	Love's Labour's Lost
	A Midsummer's Night's Dream

DELETED SCENE

CUT TO:

8 **INT. SUBURBAN LONDON STREET – DAY**   8

Terrible rain thrashing down.
Words type across the screen.
APRIL 26th.

Two young guys, in their late teens, coming
towards us through the streaming rain. Gary
and Jimmy. Gary has an umbrella, but Jimmy
just has his coat pulled over his head. A
taxi heads past them. Jimmy tries to hail
it, but it doesn't even slow down. Jimmy now
hesitating to a halt, looking around the
downpour.

                    JIMMY
        I'll be two minutes.

                    GARY
        What?

                    JIMMY
        Just going back – my mum's got an
        umbrella.

                    GARY
        You can share mine.

                    JIMMY
        (Already heading back) Two minutes!

                    GARY
        (Yelling after him) It's not gay,
        sharing.

                              CUT TO:

Few minutes later. Gary, miserable under his
umbrella. Checks his watch. Where is he? On the
sound of a doorbell.

                              CUT TO:

                                   9

9 **INT. JIMMY'S HOUSE – DAY**

A middle-aged woman – Jimmy's Mum – is pulling
open the door, to reveal Gary, still under his
umbrella, the rain still pouring.

                    GARY
        Where's Jimmy?

                    JIMMY'S MUM
        I thought he was with you.

                    GARY
        Came back for an umbrella.

                    JIMMY'S MUM
        No, he didn't.

---

very influential, and they became the template for that silhouette and that idea of the very aquiline profile. So we had to come up with our own version of that, despite my not having the right nose... We couldn't have him in the deerstalker straight away. I was quite keen on slicked-back hair. We tried all sorts of different hair, especially in the pilot, but we ended up with this curly mop that sets hearts aflutter, apparently.

'We first meet Sherlock Holmes in a morgue, which is an extraordinary place in any circumstances, but to first meet your hero there is exceptional. You fully see his face as he's leaning over a body bag and unzipping it, and you see it upside down as if you were the corpse looking out of the body bag. Sherlock is probably the least sympathetic face you could first look upon on your first day as a dead person, but it's a wonderful thing to play.

I **need to know** what **bruises** form in the next twenty minutes. **Text me.**

'People do ask what research I did for the role. There's a certain amount of criminal pathology that interests me – the procedural stuff and what you would do at a crime scene, the realities of the things that happen to us and the medical things involved – but primarily I always go back to the written word. Sherlock has multimedia at his disposal and you have the modern scenario of a crime scene and all of the forensics that that involves, and obviously we all have our cultural references to *Silent Witness*, to *CSI*, to *Cracker*, to Morse... But it's different, because here you have a man who can

look at a crime scene, use his PDA, tap into his computer, but link a narrative intuitively on first receiving all of that information, and that's something that no computer can do. It's something that a lot of our best-loved fictional detectives take an entire three-part series to do, and it's something that he can do in the blink of an eye. He's by no means going to get it right all the time – pretty near, but there are certain things that even he can't quite guess right first time...

'One of the major attractions is the idea that his obstacles are infinite. They can be equally as traditional as the original stories; they can be masterminds like Moriarty. But there's also the modern aspect of it, which is very exciting: there's terrorism, biological warfare, bombs or hijacking or any kind of siege situation... You've got political drama, corruption on every level, you've got potentially a corrupt police force, who knows, maybe the cancer is within... There's a lot more white-collar crime now, which is equally fascinating and may involve his brilliance as a logician and somebody who can crack codes and

understand patterns mathematically to deduce what's going on and who's behind a virus or some kind of attempt to hoodwink financial institutions... There are lots of very exciting modern foes he can be pitted against which is great.'

'A COLLEAGUE? HOW'D YOU GET A COLLEAGUE?'

Having found their ideal Sherlock so quickly, Steven, Mark and Sue now needed to cast their second lead, and that took a little longer. 'We saw some fantastic people,' says Sue. 'But once we put the two of them together we all just said, "Well, that's it, then, isn't it?" You could just see it in the room. It was electric really.'

'We had been saying "tall and short", "thin and round" – everything has to be opposite,' notes Steven. 'You can't have two tall, strange-looking men. There has to be a contrast between them. We saw a bunch of Watsons, and we took some of those and we put them next to Benedict and they were all fine. And then Martin stood next to Benedict, and they immediately looked like Sherlock Holmes and Dr Watson. Martin makes being ordinary a poem. He is an ordinary-looking man and he specialises in playing very ordinary people. And John Watson is a very ordinary man. Martin makes that funny and interesting and fascinating, but he's not making Dr Watson more colourful to make him interesting. He's making him absolutely truthful and honest. And the way Martin played the lines started to alter how Benedict was playing it. Benedict suddenly engaged in a slightly different way – a bit funnier and a bit warmer.'

PARK — DAY 17

and John turning from a Cappucc...
their ... Criterion C
d. ... help glancing at

DELETED SCENES

15 **EXT. ROOF OF SCOTLAND YARD — DAY**   15

Lestrade is stepping through a service door,
on the flat roof. He starts to light the
cigarette. He speaks lightly and casually,
knowing there's someone there to hear.

> LESTRADE
> Trying to give these up actually.
> I was thinking of a pipe. What do pipes
> do for you cigarettes don't?

A beat – and a cultured voice from off.

> SHERLOCK
> (From off) Cancer of the jaw.

Lestrade laughs, looks round. A tall, thin man is
standing with his back to us right at the edge of
the roof, looking out over London. A silhouette.

> LESTRADE
> Okay. What am I getting wrong this time?

> SHERLOCK
> No notes. No prior sign. Each of them
> in a strange location that means nothing
> to them where they've never gone before...
> That's not how I'd kill myself.

On Lestrade. Glances uneasily at the edge of
the roof, where Sherlock is standing.

> LESTRADE
> ... So. How are you doing these days?

17 **EXT. PARK — DAY**

Mike and John turning from a Cappuccino
stand, with their coffees. (The Criterion
Cappuccino Stand.) Mike can't help glancing
at John's stick.

> MIKE
> You okay?

> JOHN
> Just my leg.

> MIKE
> Bad, is it?

> JOHN
> My therapist thinks it's psychosomatic.

> MIKE
> What do you think?

> JOHN
> I think I got shot.

As they settle at a table…

> JOHN
> You're still at Barts then?

Martin John Christopher Freeman
Born 8 September 1971, Aldershot, Hampshire

AWARDS

Best Actor in a Leading Role for *The Hobbit: The Desolation of Smaug* (Stella Awards, 2014)

Best Actor in a Leading Role for *The Hobbit: An Unexpected Journey* (Stella Awards, 2013)

Visionary Actor for *The Hobbit: An Unexpected Journey* (Shorts Awards, 2013)

Best Hero for *The Hobbit: An Unexpected Journey* (MTV Movie Awards, 2013)

Best Actor for *The Hobbit: An Unexpected Journey* (Empire Awards, 2013)

Best Cast in a TV Show and **Outstanding Supporting Actor in a Drama Series** for *Sherlock* (Tumblr TV Awards, 2012)

Best Cast in a Miniseries or TV Movie for *Sherlock* (PAAFTJ Awards, 2012)

Best Supporting Actor for *Sherlock* (Crime Thriller Awards, 2012)

TV Movie/Miniseries Supporting Actor for *Sherlock* (Gold Derby TV Awards, 2012)

Best Supporting Actor for *Sherlock* (BAFTAs, 2011)

Best Male Comedy Performance for *Hardware* (Rose d'Or, 2004)

SELECTED FILM ROLES

2014	**The Hobbit: The Battle of the Five Armies** Bilbo Baggins
2013	**The Voorman Problem** Dr Williams
	The Hobbit: The Desolation of Smaug Bilbo Baggins
	Saving Santa Bernard
	Svengali Don
	The World's End Oliver Chamberlain
2012	**The Hobbit: An Unexpected Journey** Bilbo Baggins
	The Pirates! Band of Misfits Pirate with a scarf
2011	**What's Your Number?** Simon
2010	**Wild Target** Dixon
2009	**Swinging with the Finkels** Alvin Finkel
	Nativity! Paul Maddens
2007	**Nightwatching** Rembrandt
	The All Together Chris Ashworth
	Hot Fuzz Met Sergeant
	The Good Night Gary Shaller
	Dedication Jeremy
2006	**Breaking and Entering** Sandy
	Confetti Matt
2005	**The Hitchhiker's Guide to the Galaxy** Arthur Dent
2004	**Shaun of the Dead** Declan
	Call Register Kevin
2003	**Love Actually** John
2002	**Ali G Indahouse** Ricky C
2001	**Fancy Dress** Pirate

SELECTED TV ROLES

2014	**Fargo** Lester Nygaard
2010–2014	**Sherlock** John Watson
2009	**Micro Men** Chris Curry
	Boy Meets Girl Danny Reed
2007	**The Old Curiosity Shop** Mr Codlin
	Comedy Showcase Greg Wilson
2005	**The Robinsons** Ed Robinson
2004	**Pride** Fleck
2003–2004	**Hardware** Mike
2003	**Charles II: The Power and the Passion** Lord Shaftesbury
	Margery and Gladys DS Stringer
	The Debt Terry Ross
2002	**Linda Green** Matt
	Helen West DC Stone
2001–2003	**The Office** Tim Canterbury
2001	**World of Pub** various
	Men Only Jamie
2000	**Black Books** Doctor
	Lock, Stock... Jaap
	Bruiser various
1999	**Exhaust** The Car Owner
1998	**Picking up the Pieces** Brendan
	Casualty Ricky Beck
1997	**This Life** Stuart
	The Bill Craig Parnell

SELECTED STAGE ROLES

2014	**Richard III**
2010	**Clybourne Park**
2007	**The Last Laugh**

'Finding John Watson was a much more involved process,' Mark concurs, 'because we had to find a physical contrast and an emotional contrast. But Martin Freeman just knocked it out of the park. He's such a fantastically believable, truthful actor. John Watson is a doctor and a soldier who has been through the mill and come back wounded and a shadow of his former self. And Martin has a fantastically haunted style.'

We are very different,' says Martin. 'I'd liked Benedict from a distance, I'd liked his work for a long time, and I was looking forward to working with him, but there's no guarantee that you'll work well together. Thank god we have, really! We're quite different actors, but I think we both want to arrive at the same place.

'I thought it was very good casting when I heard that Benedict was doing it because he has a physical presence about him – you instantly believe that this is Sherlock Holmes. But he's quick as well and he can handle the big dialogue, and Sherlock's got a lot to say, loads of stuff to dazzle us with. He does still have flaws, he's not god, he's not an absolutely perfect human by any stretch, but he does have this way of reasoning and analysing which is second to none.

'None of the previous Watsons informed me at all, apart from showing what I *didn't* want to do. Nigel Bruce and Basil Rathbone were my first and maybe favourite Watson and Holmes, but I knew I couldn't and shouldn't do that. It's great to have an opportunity to play someone that isn't the bumbling Watson, that isn't just the sidekick. Obviously, Sherlock's the main man, of course he is, but there's so much for me to do. Just from a selfish point of view, I want to do lots of good stuff, lots of cerebral stuff and lots of action stuff.

'I really like the original Doyle stories, and I suppose it all feeds into what we do but I don't consciously take on anything from that Watson. I feel I'm doing Steven

and Mark's Watson, not Conan Doyle's. That's not to take anything away from Conan Doyle, we wouldn't be here if it wasn't for him. But I'll crawl over broken glass for a good script and these are really, really good scripts. Even at the pilot stage, it wasn't a script that I felt I'd read or seen a thousand times before. I was a bit suspicious initially of an updated Sherlock Holmes, just because – modern popular culture being what it is – it would be easy for it to feel very self-satisfied, very pleased with itself for being anachronistic. But *Sherlock* manages to do it in a way that isn't too self-conscious or showy.'

'WE'D BETTER UPGRADE THEIR SURVEILLANCE STATUS'

'It's the single most interesting thing that's happened to John Watson since he got invalided home,' Steven declares. 'And that's what he's lacking. He's lacking anything interesting happening to him, so he meets a psychopath in a lab – "That'll do"!'

Sue thinks John makes Sherlock more human. 'I always have this image of Sherlock at a dinner party. You'd want Sherlock at your dinner party

because he'd be entertaining, but you also know he'd be the one that would shock everybody, be rude, not care, and probably not like the food. John would make him palatable to other people. And Martin's a phenomenal actor – I'm not sure that everyone knew how good he was until he was in *Sherlock*. He provides our view of this exotic creature, and Martin is fabulous at that. When they first meet, John could be us: "God, that's amazing." "How extraordinary." "Oh, I didn't expect..." And that worked very well in the first series. As it's progressed, we have moved on from John being the "I don't understand" guy, of course. In that way we have to find other people to be surprised by Sherlock.'

Martin believes that when John meets Sherlock he sees what he's been missing since leaving the army: 'excitement, purpose and momentum through life, a reason to get up and do things and be a man of action again. And in Sherlock he finds the perfect foil for slightly dangerous, slightly grisly stuff – Sherlock is his best bet for some quick, easily gettable thrills.

'John and Sherlock are an extraordinary mismatch,' says Benedict. 'They're the perfect odd couple. Sherlock has a brain which works on the principle of deduction and he makes decisions very quickly. John is a man of action, and he's also a thrill-seeker, though he doesn't necessarily know it until he returns to civilian life and recognises that part of his life is empty. What happens in *A Study in Pink* is that a man is brought out of a very inward depressed state by this extraordinary, slightly maverick talent – someone who is beyond the law but working for the good.'

'There's a telling line where Sherlock talks about genius needing an audience, and he's applying that to killers but you know that John takes that as meaning Sherlock himself. He does genuinely want John's help and medical opinions and so on, but he also wants someone to watch him in action.'

'They lock together so well,' says Mark. 'Just watching the scene in *A Study in Pink* when they first meet and Sherlock takes command and immediately assumes they're going to be flatmates – I think it's thrilling. And it's interesting that, even with his rage after his Afghan experience, John doesn't say "No". Because he's intrigued – *Who is this man...?'*

'Usually when the executive producers are on the set you know that either you've done something wrong or it's a big important day,' Benedict explains. 'But it's slightly confusing with Sue and Steven and Mark because they're on set a lot... I think the main reason is that they absolutely love it. They were all there for when John and Sherlock are meeting for the first time.'

DELETED SCENES

25 EXT. RAILWAY STATION - DAY   25

A queue at a taxi rank. In the queue, shuffling
along, Jennifer Wilson. She's dressed entirely
in pink, and is talking on a pink-covered iPhone.

                    JENNIFER
          One hour, I'll be there. Honestly, I'll
          be there. You get the drinks in.

As she shuffles forward in the queue, out of
frame, we fade down to black.

Fading up on:

                                              CUT TO:

26 INT. LAURISTON GARDENS - DAY   26

The pill bottle. It stands on bare floorboards.
We hold on it for a moment ... then a pink-
fingernailed hand reaches into shot, takes it...

                    SALLY
          (Calling) Coming!
          (As she moves away) Stay away
          from Sherlock Holmes.

She heads towards Lestrade.

On John, staring after her, thoughtful.
Calls out:

                    JOHN
          Bye!

On John, grave, thoughtful. He turns, starts
to limp away down the street - and looks up,
something catching his eye. John's POV. On the
rooftops of houses opposite silhouetted against
the moon - Sherlock Holmes. He's standing there
perfectly calmly, oblivious to his position.
He has his PDA in one hand, and is looking one
way, then the other, as if scanning the streets
below him...

On John, staring up. What the hell's he doing??
But for a moment he's held there, staring,
fascinated - and then there's a telephone
ringing. He glances round. There's a solitary
phone box, a little distance from him, and the
phone is ringing.

Instinctively, he glances back at Sherlock,
like he almost expects it to be him - but no,
Sherlock is still scanning the horizon. Now
he's ducking out of sight, off somewhere else.

John turns and walks on. We hold on the
telephone box. As he John heads away, the
telephone stops ringing...

David Nellist (Mike Stamford) and Martin Freeman at the Criterion restaurant, the scene, in Doyle's *Study in Scarlet*, of the chance meeting with Stamford that leads to Watson first meeting Sherlock Holmes (above left)

'It's extraordinary how seldom that scene at Barts has been done,' Steven points out. 'To actually have the first meeting of Sherlock Holmes and Dr Watson where Sherlock Holmes instantly deduces that he's just come back from Afghanistan, to actually do that on film is very rare. I think it *has* been done at some point, but we're among the first to do it.'

'I got chills,' says Mark. 'But it's one of those strange things that almost every version begins late in the day in their relationship: the pattern is established: they've known each other for years, they're intimate friends, Mrs Hudson brings the client up the stairs... which is absolutely what you want to do. But this is the very first meeting, and it was thrilling to watch it actually happen. And it's still in the early-days territory of sounding each other out so it was a lot of fun because you're not automatically playing the same old game.'

'So,' Steven sums up, 'you've got this egomaniacal, slightly autistic psychopath and this incredibly decent hard-working soldier, the two most opposite people who could ever possibly meet each other, who really rather adore each other and end up sharing a flat...'

'WE'VE JUST MET AND WE'RE GOING TO LOOK AT A FLAT??'

Sherlock's next main player, of course, was a certain world-famous London address: 221B Baker Street. According to Sue, 'In the beginning, we looked at whether 221B should be a modern flat, perhaps somewhere in the docks or in a converted warehouse. But we quickly thought no, it wouldn't – most people in London still live in Victorian houses. So it seemed to make sense to keep 221B where it had always been, but to give it a modern feel.'

At which point, Arwel Wyn Jones enters the story. Arwel has been Production Designer on all three series of *Sherlock*, so was involved right from the start. He's in charge of the *Sherlock* Art Department and the overall look of the series. In 2012, he was awarded a BAFTA for his work on the show, and he has worked on many of the most high-profile television programmes to have emerged from BBC Wales in the last ten years, including *Doctor Who*, *Torchwood*, *The Sarah Jane Adventures*, *Baker Boys*, *Sugartown*, *Upstairs Downstairs* and *Wizards vs. Aliens*. For the

From 'A Study in Scarlet'
by Sir Arthur Conan Doyle

[...] He was busily engaged at it when the cabman entered the room.

'Just give me a hand with this buckle, cabman,' he said, kneeling over his task and never turning his head.

The fellow came forward with a somewhat sullen, defiant air, and put down his hands to assist. At that instant there was a sharp click, the jangling of metal, and Sherlock Holmes sprang to his feet again.

'Gentlemen,' he cried, with flashing eyes, 'let me introduce you to Mr Jefferson Hope, the murderer of Enoch Drebber and of Joseph Stangerson.'

From 'A Study in Scarlet'
by Sir Arthur Conan Doyle

'I've got a good deal to say,' our prisoner said slowly. 'I want to tell you gentlemen all about it.'

'Hadn't you better reserve that for your trial?' asked the inspector.

'I may never be tried,' he answered. 'You needn't look startled. It isn't suicide I am thinking of. Are you a doctor?' He turned his fierce dark eyes upon me as he asked this last question.

'Yes, I am,' I answered.

'Then put your hand here,' he said, with a smile, motioning with his manacled wrists towards his chest.

I did so; and became at once conscious of an extraordinary throbbing and commotion which was going on inside. The walls of his chest seemed to thrill and quiver as a frail building would do inside when some powerful engine was at work. In the silence of the room I could hear a dull humming and buzzing noise which proceeded from the same source.

'Why,' I cried, 'you have an aortic aneurism!'

From 'A Study in Pink'
by Steven Moffat

SHERLOCK (V.O.)
Who hunts in the middle of a crowd?

Thud-thud! Closer on Mrs. Hudson - but now drifting over her shoulder to ... The man standing behind her. A shadow slants across him, concealing his face - but we're closing in on the badge hung round his neck, gleaming on his chest.

[...] And then something else, being raised into shot. A pink phone! (The same pink iPhone prop as used in The Great Game.)

Normal speed again. Sherlock is staring at the shadowed figure. What's going on, what???
The Taxi driver presses a button on the phone. Then turns and heads away down the stairs.

From 'A Study in Pink'
by Steven Moffat

SHERLOCK
Is this a confession?

TAXI DRIVER
Oh, yes. And I'll tell you what else -
if you go and get the coppers now,
I won't run, I'll sit quiet and they
can take me down. I promise. [...]

SHERLOCK
You don't have long. Am I right?
The Taxi Driver smiles, affable. He taps his head.

TAXI DRIVER
Aneurism - right in here. Any breath
could be my last.

SHERLOCK
And because you're dying, you've just
murdered four people.

TAXI DRIVER
I've outlived four people. That's the
most fun you can have, with an aneurism.

Sherlock pilot, he shared the design credit with another BBC Wales veteran, Edward Thomas, but took over for the Series One remount of *A Study in Pink*.

'We wanted to create their "den",' Arwel recalls. 'Somewhere that you, as a viewer, would want to go to and spend time with them. We wanted them to be based somewhere you'd like to go into yourself – go and pick things up and play with what's in there. We also wanted interesting backgrounds that would set Sherlock and John off as interesting characters.'

'The interior of Baker Street was very important to get right,' says Mark. 'We wanted a place that's cluttered but not squalid; a sort of bachelor clutter. It's a two-blokes kind of flat but it's also very welcoming. So we wanted the flat to be very cosy and homely. We wanted to make sure that it wasn't just a Victorian set redressed; in the pilot we had a Victorian fireplace, but we changed it to something

more 1950s. Sherlock has completely converted the kitchen into his laboratory – his interests and obsessions spread out like mould through the house.'

The furniture and décor inside the flat have a modern feel but, as Sue points out, 'It's not really modern furniture, it's *fine* furniture. And the wallpaper *is* modern, but it feels as though it could have been there for ages. It's quite classic, quite bold but it could be something that has been there for years…'

Arwel is proud of – and relieved by – the success of that particular element of the 221B studio set. 'The famous wallpaper in the living room behind the sofa – no one was really sure what I was doing. When Ed Thomas, for example, was walking through the studio, he just looked at it, shook his head and said, "I hope Arwel knows what he's doing!" Even the director, Paul McGuigan, who's a big fan of wallpapers, kept asking me, "Are you sure about this?" And I was

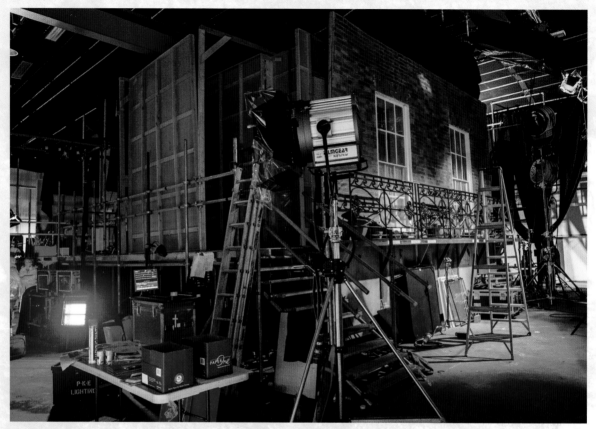

The Art Department built an actual exterior wall for the interior studio set, carefully matching the brickwork at the North Gower Street location.

The tea service used in *The Reichenbach Fall* was designed by Ali Miller. A new set used by Mrs Hudson in Series Three was by chance also an Ali Miller design, which Arwel only discovered when the Sherlockology fan website asked him about it.

More and more items will be pinned to Sherlock's 'crime wall' as an episode progresses but, with scenes shot out of order, its contents need to be carefully planned, mapped out and recorded at every stage.

The 221B exterior in London's North Gower Street (above left) and the Sherlock Holmes Museum on the real Baker Street (above right)

going, "Yeah... no, not really...". But I've been to *Sherlock* conventions since and seen purses, skirts, dresses, shirts – all done copying the same pattern; it's the background on various websites and everything.

'So we had quite a bit of fun with some different finishes and textures and everything inside. We also had to match it to an exterior location, obviously, in London. So certain elements were dictated by the exterior...'

'Finding a location for 221B was quite interesting,' Sue admits. 'We wanted an authentic feel, we wanted the window, the door, a café next door... We looked at Baker Street itself, and that would have been impossible. We couldn't have filmed there – it's five lanes wide, and it's full of Sherlock Holmes pubs and museums everywhere you look! We looked in Wales, we looked in Bristol, we looked in London. Where we shoot it is actually not that far from the original Baker Street.'

'Our Baker Street is in North Gower Street,' reveals Mark. 'It looks like Baker Street, but has all of the virtues and none of the vices. There aren't thousands of tourists trying to get into Madame Tussaud's, and it's quiet.'

Quiet? Well, it used to be, says Sue. 'When we shoot now in London, it seems to be a huge party. The fans all turn up – I don't know how they know – and people come from far and wide. They are very well behaved, but it's a party.' And we'll be attending some more *Sherlock* street parties later on...

'IT'S A CRIME SCENE, I DON'T WANT IT CONTAMINATED'

Another key location for *A Study in Pink* was the house at Lauriston Gardens where Sherlock and John examine Jennifer Wilson's corpse. Steven's script gave only general guidelines about the state of the crime scene:

'Dark, abandoned. Not too run down, but cold and empty ... A dark, narrow hallway, peeling wallpaper ... A grimy disused kitchen ... The room around them, dark, sombre, peeling wallpaper. And in the centre, a slash of pink.' Then Arwel and his team got to work...

'Before I got my hands on it, it was quite a nice house, up for sale. But we needed a murder scene, somewhere that our villain could take an unsuspecting victim, knowing it was empty, and then walk away without being seen. We went to town on distressing the walls, the floors, everything, just to give us texture and ambience. As soon as you walk in, you get the feeling of a haunted house. We had done something on a small scale for the pilot, then when we redid the episode I just wanted to have a bit more scale, a bit more fun with it.'

Sherlock was conceived and announced as a series of 60-minute episodes, and the BBC's then Head of Fiction, Jane Tranter allocated what Mark describes as 'the last bit of money for the year for drama' to the making of a pilot episode. Directed by Coky Giedroyć, this first version of *A Study in Pink* was shot in January 2009.

DELETED SCENES

Sherlock Series One
A Study in Pink

47 **INT. JOHN'S BEDROOM - NIGHT** 47

The same dull room we saw before. John is entering. He goes straight to the desk, yanks open the drawer. The gun!

CUT TO:

48 **INT. LIMOUSINE - NIGHT** 48

John climbs into the back. The woman barely glances up from her Blackberry.

JOHN
Sorry. Just had to take care of something.

WOMAN
Get your gun okay?

JOHN
... yeah.

Sherlock Series One
A Study in Pink

54 **EXT. BAKER STREET - NIGHT** 54

SHERLOCK
This is his hunting ground.
Right here in the heart of the
city. We now know the victims
were abducted, and that changes
everything. Because all of his
victims disappeared from crowded
places, from busy streets - but
nobody saw them go. They walked
out of their lives with a complete
stranger, and trusted him right to
the moment they swallowed his
poison. He can do the impossible,
this one - he needs to take a bow.

JOHN
If it is a 'he'. The pink lady
wrote "Rachel"...

SHERLOCK
Yes. That's odd. 'Til we know who
Rachel is, no point in speculating.
Mustn't theorise in advance
of the facts.

Sherlock skips down off the wall.

SHERLOCK
Think, though, think!
Who do we trust, even if we don't
know them? Who passes unnoticed
wherever they go? Who hunts
in the middle of a crowd?

When Arwel Jones and his team recced the location for Lauriston Gardens – Field's House in Newport, Wales – the property was up for sale. 'It was all whites, creams... the hallways were all magnolia. We turned it into this decrepit place, everything falling down. And then we had to put it back to how it was. So we spent a day masking things off and then painting it with an airless sprayer. We did the whole lot – top to bottom – in magnolia in three days. By the end of it, our chargehand painter, Steven Fudge, was completely magnolia. I wish I had a photo of it!'

DELETED SCENES

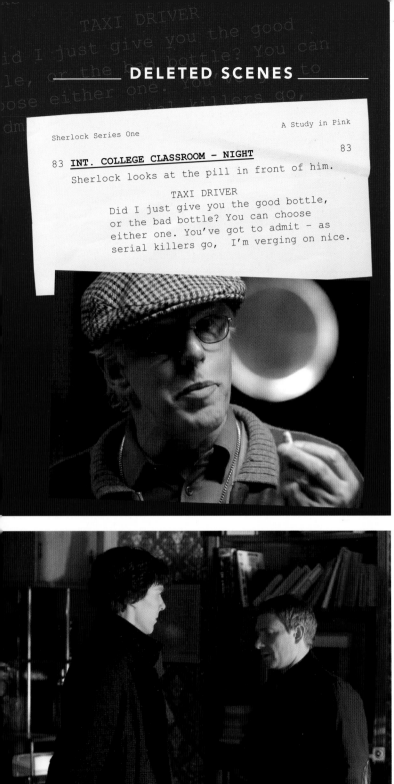

Sherlock Series One   A Study in Pink

83 INT. COLLEGE CLASSROOM – NIGHT   83
    Sherlock looks at the pill in front of him.
                    TAXI DRIVER
        Did I just give you the good bottle,
        or the bad bottle? You can choose
        either one. You've got to admit – as
        serial killers go, I'm verging on nice.

By this time, Jane had moved on and her replacement as BBC drama chief was Ben Stephenson. He asked for three 90-minute episodes.

'Everybody liked it, we were all very proud of it, but the format change meant we had to rework a lot of things,' explains Mark. 'What we had been thinking about in terms of story progression across a series now had to be telescoped, bringing all the Moriarty stuff up front much earlier. But we also had to think much bigger! Ninety minutes is movie-length, so essentially you've got three movies – a miniseries rather than an ordinary series. We still wanted to start with *A Study in Pink* as our introduction, but it was immediately obvious it would not be as simple as stapling half an hour of story to the end or in the middle. We had to expand the story, without just padding it. It's got a much bigger scale to it now.'

'We had to take that story and expand it without making it slower,' notes Steven. 'That also allowed us to change our minds about some things. One thing that was very significant for us was realising that the scenes that worked best in the pilot were where the modern world was really apparent, was really surrounding our characters. There had maybe been a touch of tentativeness – if you stand Benedict and Martin in half-light against a Victorian wall, you wouldn't know it had been updated. Then we realised that you should know in every shot that this is a modern-day Sherlock Holmes, because that's when the show has the most energy and is the most exciting. And I think we'd been a little bit too traditional on our 221B set, so we pulled it back to make it a bit more modern.'

'We felt it really benefited from seeing London, so we shot more of it on location,' Sue adds. 'And we made changes to the main studio set. We took out a bit in the middle that they had to keep walking up

and down. We built another room. In the pilot, Mrs Hudson owned the sandwich shop and the flats above; now she's just the landlady of the flat.'

'The upstairs kitchen in the pilot was rather odd,' Mark adds. 'The idea had been that it was part of the café. So it ended up like a proper restaurant kitchen, all stainless steel, which had been converted into a domestic kitchen that Sherlock had then cannibalised into his laboratory. Arwel did a fantastic job but in the pilot it just looked a bit weird. So we went for a much more domestic kitchen, right from the start.'

On the technical side, a larger budget allowed for a different camera, 'far superior', Sue notes, 'to the one we could afford for the pilot'. And the personnel,

in front of and behind the cameras, remained mostly the same. 'There were a couple of people who weren't actually available, but a lot of the crew were the same, and the composers were the same. We had a new director of photography, Steve Lawes, and Coky Giedroyć wasn't able to come back, so Paul McGuigan became the new director.'

One of Paul McGuigan's most significant contributions quickly had a major impact on the series. 'A Study in Pink was shot last because Steven was writing it while we were editing the third episode, The Great Game,' says Sue. 'And Paul said that he didn't want to use close-ups of mobile phones – and that he was going to put text on screen. Steven saw that in The Great Game and realised he

could use it as a sort of scripting tool, using text to enhance the story. So that was something that evolved from what we learnt from the first recording block.'

An **exchange of glances** between Lestrade and John. Lestrade **rolls his eyes**, used to this. But John is **fascinated** – what the hell is Sherlock doing? On Sherlock. Stepping to the body, eyes flicking, absorbing every detail. Sherlock's POV. **A blizzard of details** – fast, close. Close on outflung hand. The wedding and engagement ring. The word **MARRIED** pulses across the screen – just appears, floats, fades.

'A QUIET SPOT FOR A MURDER'

The original version of the confrontation between Sherlock and taxi driver Jeff Hope took place in 221B, but the action was now relocated to Roland-Kerr further education college. 'You want to be out there, you want to be somewhere less safe,' Steven affirms. 'In the pilot we spent an awful lot of time in that room in Baker Street not knowing what John was up to, yet so much of the story is seen from John's point of view. So we were now able to show what John is doing, to see him desperately trying to rescue Sherlock. It made the climax a bigger event in the story.'

From 'The Problem of Thor Bridge'
by Sir Arthur Conan Doyle

A problem without a solution may interest the student, but can hardly fail to annoy the casual reader. Among these unfinished tales is that of Mr James Phillimore, who, stepping back into his own house to get his umbrella, was never more seen in this world.

From 'A Study in Scarlet"
by Sir Arthur Conan Doyle

[…] Across this bare space there was scrawled in blood-red letters a single word—
RACHE.
'What do you think of that?' cried the detective, with the air of a showman exhibiting his show. […] 'Why, it means that the writer was going to put the female name Rachel, but was disturbed before he or she had time to finish. You mark my words, when this case comes to be cleared up you will find that a woman named Rachel has something to do with it. It's all very well for you to laugh, Mr Sherlock Holmes. You may be very smart and clever, but the old hound is the best, when all is said and done.'
[…] 'Poison,' said Sherlock Holmes curtly, and strode off. 'One other thing, Lestrade,' he added, turning round at the door: '*Rache* is the German for "revenge"; so don't lose your time looking for Miss Rachel.'

From A Study in Pink
by Steven Moffat

SALLY
The body of Beth Davenport, Junior Minister for Transport, was found late last night on a building site in Greater London. Preliminary investigations suggest that this was suicide. We can confirm this apparent suicide closely resembles those of Sir Jeffrey Patterson and James Phillimore. In the light of this, these incidents are now being treated as linked. The investigation is on-going, but Detective Inspector Lestrade will take questions now.

From A Study in Pink by Steven Moffat

ANDERSON
She's German. [...] Rache is German for Revenge. She could be trying to tell us something.

[...] LESTRADE
She's German.

SHERLOCK
Of course, she's not German. [...] She must have a phone or an organiser - we can find out who Rachel is.

LESTRADE
She was writing Rachel?

SHERLOCK
No, she was leaving an angry note in German - of course she was writing Rachel. No other word it can be.

'Part of the denouement,' says Benedict, 'is Sherlock realising who it is that saved him, what that means to him, and what that means for their relationship. He starts to outline this steady shot, this military career man with morals, this man of pride and principles, and it smacks him in the face the minute he sees John that that's who is going to be his partner his chronicler and his friend. So it's a very big moment, and it comes out of him nearly convicting the guy who saved him.'

Martin agrees. 'That's probably the final cementing of the friendship that has developed throughout the episode. Sherlock now knows that John is a good ally and a force to be reckoned with in his own life.'

Steven reckons that this goes to the heart of their relationship. 'John Watson saves Sherlock Holmes's life in so many ways. Sherlock would have been a lonely freak and actually dead at the end of this episode if John had not come into his life. The story here is that Sherlock learns to value someone. At the beginning, Sherlock regards John as a kind of acquisition, a sort of pet who'll sit in the corner and do what he's told. To a degree there's an element of that throughout their relationship. John reminds Sherlock that he's mortal and that he's putting himself in danger.

'Which is how it should be,' says Mark. 'But John humanises Sherlock so much that you don't find him objectionable. He's a one-off, and he regards everyone else as stupid, even his best friend. But his friend can then become a wonderful touchstone for his brilliant mind, and provide a way of dealing with people for a man who doesn't even know how to say "good morning".'

'As it often is with blokes,' Steven says, 'once the friendship is in place, it never changes. Their relationship will be the same in twenty years; they just become immediately how they're going to be with each other for ever.'

'The combination of John and Sherlock is fascinating,' notes Benedict. 'One of the best achievements that Steven has got out of this script – and it's a truly moving one – is that by the end of the first episode they have a one-word modern male relationship. "Dinner?" "Starving." "There's a good Chinese..." That's very twenty-first century, that's very bachelor, that's very everyday, and yet it's really earned by the end of the episode, so you believe it and you believe that they will help each other through thick and thin.'

3

WRITE TIME, RIGHT PLACE

Codes and ciphers, from first draft to first filming...

'I SAID YOU KNEW SOME GOOD RESTAURANTS'

The original brief for writing *Sherlock* was to have as much fun as possible. Mark Gatiss and Steven Moffat have this schoolboy infatuation with Sherlock Holmes, and it's great for me, because there's two of them and there's three films each series, so I was invited to be part of a schoolboy gang.

'It's the Sherlock Holmes Club. So the brief was to have as much fun as possible in writing an adventure – not a thriller. Steven kept saying this to me: it's an adventure, and the more vivid and strange you can make the adventure, the better. So I was able to have people running across rooftops and fighting in a railway tunnel with crossbows, Chinese acrobats, people breaking into London banks by running up the sides of walls...

It's the sort of thing I will never get a chance to write anywhere else.'

Sherlock's second episode brought a new name to the writing team: Stephen Thompson. Steve has contributed scripts to several series, including *Doctor Who*, *Doctors*, *Silk*, and *Upstairs Downstairs*. He is also a prizewinning playwright – his first play, *Damages*, won the Meyer-Whitworth Award for new writing in 2004 – and it's thanks to his stage work that he first got his break into *Sherlock*. His second play was *Whipping It Up*, originally performed at London's Bush theatre in 2006, starring Richard Wilson and Robert Bathurst. *The Guardian*'s Michael Billington called it 'a pungent satire on the parliamentary whips' office', and commented: 'It is always good to see promise fulfilled.'

'Steven Moffat saw *Whipping It Up* when it transferred to the West End. We met afterwards and he invited me to dinner. Mark Gatiss was there, too. And – of course – we ended up talking about Sherlock Holmes, the original stories and all the film versions. When they then started talking about updating it, I had the usual reaction, to be honest: "Come off it!" But they asked me to write for it, which is a fantastic way to get a gig! And by the time they'd completed the pilot

HOLMES FROM HOLMES

From 'The Adventure of the Dancing Men'
by Sir Arthur Conan Doyle

'These hieroglyphics have evidently a meaning. If it is a purely arbitrary one, it may be impossible for us to solve it. If, on the other hand, it is systematic, I have no doubt that we shall get to the bottom of it. But this particular sample is so short that I can do nothing, and the facts which you have brought me are so indefinite that we have no basis for an investigation. I would suggest that you return to Norfolk, that you keep a keen lookout, and that you take an exact copy of any fresh dancing men which may appear. It is a thousand pities that we have not a reproduction of those which were done in chalk upon the window-sill. Make a discreet inquiry also as to any strangers in the neighbourhood. When you have collected some fresh evidence, come to me again.'

From 'The Blind Banker'
by Steve Thompson

```
                SHERLOCK
The world runs on codes and ciphers, John...
that million pound security system at the
bank... the pin machine you took exception
to... cryptography inhabits our every
waking moment [...] But it's all computer
generated. Electronic codes – electronic
ciphering methods. This is different: it's
an ancient device. Modern code-breaking
methods can't unravel it.
```

and showed that to me, I'd completely bought it.

'When we started, none of us truly knew how it was going to be. It takes a while to work out what a show will be. But Steven and Mark are terribly easy guys to work with. Most television requires an awful lot of consultation and collaboration, endless meetings... On *Sherlock*, the three of us sit around in restaurants chatting about stuff that we like! So there isn't a brief, as such (aside from the instruction to have fun with it) – we generally start out asking each other: "What's your favourite story?"'

For the first series, Steve's inspiration was 'The Adventure of the Dancing Men,' the third story in Conan Doyle's

The Return of Sherlock Holmes. 'I wanted to do "Dancing Men" because it's about a code, and I'm hugely interested in codebreaking. I'm a mathematician by background – I was a maths teacher until 2003 – and you don't get a lot of opportunities to write about it in drama. So *The Blind Banker* is about solving a code, and I was able to fill the script with numbers and data and patterns of codebreaking.'

The story gets going in what Steve's script calls one of 'the biggest banks in the land ... A gigantic cathedral of steel and glass – the most high-tech, swanky new building in the city', a set of modern imagery that's contrasted strongly with the story's Chinese Tong elements. 'Mark

---

DELETED SCENE

Sherlock Series One

The Blind Banker

1 <u>**INT. MUSEUM - ANTIQUITIES ROOM. DAY**</u>   1

                        SOO LIN
            The deposit left on the clay
            creates this beautiful patina,
            over time. Some pots - the clay
            has been burnished by tea made
            over four hundred years ago.

    A party of school children watching her. She offers
    the cup to a BOY. He takes it nervously and sips.

                        SOO LIN
            You drink from the pot
            that served Tan Lun himself.
            Great General of the Ming Dynasty.

Pretty much every element of set dressing must be sourced or created by the Art Department. Before they could deface it, they had to paint the portrait of Sir William Shad and devise the graffiti itself. Other original artwork designed by Arwel's team included CCTV computer displays and even the cheque paid to Sherlock by Shad Sanderson bank.

Sherlock Series One

The Blind Banker

5 EXT. EDDIE'S FLAT. NIGHT   5

Isle of Dogs. 1am.
A taxi pulls up outside an apartment block...
Plush city flats, each with a private balcony.
A man jumps out - EDDIE - early 30's, chalk
pin-stripe, red braces. He can only be a
banker. Throws a twenty at the DRIVER.

                    TAXI DRIVER
          You wanna receipt?

But EDDIE doesn't stop to reply. He's in a
blind panic. He rushes up to the apartments,
drenched in sweat, and punches the key pad.
Doors open. He bolts inside.

6 INT. EDDIE'S FLAT. NIGHT   6

Ping! The elevator doors slide open. 6th floor.
EDDIE rushes out, fumbles for his key and jams
it in the lock.

                    EDDIE
          Come on. Come on.

                              JUMP CUT TO:
Slams the door behind him, breathing fast.

                              JUMP CUT TO:
Bolts the door and puts the chain on. Dashes
around his flat, searching for something.

His flat is sparse - parchment-coloured walls;
a pristine kitchen. No furniture. The sterile
lifestyle of a City trader.

In the kitchen drawer he finds it!
A gun - 9mm, semiautomatic. He kisses it -
bathed in relief. And then he hears something
terrifying - In the distance - a drum. A
single rhythmic monotone. Tribal. Menacing.
Dashes into the bedroom.

                              JUMP CUT TO:
No bed. Just a mattress. A large pile of books
stacked in the corner. And a suitcase. The
window is open. Pale muslin curtains billow.
The drum still echoes out in the street. EDDIE
jams a chair against the door. He collapses on
the bed. The sound of the drum bores into his
brain - Blind terror.

suggested incorporating those, to give the episode a really strong visual flavour. I spent some time at the Fitzwilliam Museum in Cambridge, researching ancient Chinese artefacts, languages and number systems – investigating strange worlds you'd never explore under any other circumstances. That stage is a bit like cramming for an exam: I suddenly became an expert on antique earthenware teapots. The Circus and the circus acts, though, were just me having fun.'

With his research complete, Steve started writing. 'I write a draft and then Steven, Mark and I enjoy a series of long lunches with Sue Vertue, hacking through the script. It feels quite leisurely at that point. It's supposed to be quite a panicky process, but on *Sherlock* it's all rather "Shall we order dessert?" It's hugely collaborative, we're constantly swapping ideas, and we're shameless about stealing things from elsewhere. It's usually a bit of a giggle. Although we learned quite quickly to keep our voices down – when you're discussing the top-secret plots of *Doctor Who* or *Sherlock* in a restaurant, there's bound to be someone trying to listen in – it's all too easy to find that somebody's tweeted an entire plot!'

'The thing that riveted me about Sherlock Holmes,' says Steven Moffat, 'was, more than anything else, the deductions – they are so exciting. There is a brilliant sequence in *The Sign of Four* where he deduces a man's entire life just from looking at his pocket watch. We had a very similar sequence in *A Study in Pink*, using a mobile phone because that's the modern equivalent of a pocket watch, something that's on you all the time that would start to reflect your personality. Those deductions are extremely difficult to think of; it's a very, very hard part of writing *Sherlock*, and we spend ages on it, swapping ideas. Sue came up with a brilliant set of deductions for *The Blind Banker*: Sherlock glancing round Van

Coon's flat and realising the man is left-handed, just from the butter on the knife, the location of the tea stains on the armchair, the position of the notepad next to the phone...'

The gangsters in *The Blind Banker* communicate using a code, with symbols disguised as graffiti in strategic places around London. 'The code is a book code,' explains Steve Thompson. 'A book code is an old device, its hundreds of years old, people did write them. In a book code you specify two numbers that identify a specific page in the book and a specific word on that page. To decipher it, you have to know what book it is. So Sherlock eventually works out that it has to be a book everyone owns.

'I'll usually go through two or three drafts before the director comes on board, and there'll often then be another couple of drafts to deal with technical or budget requirements and so on. So we probably go through five or six drafts in total. It'd be easy to keep tweaking and rewriting for ever, but *Sherlock* is very tightly timetabled, because we need to work around things like Benedict and Martin's availability. So, as Steven often says, no script is ever properly finished – it's just transmitted.'

'IN LONDON FOR ONE NIGHT ONLY'

'T he usual rhythm,' says Steve Thompson, 'is I go for the first morning's filming then I leave. It's good manners to turn up and shake hands with everybody, and ask nervously if there are any script problems. It's really exciting but, as the writer, turning up can be a bit of a double-edged sword: you can get embroiled in lengthy discussions and quite often have to do rewrites on the spot. So I find it easier to be at the end of a phone, ready at the computer to make any revisions.

'But one thing does stand out whenever I do visit a location or studio – the London taxi drivers. You tell them where you're going, they ask what you do, and then they want to know what you've written that they might have seen. *Doctor Who*? 'Don't watch

it, mate.' *Upstairs Downstairs*? 'Not seen it, mate.' *Sherlock*? They go *wild* for *Sherlock*. It's more adoration than I've ever had! I'm struggling with a script for something else and they just don't care. But they love *Sherlock*. It's completely different in Cardiff – every show in the world is made there now, and everyone there is brilliantly blasé about television. Just about everybody has had a TV show filmed in their street: *Doctor Who*'s filming at one end, *Sherlock* at the other, and *Casualty* is filming at the ravine or the beach that all the other programmes are queueing up to use.'

As a BBC Cymru commission, the series is mostly filmed in Wales. The set builds, principally for 221B Baker Street, were in the BBC's Upper Boat Studios in Treforest Industrial Estate, north-west of Cardiff, although those facilities have now been closed down following the opening of the Roath Lock Studios in the BBC Drama Village in Cardiff's docklands.

'We try to do as much as possible in Wales,' Arwel Wyn Jones notes. 'But obviously with Sherlock Holmes being so tied in to London, there are certain elements we have to do in London. We could never con anyone into thinking Cardiff is London for some of the exterior streets, like Baker Street. We've tried to show London in a different way, but still you need those landmarks and that skyline, just to get the scale and the familiarity.' Having established that London setting, it's then easier for the team to make use of 'certain Cardiff

Sherlock Series One   The Blind Banker

7 **INT. LOCAL SUPERMARKET. DAY**   7

   JOHN in Tesco Extra buying groceries. Gets to
   the checkout. He runs his shopping through the
   self-service scanner. The electronic voice
   takes him step-by-step through the process.

                    ELECTRONIC VOICE
                 Please place your items
                 in the bag provided.

Sherlock Series One   The Blind Banker

15A **INT. 221B BAKER STREET. DAY**   15A
                    SHERLOCK
          In a manner of speaking. Took me
          less than a minute to guess yours.
          Not exactly Fort Knox.

                    JOHN
          You guessed my password!?

                    SHERLOCK
          There are forty-three.

                    JOHN
          What?

                    SHERLOCK
          Types of password. That people like
          you commonly use.

                    JOHN
          What does that mean? 'People like
          me'.

                    SHERLOCK
          Ordinary.

                    JOHN
          Stupid. Better change it.

                    SHERLOCK
          There's no point.

                    JOHN
          No. I suppose.

          SHERLOCK clicking on JOHN'S Blog page -

                    SHERLOCK
          I see you've started a blog -

                    JOHN
          (Suddenly wary) You - you read it?

                    SHERLOCK
          'Imperious'. Not a word I've
          ever been called before.

                    JOHN
          I said some nice stuff about you too -
          I said you knew some good restaurants.

                    SHERLOCK
          'Pompous' has a 'U' in it.

                    JOHN
          Right. Thank you.

          JOHN snatches the computer away and snaps it
          shut.

          JOHN collapses in the chair and examines   CUT TO:
          today's mail. Plenty of bills.

                    JOHN
          I need to get a job.

SHERLOCK S...
JOHN exploring the railway track...
There are a few homeless people on cardboard
beds. JOHN picks his way past them in the gloom,
trying not to look awkward.
JOHN ... you?

Sherlock Series One   The Blind Banker

70 **EXT. MUSEUM. NIGHT**   70

Coming out of the museum –

                    SHERLOCK
        We have to get to Soo Lin Yao –

                    JOHN
        If she's still alive! That cipher –
        it means he's planning to kill her next.

                    SHERLOCK
        That's why I found him in that flat
        – he was waiting for her.

A voice behind.

                    RAZ
        Sherlock!

They turn. RAZ is there – dirty hoody
and trainers.

                    JOHN
        Well, look who it is –

                    RAZ
        I've found something you'll like.

                    SHERLOCK
        They've been here. The exact same
        paint. John, go up on to the railway
        line. Look for that same colour. If
        we're going to decipher this language
        we're going to need more evidence.

                    JOHN
        Where are you gonna g – ?

Turns to RAZ – but the lad has gone again.

                    JOHN
        Could have predicted that.

74 **EXT. SOUTH BANK. NIGHT**   74

        JOHN exploring the railway tracks to the
        north. There are a few homeless people on
        cardboard beds. JOHN picks his way past them
        in the gloom, trying not to look awkward.

                    JOHN
        Er – 'Scuse, can I squeeze past you?

A HOMELESS GUY grunts – looks threatening.

                    HOMELESS GUY
        This is my place.

                    JOHN
        I just want to look at that wall –
        Can you move a little bit?

                    HOMELESS GUY
        Five pound.

                    JOHN
        What?

                    HOMELESS GUY
        You want me to move. Five pound.

                    JOHN
        OK.

JOHN digs into his pocket.

                    HOMELESS GUY
        Ten.

                    JOHN
        What happened to five?

                    HOMELESS GUY
        Too quick to say 'Yes'.

                                        CUT TO:
SHERLOCK continues south. The moon illuminates
graffiti – grey in the light.

109 **INT. HIDEOUT. NIGHT**   109

> JOHN
> Ah. Did I really say that? (Breath.
> She smiles) I s'pose there's no point in
> persuading you I was doing an impression –

She produces a small revolver and presses it
to JOHN'S temple. He squirms.

> THE OPERA SINGER
> Sherlock Holmes – you're my pin-up.
> Did you know?

Holds up her phone – shows him the photos
she has taken – dozens and dozens of photos
of JOHN.

> THE OPERA SINGER
> Your friend John writes a fascinating
> blog – I read it every day. I've made an
> intricate study of you. But you – you
> know nothing about your most devoted
> fan. (Breath) I am Shan.

Beat. JOHN stares at the diminutive woman.

> JOHN
> (Surprised, bewildered)
> You're Shan? 'The mountain'?

> THE OPERA SINGER
> (A silvery laugh) Shan is two words
> in Chinese. It also means 'The
> elegant'.

Surfs the internet on her phone.

> THE OPERA SINGER
> 'There is no puzzle, no enigma that
> my friend Sherlock cannot solve'.
> Let us put it to the test.

She cocks the trigger.

> THE OPERA SINGER
> (Light, gentle) Three times we've tried
> to kill you and your companion: the flat
> in Chinatown; the museum; tonight at the
> theatre. What does it tell you when an
> assassin cannot shoot straight?

> THE OPERA SINGER
> Blank bullets. Fired at the museum.
> And the fight in Soo Lin's flat – your
> companion was allowed to go free. If we
> wanted to kill you Mr Holmes we'd have
> done it by now. We just wanted to make
> you inquisitive. (Brandishing the gun)
> Nothing like firing a gun at someone –
> to make them think they're on the trail
> of something special. We haven't found
> what we seek, but no matter. Now we have
> our own sniffer dog. Sherlock Holmes.

She sniffs at him gently.

> THE OPERA SINGER
> The rat who gnaws at the tail of
> the cat only invites destruction.

> JOHN
> Proverb?

> THE OPERA SINGER
> (Beat. Her smile diminishing)
> Do you have it?

in London speaks volumes because silly little things like the lamp-posts and post boxes and taxis and red London buses send such vivid signals. The visual impact on the story of those few days in London is hugely important. Tower 42, in particular, was amazing – there's a huge drama to it in its size and scale. I'd written pages trying to describe this shiny modern building, and the location they chose was perfect.'

INT. **SHAD SANDERSON.**
DAY 18
SHERLOCK and JOHN inside. A vast high-tech atrium. **Glass lifts**; internal windows; multiple trading floors. All illuminated in bold colours – **reds** and **blues**. (Like Bloomberg's New York HQ – more like a nightclub than a bank.) Banks of **digital clocks** herald the time in New York, London and Tokyo. London hits 12pm; Hong Kong hits 8pm; New York hits 7am. Simultaneously. Employees wave their badges at electronic eyes. **Security doors** swing open. (You can't get to the lavatory here without a pass.)

JOHN
When you said we were going to the **bank...**

121 **INT. MUSEUM - ANTIQUITIES ROOM. DAY** 121

Chinese Antiquities Room. The mannequin of
the Empress in gold and black.

The MUSEUM DIRECTOR, SHERLOCK and JOHN stare
at her. The mannequin's costume has been
fashioned to resemble her exactly as she was
at her wedding - a thousand years ago. The
mannequin wears a plastic green reproduction
hair pin as part of the ensemble.

> MUSEUM DIRECTOR
> Empress Wu Zetian. Only woman to
> rule Imperial China. This costume
> is a mock-up of course. She lived
> fourteen hundred years ago. Nothing
> of hers has survived.

> SHERLOCK
> You're sure about that?

> MUSEUM DIRECTOR
> You hear rumours. The Chinese are alway
> uncovering new artefacts. Anything of
> hers would be worth - millions.

SHERLOCK produces the pin.

> SHERLOCK
> I wonder - could you find a place
> for this, somewhere in the display?

Out on the MUSEUM DIRECTOR, eyes wide.
She looks at the pin and immediately knows
its true value.

122 **INT. MUSEUM - ATRIUM/ENTRANCE. DAY** 122

SHERLOCK and JOHN leaving. ANDY waiting
for them by the exit.

> ANDY
> Almost the last thing she said to me -
> you have to look hard at something to
> see its value. I knew she was a sweet
> girl. But truly - I never knew how
> brave she was as well.

JOHN smiles sadly. Walks past. And then
comes back.

> JOHN
> That list of benefactors - on the
> gallery wall. What sort of donation
> would I need?

He hands ANDY the envelope from SEB.
ANDY opens it. His eyes widen.

> ANDY
> This would certainly cover it. What name?

> JOHN
> Three words.

> ANDY
> Of course. 'Holmes and Watson'.

> JOHN
> No. No.

123 **INT. MUSEUM. DAY** 123

Close-up of the wall of Benefactors.
"With grateful thanks for valuable donations
to the National Antiquities Museum - "
A sculptor is chiselling a new name into
the list. 'SOO LIN YA -'

Photographs taken by the director and location managers during their recces for *The Blind Banker*:
the National Museum of Wales, Cardiff (above and below left) and Swansea's Central Library (below right)

A Newport shop redressed as the Lucky Cat (top); and the Royal Bank of Scotland, Bishopsgate, London (above)

4

THE GAME IS ON

Directing and editing Holmes, and casting Moriarty

'THIS IS A FUN ONE...'

'It was terrifying to write *The Great Game*,' recalls Mark Gatiss. 'A terrifying challenge because it was the series finale.

'I had already written a 60-minute script which was going to be the second episode in the original conception. It was about a lost painting by Vermeer that Sherlock is convinced is fake. What took him an hour to figure out in that original format, I was able to telescope into ten minutes in the movie-length version. My favourite parts of that adventure could then happen in a very short period of time – you're just motoring along against a ticking clock.'

Another ticking clock meant that Mark's script for the Series One finale was the first to go into production, with Steven Moffat's opening episode being filmed last. At the helm for both stories was Paul McGuigan, the renowned director of award-winning movies like *Lucky Number Slevin*, *Gangster No. 1* and *Push*.

'I was working in Los Angeles, and my agent called to say that Mark Gatiss, Steven Moffat and Sue Vertue wanted to talk to me about a BBC show called *Sherlock*, so I went to meet them in London. They'd done the 60-minute pilot episode, but the series was now a run of 90-minute movies, so they wanted to reshoot the whole thing – would I be interested? I'd not really done television at that point; I'd done a pilot in the USA, but I'd mostly done films. They showed me the pilot, and we talked it through. I felt that 60 minutes wasn't really long enough: it's too short a format to delve into the characters and bring a sense of style to it. When you're doing a pilot, you want to introduce the characters, but you also want to tell a story. Sherlock's a very particular character to introduce, with all his little foibles and mannerisms, so you need time to do that but also to create a compelling story within that introductory episode. So the move to 90-minute versions was very important. And when I read the first scripts, it was a no-brainer.

'The gap between film and television has narrowed over recent years. We're now getting used to high-quality TV production, where before we used to make excuses for it. The two are now more equal in intent and cinematic ambition. The great thing about TV, though, is that you can tell longer stories and, of course, it attracts great writers. The film director is king – on television, it's the writer, so you have to get your head around that.

'I'd just come off a film where I was not happy with the writing. Sometimes in the movie world you feel you can make a script better as you go along, but I'd made a promise to myself that I'd only get involved with people when I was excited by the writing. So I was interested in coming to tell these stories on TV, and Mark, Steven and Sue were very encouraging of me bringing my cinematic sensibilities to the storytelling. My job was to bring it alive, to make it much more visual.'

Paul had been a big fan of the original Conan Doyle stories when he was younger, and now he set about getting to know them again. 'I bought every story, and I sat and read them aloud to my girlfriend. It was really interesting. What's good about Doyle is he knows when to pull the story tight. They're quite short, and usually nothing really happens until the last paragraph, then everything happens! I remembered as I read them again what I had imagined they would look like. Reading them, your imagination is much more powerful than any realisation on a screen, so it was important for me to tap into what I imagined the world to be and not to be to influenced by the movies or TV series that had gone before.'

Paul's input swiftly made itself felt as the series went into production. 'My first move, while Mark and Steven were still working on their scripts, was to get in touch with Arwel Wyn Jones, and we worked closely together redesigning 221B Baker Street [see pages 52–8]. I don't think anyone's instinct was to make 221B a loft or a modern flat – we weren't after minimalism or high-tech, we wanted familiarity. We all agreed the modernity should not be forced. I also did some

location-scouting in Cardiff, but Cardiff doesn't hold up that well for London – there's really only one street – so we made the decision to do quite a bit more of it in London. Sue and I went to London and scouted out where we'd shoot. They'd already shot Baker Street scenes in North Gower Street, and we decided to use more of that, and to open it up more. I liked the idea of seeing the scope of London – it's a big character in the piece, and I wanted to avoid it feeling insular.'

So work began on Mark's episode. 'Steven Moffat is notoriously the last one to hand any scripts in,' observes Paul, 'which is a smart move on his part. Doing Mark's story first, we didn't have to introduce everything straight away, so we could put our toe in the water. For Steven's first story, though, we had to be confident about who Sherlock was and how we were going to present it. In the first five minutes of *A Study in Pink*, we threw everything at it – Sherlock-vision, text, freeze-frame stuff, phone stuff, "wrong, wrong, wrong" at the press conference... I wanted people to relax after that and get the language of the show. So having done that and *The Great Game*, when we get to Series Two, we can

DELETED SCENE

3 **INT. LUCY'S HOUSE. NIGHT.**   3

A very tidy, slightly beige house. A young man, WESTIE, and his girlfriend LUCY are watching TV. Westie looks troubled, distracted,

                    LUCY
      It's all right. Honestly. I know it
      wasn't your thing. Next time we'll
      watch something with zombies.

                  WESTIE
      What? Oh. Yeah.

                  LUCY
      What is it, love? You've been funny all –

Westie gets up, goes to the window. Orange street light bleeds over his face.

             LUCY (CONT'D)
      What's the matter? Westie?

                  WESTIE
      Lucy, love. I've got to go out.

                  LUCY
      What?

                  WESTIE
      Got to see someone. It's important.
      Dead important.

                  LUCY
      You're kidding, aren't you? It's so late –

                  WESTIE
      I'll get a cab. Won't be long.

                  LUCY
      What? Who are you going to see?

                  WESTIE
      It can't wait. Sorry. Should've sorted
      it (ages ago) –

He shakes his head.

             WESTIE (CONT'D)
      Sorry.

He grabs his coat then dashes back and kisses her.

             WESTIE (CONT'D)
      Love you.

                  LUCY
      Westie!

                  WESTIE
      I won't be long.

And he's gone. The front door slams. She's alone. The TV blares on.

19 <u>**INT. BAKER STREET. KITCHEN-LAB. NIGHT.**</u>   **19**

SHERLOCK is bent over a microscope. Three
cups of cold tea stand next to him.

                    MRS HUDSON (O.S.)
            Don't know why I bother.

Sherlock doesn't look up from the microscope.
MRS HUDSON comes into view with a fresh cup on
a tray.

                    MRS HUDSON (CONT'D)
            I'm not your housekeeper.

Sherlock suddenly sits back, eyes glittering
with triumph.
                    SHERLOCK
            Poison.

                    MRS HUDSON
            (softening) I know. It's the caffeine.
            How about Camomile?

                    SHERLOCK
            Clever. Clever.

                    MRS HUDSON
            What are you on about?

JOHN enters. Sherlock looks up, thrilled.
                    SHERLOCK
            Clostridium botulinim. One of the
            deadliest poisons on earth!

47 <u>**INT. MANSION. DAY.**</u>   **47**

RAOUL brings in tea on a tray.

                    KENNY
            Thank you, Raoul.

The cat winds itself round Raoul's ankles.

                    KENNY (CONT'D)
            So will he be long, your photographer?
            I don't want to be rude but you'll have
            to be quick. I've got the funeral to
            arrange and all sorts...

                    JOHN
            Of course, of course. It'd be an
            interesting angle, that's all. "Connie's
            brother rebuilds life after tragedy".

                    KENNY
            Oh yes. I like that.

Doorbell rings.

                    RAOUL
            Excuse me.

                    JOHN
            That'll be him.

have Sherlock on a sofa in a field, and nobody questions it. You have to be brave and say to audience: This is our show.'

As Mark's draft scripts came through, Paul realised that there were 'a lot of scenes to do with phones and computers and so on. That was the most important turning point for us. I said, "I'll only do this if I can bring my own style to it." I was quite adamant that I wasn't going to shoot screens on phones – that'd be a total waste of my time, everyone knows what a phone screen looks like, and *Sherlock* should be so much more inventive. The first thing I came up with was how to let the audience into Sherlock's mind. So you first see the crime scene from a proscenium view. Then, when you see it again, when Sherlock's making his deductions, you see what he's seeing, which opens up the scene in a new way.

'So I worked on the methodology of that a lot, getting the writers and producers excited about the possibilities. That opened up their writing and allowed them to think about it in a different way as well. The realisation that a lot of the dramatic moments were said to a phone screen or a computer – which is *not* dramatic – pushed us towards the onscreen text idea. We knew there'd be no point putting text onscreen afterwards as an afterthought; we needed to actually frame it. So Steve Lawes, the Director of Photography, shot them in thirds of

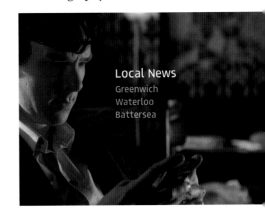

Local News
Greenwich
Waterloo
Battersea

frames: one-third Benedict or Martin, two-thirds space for the framing of the text. Text would also move within the environment so it felt like a deliberate thing, rather than something that was splattered on afterwards.

'I knew we had something special when I saw the final version of *A Study in Pink*, and watched that early scene when Lestrade comes bounding up the stairs to ask Sherlock, "Will you come?" In the first edit, the music used was quite dark. I turned round to Charlie Philips, the editor, and said: "We're making a big mistake here, because this *excites* Sherlock – we should make the music go against type. So we replaced it with this upbeat music. Rewatching it was great because we'd not seen a show before where death and murder become *exciting*. That was unexpected. Watching that later with a group of people, I thought, "This might do all right."

Charlie Phillips was the editor for five episodes of the first three series of *Sherlock*: *A Study in Pink*, *The Great Game*, *A Scandal in Belgravia*, *The Hounds of Baskerville* and *The Empty Hearse*. 'The rushes arrive daily,' he says. 'They arrive in the late afternoon but take all night to process, so I start working on them the following morning. Essentially, I'm working scene by scene as the episode is shot. I ask for the whole of the day's rushes in the order they were shot in. I then watch all of them in chronological order – I get to watch the day's events, and hear the little bits of chatter before and after the clapper board, and that's all very useful because you can see what's being changed as they develop each take. That means I get a clear idea of what it is they want. And I can use the information to cut closer to what the director actually wants, and assemble the scenes very quickly.

'Before *Sherlock*, I had never worked with Paul McGuigan, but I had worked with Sue Vertue on a number of occasions, and she wanted me to do it. I'd done a couple of comedies with her, and I had come in to do the visual effects for a couple of episodes of Steven Moffat's *Jekyll*, which were an early concept of what we went on to do on *Sherlock*. So Paul interviewed me and, in that first interview, I began to get some understanding of what he was going to try and do. Mostly he was talking about the idea that we could get a much deeper insight into what Sherlock was seeing by revisiting it in his

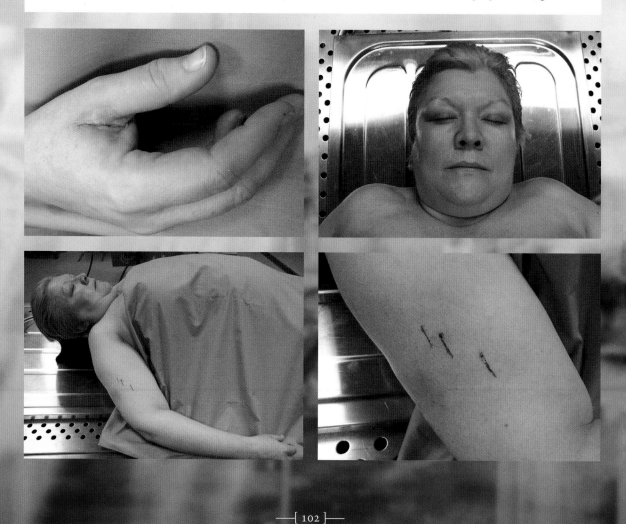

description to John of what was going on. He talked about using a stills camera to get details that would flash onto the screen and be a Sherlock's eye view on what we'd just seen.

'The first time that happened was in *The Great Game*, when we got a detailed look at Connie Prince's body on the slab in the morgue. When I look back at that, it's not quite as refined as other sequences that we've made since because we were designing it as we went. *The Great Game* was the first episode that was shot and therefore the first that was edited, and that was the point at which we came up with a lot of the stylistic ideas that we thought would work. Paul's Director of Photography, Steve Lawes, had a phone app that could join images

together to make a film, and he'd taken some pictures of one of the clapper loaders, walking round them and taking film. He'd got this stop-motion thing going on, and he asked if I could do something like that if I was given the stills. Absolutely I could, because I was already aware that you could take stills and then load them into the editing software and create a moving image. So they took stills and I stuck them in and manipulated the speed at which they went. You could gradually ramp up the speed of something and then freeze it at the pertinent moment. While they were shooting, Paul would come in every now and then to see what I was working on, and that meant he could go away and shoot something that would

work better, and we gradually built it like that – backwards and forwards, me working on the rushes, and him saying, "It'd be good if we shot it like this..." They were early successes, where we could see that something was really going to work well.

'The script for *The Great Game* required people to see and understand the texts that were passing between John and Mycroft and Sherlock – we'd have needed about thirty-five close-ups of mobile phones held in hands with the correct text on the screen. And Paul hates cutting to something out of nowhere in close-up just to tell the story. He desperately needs things to appear organically, to pan to them, to zoom to them across the screen in a natural way, and

there was no way to make that look elegant with all these mobile phones. And so he just rejected the idea of showing texts on phones. They had been shooting for about two weeks when I asked him when we were going to get these shots – because I was cutting and assembling the scenes and the shots were all missing – and he said we weren't going to do that: "Let's just put it on the screen." And I was slightly horrified…

'The first one I did was when John is in the dead security guard's flat, and he receives a text from Mycroft. Paul had got this shot of Martin Freeman in the flat with this beautiful bit of Arwel Wyn Jones wallpaper next to him, and it was a lovely bit of framing with Martin to one side and the wallpaper dominating the right-hand side of the screen. And I thought, what if I put the text on the wallpaper – John pulls his

phone out and the text appears there – so you understand that the text isn't actually on the wallpaper, it's in John's head, but it's an organic part of the scene, following Paul's style. And then as John puts his phone away he walks in front of the text so that he wipes it out, if you like. And then, as we cut wide, I made the text smaller on the wall.

'Then I started doing different things: I hung the text in the air, and tracked it onto movement in the camera – a movement of John's arm, say – so it tracked the image and looked like it was there in the frame and wasn't just stuck on top. These all worked really well and began to seem like a style. And Paul began to shoot stuff where he knew we could put text in. A classic one is John sitting in his bedroom, reading a text that Sherlock has sent – Paul actually shot that with

space to put the text quite large behind John.

'At the same time, we began to investigate transitions from one image to another. I began to look at ways of tracking bits of image and wiping them in, or using wipes to introduce bits of incoming image into an outgoing image. So the texts and those wipes developed at the same time. I just used one font. I always assumed that what I did would be recreated like everything else I do in the offline edit; I couldn't produce full-quality stuff. I felt that we were designing the style of it, and I didn't want that to be messed with. So we brought in Peter Anderson Studio to make the text and give it a unified typeface.

'I then had enormous fun with Paul, adding text to Sherlock's initial investigation of the woman's corpse in *A Study in*

Pink. Paul had this pole camera – a camera on a kind of crane – which he'd lifted up through the floor into the room. That gave us a flow of transitions that we could match the text to – circular round her ring, and so on. How we displayed the text became quite critical, so I made sure that the online editor, Scott Hinchcliffe at Prime Focus, knew this had to be copied precisely. It wasn't just a guideline, it was exactly what we wanted. Scott was the ideal person – he recreated everything I did, and some of it was incredibly complicated.

'Sometimes I was building extra picture around the original picture so that I could move it without revealing the black edges of the screen, and that allowed me to track it in to another image.

'Similarly, my sound is generally quite complete. The scene in the Planetarium where the machinery starts rewinding and flashing – I did all the sound for that, the rewind noise, the fast-forward noise, using plugins in the editing software. And then I gave it to Bang Audio in Cardiff: "Sorry, you have to recreate *this*."'

When the first episode of *Sherlock* was broadcast, viewers and critics were impressed by the novelty of the appearance and style of the text, and the way it succinctly contributes to telling the story. But it's not widely understood that it was developed in an edit suite; a lot of people assume that it was developed afterwards as a visual effect. 'That would be impossible,' declares Charlie.

'You couldn't get that integrated storytelling from VFX if you did them afterwards; the process has to be that it's done in the edit, and then it's finished off. And in fact, more was done in this edit because I have a history as an online, finishing editor, doing text and visual effects and pictures flying around, before I became an offline, storytelling editor. I never leave that to visual effects; in some form, I always do it myself, and as close as possible to the end result I want. Which means that anyone who works with me finds that it's less a creative process on their part and more of a *recreative* process, recreating what I've done faithfully.

'For me, it's one of the best things to have worked on at that time in my life. I was ready for it.'

HOLMES FROM HOLMES

From 'The Adventure of the Bruce-Partington Plans'
by Sir Arthur Conan Doyle

'I have it,' I cried, and plunged among the litter of papers upon the sofa. 'Yes, yes, here he is, sure enough! Cadogen West was the young man who was found dead on the Underground on Tuesday morning.'

Holmes sat up at attention, his pipe halfway to his lips.

'This must be serious, Watson. A death which has caused my brother to alter his habits can be no ordinary one. What in the world can he have to do with it? The case was featureless as I remember it. The young man had apparently fallen out of the train and killed himself. He had not been robbed, and there was no particular reason to suspect violence. Is that not so?'

From 'The Great Game'
by Mark Gatiss

```
                    MYCROFT
(holds up some documents)
Andrew West. Known as 'Westie' to his
friends. Civil servant. Found dead on
the rails at Battersea station this
morning. Head smashed in.

                    JOHN
Jumped in front of a train?

                    MYCROFT
That seems the logical assumption.

                    JOHN
But?

                    MYCROFT
But?

                    JOHN
Well, you wouldn't be here if
it was just an accident.
```

'I also enjoyed the scene where they chase the taxi across London in *A Study in Pink*: this big chase, only about four lines – how are we going to do this in just one night? I was proud that we'd already set up this language while we were making *The Great Game* so we could do things that were quite unusual. The idea was to do it through Sherlock's mind: he could work out where the stop signs were, the one-way streets, the signs. So I went out on my own with a 5-D camera, and I shot all the signs, and I shot all these weird angles. And then on that one night we just got the guys to run the whole night –

"Just keep running! I'll cut it together!" – through Soho. That scene has the correct impact, good storytelling impact, and it brings together all the elements: storytelling, great acting, action, onscreen text, peeking inside Sherlock's mind, showing the audience what he thinks and how he thinks and how quickly he thinks – giving him superhuman powers, almost. I'm pleased by that – if we hadn't got that right, the audience would have felt cheated. They were excited by his intellect, they understood it. Sometimes intellect in movies is smoke-and-mirrors – "He sounds like he's clever, but I don't actually see him being clever." To see it is very satisfying on film. Charlie and I spent quite a bit of time putting that together in the edit suite.

'In filmmaking, they say that twenty per cent of what you shoot won't end up in the movie. On such a tight schedule and with a television budget, even a good one, you can't really afford to have days making *Sherlock* where you're not using everything. We try to make it as tight as possible. We all talk through the scripts many times – in restaurants mainly (and then forget what we said about it and have to go back and do it again). Once it's all

From 'The Adventure of the Bruce-Partington Plans'
by Sir Arthur Conan Doyle

'What were the technical papers?'

'Ah, there's the point! Fortunately, it has not come out. The press would be furious if it did. The papers which this wretched youth had in his pocket were the plans of the Bruce-Partington submarine.'

Mycroft Holmes spoke with a solemnity which showed his sense of the importance of the subject. His brother and I sat expectant.

'Surely you have heard of it? I thought everyone had heard of it.'

'Only as a name.'

'Its importance can hardly be exaggerated. It has been the most jealously guarded of all government secrets. You may take it from me that naval warfare becomes impossible within the radius of a Bruce-Partington's operation. Two years ago a very large sum was smuggled through the Estimates and was expended in acquiring a monopoly of the invention. Every effort has been made to keep the secret. The plans, which are exceedingly intricate, comprising some thirty separate patents, each essential to the working of the whole, are kept in an elaborate safe in a confidential office adjoining the arsenal, with burglar-proof doors and windows. Under no conceivable circumstances were the plans to be taken from the office. If the chief constructor of the Navy desired to consult them, even he was forced to go to the Woolwich office for the purpose. And yet here we find them in the pocket of a dead junior clerk in the heart of London. From an official point of view it's simply awful.'

'But you have recovered them?'

'No, Sherlock, no! That's the pinch. We have not. Ten papers were taken from Woolwich. There were seven in the pocket of Cadogan West. The three most essential are gone—stolen, vanished. You must drop everything, Sherlock. Never mind your usual petty puzzles of the police-court. It's a vital international problem that you have to solve. Why did Cadogan West take the papers, where are the missing ones, how did he die, how came his body where it was found, how can the evil be set right? Find an answer to all these questions, and you will have done good service for your country.'

'Why do you not solve it yourself, Mycroft? You can see as far as I.'

'Possibly, Sherlock. But it is a question of getting details. Give me your details, and from an armchair I will return you an excellent expert opinion. But to run here and run there, to cross-question railway guards, and lie on my face with a lens to my eye—it is not my metier. No, you are the one man who can clear the matter up. If you have a fancy to see your name in the next honours list—'

From The Great Game
by Mark Gatiss

MYCROFT
The Ministry of Defence has been working on a new missile defence system. The Bruce-Partington Program, it's called. And the plans for it were on a memory stick.

JOHN
That wasn't very clever.

MYCROFT
(withering) It's not the only copy. But it is secret. And missing.

JOHN
(delighted) Top secret?

MYCROFT
Very. We think West must've taken the memory stick and we can't possibly risk it falling into the wrong hands. You've got to find those plans, Sherlock. Don't make me order you.

SHERLOCK
Like to see you try.

Silence.

MYCROFT
Think it over.

Mycroft winces slightly, touches his jaw, then takes John's hand again.

MYCROFT (CONT'D)
Good bye, John. (pointed) See you very soon.

shot and we're editing, a couple of scenes might be edited out, simply because they *should* go. Mark and Steven understand that better than anybody – they're total masters at it. They understand Sherlock Holmes so well, and they also know the structure of television very well. You learn a lot from them because they doesn't waste things, and they're very conscious of the time we have to do it in, so they don't feel that their characters have to have big soliloquys. Sherlock does have ten-page scenes, but they become the powerhouse scenes, every sentence is used and there's a rhythm to it. Sometimes we get scripts that feel a little long, but I'll fight to keep them that long because I know that people want to hear Sherlock talking a lot, and they're fascinated by how this man speaks and the rhythm he speaks in. We try to get Benedict Cumberbatch to learn the lines really fast, so the connection between the writers and Benedict is really important. Benedict has been able to translate Steven and Mark's words in such a way that they're just impulsive and it feels like he's not reading it. That's what ultimately makes it very streamlined.

'I'm also very proud of Martin Freeman's work. Dr Watson is a part that's never been realised properly, it's always been the bumbling idiot. I was very proud of how he did that. John Watson, to me, is the harder role, and I think Martin's performance makes that show. A problem we had when we first presented it to the BBC was we were introducing a lead character who's not a very nice man, who says inappropriate things, who's a bit self-obsessed and has a superiority complex – factors that make someone you don't really want to watch. The BBC were worried he might be too unpleasant. Our reply was that Martin is playing a character who is basically us watching Sherlock. So when Sherlock says something really stupid and dumb,

'These are the only photos taken during Series One of me as Mycroft, as it was all secret!' reveals Mark Gatiss.

Mark Gatiss   Born 17 October 1966, Sedgefield

SELECTED FILM ROLES

2015	Frankenstein Dettweiler
	Our Kind of Traitor Billy Matlock
2006	Starter for 10 Bamber Gascoigne
2005	The League of Gentlemen's Apocalypse
	Various characters
2003	Bright Young Things Estate agent

SELECTED TV ROLES

2014	Game of Thrones Tycho Nestoris
2012	Inspector George Gently Stephen Groves
	Being Human Mr Snow
2011	The Crimson Petal and the White
	Henry Rackham Junior
	Doctor Who Gantok
2010–2014	Sherlock Mycroft Holmes
2010	The First Men in the Moon Professor Cavor
	Worried About the Boy Malcolm MacLaren
	Midsomer Murders Rev Giles Shawcross
2009	Agatha Christie's Poirot Leonard Boynton
2008	Sense and Sensibility John Dashwood
	Crooked House Curator
	Psychoville Jason Griffin

2007	Jekyll Robert Louis Stevenson
	Doctor Who Professor Lazarus
	The Wind in the Willows Ratty
2006	Fear of Fanny Johnnie Cradock
2005	Funland Ambrose Chapfel
	The Quatermass Experiment John Patterson
2004	Agatha Christie's Marple Ronald Hawes
	Catterick Peter
2003–2005	Nighty Night Glenn Bulb
1999–2002	The League of Gentlemen Various characters
2001	Randall & Hopkirk (Deceased) Inspector Large
	Spaced Agent

SELECTED STAGE ROLES

2013	Coriolanus
2012	55 Days
	The Recruiting Officer
2010	Season's Greetings
2007	All About My Mother
2005	The League Of Gentlemen Are Behind You
2003	Art
2001	The League Of Gentlemen

Andrew Scott   Born 21 October 1976, Churchtown, Dublin, Ireland

AWARDS

Actor in a Supporting Role for *Sherlock* (IFTA Award, 2013)
Best Supporting Actor in a Drama Series
  for *Sherlock* (British Academy Television Award, 2012)
Outstanding Achievement in an Affiliate Theatre for
  A Girl in a Car with a Man (Laurence Olivier Award, 2005)

Theatregoers' Choice Award for *Aristocrats* (2005)
Best Actor for *Dead Bodies* (IFTA Award, 2003)

SELECTED FILM ROLES

2014	**Jimmy's Hall** Father Seamus
	Pride Gethin
	Locke Donal
2013	**The Stag** Davin
2012	**Sea Wall** Alex
2010	**Silent Things** Jake
	Chasing Cotards Hart Elliot-Hinwood
2009	**Anton Chekhov's** The Duel Laevsky
2003	**Dead Bodies** Tommy McGann
2001	**I Was the Cigarette Girl** Tim
2000	**Nora** Michael Bodkin
1998	**The Tale of Sweety Barrett** Danny
	Saving Private Ryan Soldier on the Beach
1997	**Drinking Crude** Paul
1995	**Korea** Eamonn Doyle

SELECTED TV ROLES

2010–2014	**Sherlock** Jim Moriarty
2013	**Dates** Christian
2012	**The Town** Mark Nicholas
	The Scapegoat Paul
	Blackout Dalien Bevan
2011	**The Hour** Adam Le Ray
2010	**Garrow's Law** Captain Jones
	Lennon Naked Paul McCartney
	Foyle's War James Devereux
2008	**Little White Lie** Barry
	John Adams Colonel William Smith
2007	**Nuclear Secrets** Andrei Sakarov
2005	**The Quatermass Experiment** Vernon
2004	**My Life in Film** Jones
2001	**Band of Brothers** Private John 'Cowboy' Hall

SELECTED STAGE ROLES

2011	**Emperor and Galilean**
2010	**Cock**
	Design for Living
2008	**Sea Wall**
2006	**The Vertical Hour**
	Dying City
2005	**A Girl in a Car with a Man**
	Aristocrats

John can tell him he's out of order. The audience is saying that at exactly the same time – so they get to have a voice through John. You can allow Sherlock to be the character that he is because you have the voice of the audience, and as a viewer you trust Martin to say the appropriate thing at the appropriate time.

'And that's the fun of the characters – the chemistry between the two, the writing, the understanding that John Watson has to say those things when we feel Sherlock has gone too far – that's what makes that show. That's what I'm most proud of. Seeing John become a character you really care for, because he *is* the audience.'

'I GAVE YOU MY NUMBER. THOUGHT YOU MIGHT CALL'

hen Paul joined the production, the two leads were in place as were most of the regular supporting cast. There was one vital piece of casting still to do, though. 'I was there for Andrew Scott's audition. I think it helps when the director's really excited, and I was really excited. Moriarty could so easily have been a moustache-twirling baddie, and that would have been totally wrong for the show…'

'Moriarty hadn't really been formed, aside from a notion that he would be somewhere in the background and that Sherlock would begrudgingly respect this person but we wouldn't know, until he said his name, who he was…' recalls Mark Gatiss. 'The idea was that when we got to the end of our first run of 60-minute episodes, Sherlock would have had a suspicion that there was someone behind a lot of the cases – not all of them – but an organising intelligence. Then, somewhere towards the end, he would meet him, and not know who he was. There were earlier versions of *The Great Game* where they

M_ THEY CANNOT TRACE THIS BACK TO ME

would swap email addresses and all you'd see would be "Oh, its JimMoriarty@gmail.com", and that's where it would end. As soon as we knew we were doing three 90-minute episodes, we had to have the debate about deferring pleasure: to what extent do you tease things out? With a miniseries of three films, we were suddenly aiming for a larger grandeur. So we decided to bring him in for *The Great Game*, after teasing hints of him in the previous stories.'

'There are lots of different interpretations of Moriarty, and I decided to look at none of them,' says Andrew Scott. 'I knew a little bit about Moriarty from the books, but when my agent first rang me about Moriarty I didn't really know what their take on him was going to be.

'As an actor, there's a certain amount of secrets that the character has to have in order to make them who they are. I suppose I'm the only person who has to feel that Moriarty is not a villain. I can't play the villainy of the man; I have to look at him as a proper human being. I have a sort of interior map of what his back story is, but I won't share it. I think there is a very dangerous reduction that can happen if you start to talk about the back story of a character – part of the reason Moriarty is so frightening is that you don't know what his background is. Because Moriarty is the prototype for an awful lot of literary villains, I had to begin again with just the essence of him, using those really brilliant scripts. I look at what's dark inside of me, rather than try and do an imitation of what someone else has done. So you see his vulnerable side and his youthful side.

'I think it really works that Benedict

[handwritten margin notes, partially legible] ...you will soon get the clearest fact of all. The bodies cannot... Try the cellars and the garden. It should not take long to...

HOLMES FROM HOLMES

From 'The Adventure of the Musgrave Ritual'
by Sir Arthur Conan Doyle

An anomaly which often struck me in the character of my friend Sherlock Holmes was that, although in his methods of thought he was the neatest and most methodical of mankind, and although also he affected a certain quiet primness of dress, he was none the less in his personal habits one of the most untidy men that ever drove a fellow-lodger to distraction. Not that I am in the least conventional in that respect myself. The rough-and-tumble work in Afghanistan, coming on the top of natural Bohemianism of disposition, has made me rather more lax than befits a medical man. But with me there is a limit, and when I find a man who keeps his cigars in the coal-scuttle, his tobacco in the toe end of a Persian slipper, and his unanswered correspondence transfixed by a jack-knife into the very centre of his wooden mantelpiece, then I begin to give myself virtuous airs. I have always held, too, that pistol practice should be distinctly an open-air pastime; and when Holmes, in one of his queer humours, would sit in an armchair with his hair-trigger and a hundred Boxer cartridges and proceed to adorn the opposite wall with a patriotic V. R. done in bullet-pocks, I felt strongly that neither the atmosphere nor the appearance of our room was improved by it.

From 'The Five Orange Pips'
by Sir Arthur Conan Doyle

Holmes turned over the leaves of the book upon his knee. 'Here it is,' said he presently:

'Ku Klux Klan. A name derived from the fanciful resemblance to the sound produced by cocking a rifle. This terrible secret society was formed by some ex-Confederate soldiers in the Southern states after the Civil War, and it rapidly formed local branches in different parts of the country, notably in Tennessee, Louisiana, the Carolinas, Georgia, and Florida. Its power was used for political purposes, principally for the terrorising of the negro voters and the murdering and driving from the country of those who were opposed to its views. Its outrages were usually preceded by a warning sent to the marked man in some fantastic but generally recognised shape — a sprig of oak-leaves in some parts, melon seeds or orange pips in others. On receiving this the victim might either openly abjure his former ways, or might fly from the country. If he braved the matter out, death would unfailingly come upon him, and usually in some strange and unforeseen manner. So perfect was the organisation of the society, and so systematic its methods, that there is hardly a case upon record where any man succeeded in braving it with impunity, or in which any of its outrages were traced home to the perpetrators.'

From 'The Great Game'
by Mark Gatiss

BANG! BANG! BANG! Three gunshots. SHERLOCK's letting fly at the wall with a revolver. He's drawn a 'smiley face' on the wall and it now has bullet holes for eyes and a mouth. The door flies open and JOHN tumbles inside. Back from a night out.

JOHN
What the hell are you doing?!

SHERLOCK
Bored.

JOHN
What?

SHERLOCK
Bored –

Bang!
SHERLOCK (CONT'D)
Bored –

Bang!
SHERLOCK (CONT'D)
Bored. I don't know what's got into the criminal classes. It's a good job I'm not one of them.

JOHN
So you take it out on the wall?

SHERLOCK
The wall had it coming.

From 'The Great Game'
by Mark Gatiss

PHONE VOICE
You have one new message.

They listen, rapt. From the phone: Beep. Beep. Beep. Beep. Beep.

JOHN
That's it?

Close on the phone: a photo is downloading.

SHERLOCK
No, that's not it.

Close on the photo: the inside of a bare, empty flat.

LESTRADE
What the hell are we supposed to make of that? An estate agent's photo and the bloody Greenwich pips!

Beat.

SHERLOCK
(grave) It's a warning.

JOHN
A warning?

Sherlock grabs the phone from Lestrade.

SHERLOCK
(realising) Some secret societies used to send dried Melon seeds. Orange pips. Things like that. Five pips! They're warning us that it's going to happen again.

and I are of the same age, and it also helps that the audience weren't too familiar with my face before. At first, some people thought, "No, I do not want Moriarty to be like this," but you just have to have the courage of your convictions: this is the way we are doing it. If you have that confidence, the audience can become quite unsettled by the character. So I have to believe that this is a person who is aesthetic and sensitive and has all those qualities to him, and you can hint at those things in the way that he dresses and the way he deals with other people. We shouldn't know what he has for breakfast or if he was damaged as a child or that kind of thing; I don't think it helps anybody. But one of my favourite

scenes to film was in the courtroom in *The Reichenbach Fall*, when the guard had to take chewing gum out of Moriarty's pocket. That gave a real insight into his playfulness and his sexuality. It was a great way to portray him, because we see him so little and we rarely see him with anybody else. So I had this little moment with one of the supporting artists, talking her through this quite intimate encounter.

'What happened, extraordinarily, was that the show was an immediate success, and not just in terms of ratings and critical response – people had an instant affection for the show, which I don't think any of us had experienced before. It usually takes a long time for a show to seep into

From 'A Study in Scarlet'
by Sir Arthur Conan Doyle

His ignorance was as remarkable as his knowledge. Of contemporary literature, philosophy and politics he appeared to know next to nothing. Upon my quoting Thomas Carlyle, he inquired in the naivest way who he might be and what he had done. My surprise reached a climax, however, when I found incidentally that he was ignorant of the Copernican Theory and of the composition of the Solar System. That any civilised human being in this nineteenth century should not be aware that the Earth travelled round the Sun appeared to be to me such an extraordinary fact that I could hardly realise it.

'You appear to be astonished,' he said, smiling at my expression of surprise. 'Now that I do know it I shall do my best to forget it.'

'To forget it!'

'You see,' he explained, 'I consider that a man's brain originally is like a little empty attic, and you have to stock it with such furniture as you choose. A fool takes in all the lumber of every sort that he comes across, so that the knowledge which might be useful to him gets crowded out, or at best is jumbled up with a lot of other things so that he has a difficulty in laying his hands upon it. Now the skilful workman is very careful indeed as to what he takes into his brain-attic. He will have nothing but the tools which may help him in doing his work, but of these he has a large assortment, and all in the most perfect order. It is a mistake to think that that little room has elastic walls and can distend to any extent. Depend upon it there comes a time when for every addition of knowledge you forget something that you knew before. It is of the highest importance, therefore, not to have useless facts elbowing out the useful ones.'

'But the Solar System!' I protested.

'What the deuce is it to me?' he interrupted impatiently; 'you say that we go round the Sun. If we went round the Moon it would not make a pennyworth of difference to me or to my work.'

From 'The Great Game'
by Mark Gatiss

SHERLOCK
Flattered? (reads from blog) 'Sherlock sees right through everyone and everything in seconds. What's incredible, though is how spectacularly ignorant he is about some things.'

JOHN
Hang on, I didn't mean –

SHERLOCK
What, you meant 'spectacularly ignorant' in a nice way? Look, it doesn't matter to me who's Prime Minister. Or who's sleeping with who –

JOHN
Or that the Earth goes round the Sun?

SHERLOCK
Oh that again. It's not important.

JOHN
Not important! It's primary school stuff! How can you not know that?

SHERLOCK
If I ever did, I've deleted it.

JOHN
Deleted it?

SHERLOCK
Listen –

He jabs a bony finger to his temple.

SHERLOCK (CONT'D)
THIS is my hard drive. Only makes sense to put stuff in there that's useful. Really useful. Ordinary people fill their brains with all kinds of rubbish. And then it's impossible to get at the stuff that matters. You follow?

JOHN
But it's the Solar System – !

SHERLOCK
What the hell does that matter? So we go around the Sun! If we went round the Moon or... round and round the garden like a teddy bear it wouldn't make any difference. All that matters is the work. Without it, my brain rots. Put that in your blog. Or, better still, stop inflicting your opinions on the world.

the audience's hearts. But by the time *The Great Game* came out, people were talking about *Sherlock*, it had these huge audience figures, everybody loved it, and that was after only two episodes. I was terrified that I was going to mess it up at the end when Moriarty makes his appearance in the last ten minutes. So my job was to try and surprise the audience. You wouldn't necessarily associate somebody like me with villainous qualities, certainly at that time. I think people were disarmed by that.

'When *The Great Game* was first broadcast, I was rehearsing a play at the Old Vic, and I wasn't able, of course, to tell anybody that I was in it. People were coming in, as all actors do, talking about *Sherlock*: "Did you see it? It's great. It's fantastic." And I had to pretend that I hadn't really watched it. Then I came in on the Monday, and Maggie McCarthy, who is a wonderful British actress, came in and was saying, "You're... Moriarty... What?! What?!" It was wonderful to see an actor who was a real enthusiast be so thrilled.

'There was a great sense of storytelling to that episode – who is it going to be, what is he going to be like... They had written a temporary scene for audition purposes. I was in a play at the time, and I was about to go on stage, and I got an email with this temporary script for the next day. And it was this extraordinary, fantastic dialogue that ended up being the swimming pool scene at the end of *The Great Game*, which was Moriarty's first proper entrance in the series.

'"I will burn the *heart* out of you": that seemed to be such a horrible image. It's very important, with a line like that, you feel that the way somebody looks doesn't necessarily reflect their interior life. I wanted the audience to feel that – whatever they were thinking about me – they weren't to feel comfortable at any stage.'

'I used to live in Bedminster,' says Mark Gatiss, 'about five minutes away from the swimming pool we used at the end of *The Great Game*. I used to swim in that pool. If this was a ropey biopic of my life, you wouldn't believe things like that: here I am swimming in this pool in Bristol in 1991, and one day we're doing *Sherlock* here... Ridiculous.'

A selection of shots from the location recce for *The Great Game*: Battersea Train Depot, London (opposite bottom right); the Thames shoreline in London (top right); Oxo Tower, London (above)

On set and filming the bombing of Baker Street (above); part of the set dressing for Connie and Kenny Prince's house (below left); the set for the 'lost Vermeer' exhibition (opposite, top left) and the painting itself (opposite below)

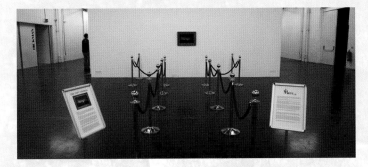

Sherlock Episode 3				
FX Cut Down Draft		03/12/2009	Construction	Props
No	**Scene**			
	3 x shots & 2 bloodbags			40
85	INT. BAKER STREET. DAY.			
	John's Laptop			
	Breakfast			
86	EXT. BAKER STREET. DAY.			
87	EXT. CORNER SHOP. DAY.			
	Carton of milk & repeats (Beans ?)			
88	INT. BAKER STREET. HALL. DAY.			
89	INT. BAKER STREET. DAY.			
	Computer graphics			
90	EXT. BAKER STREET. DAY.			
	Translight			
91	EXT. POLICE STATION. MEXICO. DAY.		500	
	Snow			
92	INT. POLICE STATION. CELL. MEXICO. DAY.			

Sherlock Episode 3				
Draft 8		01/01/2010	Construction	Props
No	**Scene**			
	Office furniture			100
	Lighting			50
	Strong box			400
	German envelope			
	i phone			
	Wilting pot plants			
13	EXT. BAKER STREET. DAY.			0
	Cab			
	Intercom			
14	EXT. BAKER STREET REAR. DAY.			
	Rusty Bell			5
	Paint Finish			

Crew schedules for *The Great Game* (above)

5

IT'S THE NEW SEXY

Scandals and supporting players...

'BOYS! YOU'VE GOT ANOTHER ONE!'

'Nobody cared,' declares Paul McGuigan. 'When we were shooting the first series in Wales and London, we were just another film crew out on the streets. Nobody knew who Benedict Cumberbatch was.'

That was in January to April of 2010. A little over a year later, in May 2011, Series Two began production in the wake of *Sherlock*'s enormous success on transmission in July and August 2010, and it instantly brought several new challenges. 'That's when "second album syndrome" hit us,' says Paul. 'Making the second series, after such massive success, you're actually worried by that success – you're hoping not just to match it but to top it. And, of course, it's only three episodes, so they're going to be much more intensely scrutinised. In America, you'll make a series of 23 episodes; and here we are making just three – it's a big ask for them all to be equally as good as each other. And it's actually three whole *movies*, each one shot in just 22 days. That's against the 65 days I had shooting

Victor Frankenstein, for example. Movies have other things they have to do, of course: more scope, more extras, more money. More demand on you for every shot to be cinematic. As much as *Sherlock*'s cinematic, you still have the constraints of doing more than one scene a day. Some days we were doing seven or eight pages because Benedict has so much dialogue. That's a lot to cover in one day.'

Challenge number two was the sudden arrival at location shoots of squads of onlooking fans. 'You do worry when you see that in the street,' admits Paul. 'From an actor's point of view, it's difficult, and for me, as director, it can also be quite tricky to have loads of people around. The *Sherlock* fans were very well-behaved, though, incredibly respectful.'

The series opener was, once again, the last into production for the year. Having established the show's visual language, the whole team was keen to keep exploring new ideas, notably in the couple of scenes that merged the characters (and furniture) from a studio set with flashbacks to an exterior location, as Sherlock and Irene Adler deduce how the hitchhiker's death came about. Inspired by the 'Sherlock-vision' techniques Paul had pioneered on the first series, Steven Moffat's script called for a stylised, dreamlike

Every episode has a scene-by-scene breakdown detailing… everything!

presentation of these scenes. Paul wanted to go even further…

'My five-dollar trick: the bed,' smiles Paul. 'I come from a very photographic background. I'd done it once in a music video, and I decided to do it again. We did it for real with a pneumatic half a bed, made up by Danny Hargreaves and his special effects team. It was really very simple. The best ideas are simple. Because we now have the visual language, as a director I can be quite creative with my solutions. Which also feeds the writers, so, when we did *Scandal*, Steven had now opened up his head with all the texts and all that stuff, and we challenge each other now. He'll say, "I'm going to give you this big scene with an aeroplane." Yeah, we can do that! So that's another great visual layer of storytelling which we didn't have when we started. And we have two layers now: we've got Sherlock's unique vision but we also have the textual interpretation of that.'

Now **FLASHBACKING** to the earlier scene, but in **SHERLOCK VISION**. PHIL is at the wheel of his car, trying to start his car – he's in **freeze-frame**.

Now SHERLOCK walks past Phil (**in reality**, still swanning about Irene's room talking to her, but **visually** now walking among the flashback.)

Over at with HIKER, also **frozen**. He's standing, seemingly **staring** at the sky

And SHERLOCK steps from **behind** FROZEN HIKER. (Again still really swanning about Irene's room, but **stitched into** the flashback.)

We cut to Irene, still sitting on the **sofa** – but now the sofa is SITTING IN THE MIDDLE OF THE **FIELD**. Beyond her, we can see Phil in the car.

This time it's SHERLOCK, not Phil, sitting at the wheel. He looks a little **dazed**, confused. The image is slightly, **twisted**, distorted – **dreamy**. And where Sherlock swanned past last time, this time it's **IRENE**.

SHERLOCK
I… I don't…

Closer on Irene – now more **stylised**, she's surrounded by **darkness**.

IRENE ADLER
Hush now, it's okay. (Kissing his cheek) I'm only returning your coat.

'WE SEE ALL THE BRAKES JAM ON IN HIS BRAIN'

I think Sherlock's biggest fear is loss of control,' observes Benedict Cumberbatch. 'There are two instances in Series Two: one in *The Hounds of Baskerville* with the poisonous fog, and the other in *A Scandal in Belgravia* when Irene Adler drugs him. It's his worst fear because he becomes utterly subjugated, he's at someone else's disposal and the horror for him, coming round, is not knowing what has happened and what he has done. I love playing scenes where he loses control. There's something very thrilling for an audience in seeing the character's

Sherlock Series Two
A Scandal in Belgravia

1 **INT. SWIMMING POOL – NIGHT**   1

                    SHERLOCK
          (Looking to the phone) Did somebody
          make you a better offer?

                    JIM
          Oh, don't you worry, we'll find the
          right moment. Because we've got a
          problem to solve together, you and I.
          Do you know what it is?

                    SHERLOCK
          I'm fascinated.

                    JIM
          The big one. The best one. The final
          problem. And the funny thing is, I've
          already told you all about it. You'll be
          hearing from me, Sherlock – but not for
          a while.

     And he turns on his heel and just walks away.
     Talking on his phone.

                    JIM
          If you have what you say you have,
          I will make you rich. If you don't,
          I will make you into shoes...

assuredness having its edges knocked off. When Irene Adler anaesthetises him, I was really keen to have that play as a weakness, as something that made him vulnerable and tied in with the drug addiction issues, because the best way to go with this character is to evolve him and continually explore what his blind spots are. When Sherlock shows human weakness and an ability or inability to learn, I think we can truly care about him.'

A Scandal in Belgravia is also renowned for a couple of very revealing scenes. 'The scenes in Buckingham Palace are fantastic,' says Benedict, 'because they're the first to really shine a light on the domestic life of Mycroft and Sherlock, and begin to explore the idea that these brothers weren't just freshly hatched super-brains, they did have a family and a home and a background. When Mycroft comes in, they're like two giggling schoolchildren, and we see their whole childhood in a nutshell. It's great to have the crystallisation of that relationship played out in the absurd circumstances of Sherlock wrapped in a sheet in the middle of Buckingham Palace.'

The opening minutes of *A Scandal in Belgravia*, of course, had to resolve Series One's cliffhanger ending, which meant returning to Bristol South Swimming Pool in Bedminster – more than twelve months after *Sherlock* had first filmed there. The building housing the 30-metre pool was constructed in 1931 and is Grade II listed, which English Heritage defines as 'nationally important and of special interest'. That protects the architecture and fabric. It doesn't, however, stop Bristol Council redecorating…

'We'd not really changed anything at that location when we made *The Great Game*,' recalls Arwel Wyn Jones. 'The posters and so on were already there, and we left them in place during the shoot. Then we went back a year later for the Series Two recce and discovered that they'd given the whole place a complete makeover. The posters were gone, the walls had been painted… So we had to change everything to match *The Great Game*, recreate all the posters and decorations [below], and then restore it all at the end of filming.' That unexpected task was not helped by the fact that the production team had no reference photos: 'We didn't take any shots of the pool scene in the first series as we wanted to keep Moriarty's identity a secret.'

DELETED SCENES

7   INT. BARTS CORRIDOR - DAY   7

SHERLOCK and JOHN heading along the corridor
towards us, SALLY DONOVAN leading the way. A YOUNG
OFFICER passes in the opposite direction.

            YOUNG OFFICER
      (To John) Loved The Geek Interpreter.

            SALLY DONONVAN
      Yeah, that was a good one.

44   INT. BUCKINGHAM PALACE - GRAND ROOM - DAY   44

            MYCROFT
      Naturally not. They all spy on people
      for money.

            SHERLOCK
      Fair point.

            JOHN
      But it's Sherlock you want - what am I
      doing here?

            THE EQUERRY
      I did wonder myself, Mycroft.

            MYCROFT
      My baby brother is a genius in his chosen
      field. But in this case, we need a genius
      with a conscience - which, typically, my
      brother has outsourced.

            JOHN
      Oh, great. I'm Jiminy Cricket.

The Holmes brothers both laugh - a rare moment
of bonding.

            MYCROFT
      Actually, that rather works.

            SHERLOCK
      It does, doesn't it?

            THE EQUERRY
      (Sharply) I do think we have a timetable.

            MYCROFT
      Of course, yes.

He has taken an ENVELOPE from his CASE, now slides
a PHOTOGRAPH from it. He passes it to Sherlock.

            MYCROFT
      What do you know about this woman?

46   INT. BUCKINGHAM PALACE - GRAND ROOM - DAY   46

On SHERLOCK as he now flicks the photo around
for JOHN, as if trying it out on him. John,
sipping his tea, almost misses.

            SHERLOCK
      - but she's clearly very attractive. John,
      you might want to dab your shirt front.
      Who is she?

And then there's The Woman... 'Irene Alder knows how to use her place in the world and her status as a woman to get what she wants. She is brilliant and, like Sherlock, she has a capacity for a very calculated use of love, affection, sexuality, charm and intellect. She dupes Sherlock, and he does fall for her, to a degree, during the game of love that they play. But, he is fully aware of what that game is, and he starts to monitor it from quite early on. That's very clear from the first moment he meets her, not at least because he scans her and he can't find anything that is readable in her naked form.'

For the first time ever, we see all **the brakes jam on** in his brain as he just **stares**. Because IRENE ADLER is standing in front of him, entirely **naked**. (NB. This shot for pre-watershed. We know she is naked but we don't see anything. Like Sherlock, we always manage to **avert our eyes**.)

'What's wonderful about the first time they meet,' says Lara Pulver, 'is that the infamous Sherlock Holmes arrives disguised as a vicar, and she decides to call his bluff. She throws him off his game by wearing her "battle dress". And that makes for such a lovely moment when, for the first time, Sherlock can't decipher anything about another person. Which intrigues and attracts him.

'It wasn't a particularly tricky scene to shoot. We were down to a skeleton crew, and Paul McGuigan was extremely

respectful in the sense that we knew we weren't showing anything and we knew that's not the reason why the scene even existed. So it was just a case of shooting it in a very specific way so that we couldn't see anything. And, six hours later, we got it!'

'It didn't take that long,' recalls Paul. 'I said to Lara, "This could take us all day or it could take an hour and a half – it's up to you." When I first read the script, it was one of those "How the hell do we do this?" scenes. It made me really nervous, I was losing sleep at night, not because of the nudity but because I'd seen all these really cheesy ways of doing nude scenes. I had images of cream buns with little cherries on the top, a saxophone playing... It's hard to get that out of your head. I still hadn't worked it out when I went on set that day. I knew that I wanted to do something that felt more organic than hiding behind cream buns! I had to rely on Lara having faith in me to shoot it in the right way. I told the cameraman to just avoid seeing anything – that's a much easier direction than "You've got to get behind the cream bun by this line." It means the actors aren't restricted and the camera's not restricted in its movement. It just relies on Lara saying, "OK, I'm going to be naked." She was very brave and she helped a lot with that scene. She knew where the camera was so she was aware of the camera as much as we were aware of avoiding her. From the first take, we knew this was the proper way of doing it because we got a lot of coverage. It's very seamless, it just dances along, and it doesn't feel like it's dictated by the nudity but by the drama, which is much more important.'

Inevitably, the UK press got more hot and bothered than the cast and crew. 'BBC under fire for raunchy pre-watershed scenes,' insisted one paper, under the snappy headline 'Sherlock and the case of nudity before 9pm'.

'It's a **mystery** that Sherlock Holmes himself might struggle to solve – how could the **BBC** think that these scenes were appropriate for a **pre-watershed** audience?'

Three people had complained about the scene on Twitter, the paper revealed, leaving the BBC reeling once again and prompting much soul-searching at Hartswood Films... 'What was most amusing,' comments Sue Vertue, 'was the fact that the papers printed all the pictures that they were saying there were complaints about. And, of course, we had checked every moment, frame by frame, and you never actually see anything. Lara was amazingly brave, and quite stunning in it.'

'THERE ARE MANY NAMES FOR WHAT SHE DOES'

'We were discussing casting for Irene Adler,' Sue says. 'We didn't know Lara at all, but her agent wanted her to audition, so we sent her the script. She made a tape, which we watched and gave some notes on, and then she came over to audition face to face.'

'I'd just finished shooting another BBC series,' remembers Lara, 'and I was on the plane back to Los Angeles, which is where I live. I was reading the *Sherlock* script on the plane, I just thought, "Turn this plane around because I want to go back and audition for this role!" When I got back home, I immediately put two or three scenes down on tape and sent them over. Hartswood came back with a lovely response, saying, "Could you fly over so

Lara Pulver Born 1 September 1980, Southend-on-Sea, Essex

SELECTED FILM ROLES

2014	Edge of Tomorrow	Karen Lord
2011	Language of a Broken Heart	Violet
2010	Legacy: Black Ops	Diane Shaw

SELECTED TV ROLES

2014	Fleming	Ann O'Neill
2013–2014	Da Vinci's Demons	Clarice Orsini
2013	Skins	Victoria
2012–2014	Sherlock	Irene Adler
2012	Coming up	Annette
2011	Spooks	Erin Watts
2010–2012	True Blood	Claudine Crane
2010	The Special Relationship	Intern
2009	Robin Hood	Isabella

SELECTED STAGE ROLES

2014	Gypsy
2012	Uncle Vanya
2008	Parade
2006	The Last Five Years

Part of the gang: Lara Pulver joins Steven Moffat and Mark Gatiss at the BAFTAs.

we could meet you?" I'd just done a ten-and-a-half-hour journey and, as much as I wanted to jump back on a plane, I knew there was no way it would be to my advantage. So I spoke to the casting director, Kate Rhodes James, and she said that Mark, Steven and Sue wanted to give me a few notes. I said, "Can I be cheeky and ask you to give me the notes – I'll use the fact that I'm eight hours behind you to re-do the tape. Then, if I'm still in the ball park, let me know and I'll get on a plane first thing tomorrow." I got a call at seven o'clock the next morning asking me to get back on a plane. So within 72 hours I turned around, came back to London, Benedict, Steven, Sue, everyone, and it was suddenly a reality. And I did a lovely session with Benedict, reading a few scenes, and we got on really well. The following morning I heard that the job's was mine and the read-through was on the next Monday. I remember turning up for the read-through and Martin had just won a BAFTA and the show had been Emmy-nominated, and everyone's confidence and enthusiasm for *Sherlock* was infectious. When I walked into the room, I just knew that I was going to have the best five weeks of my life.

'The main challenge of playing Irene Adler was for you to understand why she does the things she does. She isn't just manipulative, she isn't just selfish, she isn't just a complete narcissist. She's actually a bit dysfunctional and a bit lost and, at times, she's vulnerable. So it was interesting for me to decide when that very strong and powerful mask could slip. You never quite know whether Sherlock or Irene means what they say, because for either of them to risk being honest would also risk being vulnerable. The scene where I'm inviting him to dinner and taking his hand but he's actually testing for my pulse – that's a very intimate moment and yet you can never quite tell whether it's sincere, whether it's playful, whether it's teasing, whether it's manipulative. Then you have the moment where he deciphers the code which is probably the most honest

moment between them. And which she quickly recovers from, saying she was just playing the game…

'Each of the women in Sherlock's life obviously serves a story purpose, but what they all have in common is that they love him. If you think about Molly, Mrs Hudson, Irene Adler – they're all absolutely fascinated by and accepting of this very damaged, dysfunctional man.'

DELETED SCENES

52 **INT. BUCKINGHAM PALACE – GRAND ROOM – DAY**   52

                SHERLOCK
Hardly a difficult deduction. Photographs of whom?

                THE EQUERRY
A person of significance to my employer.

                SHERLOCK
Family member, friend, distant relative...?

                THE EQUERRY
We prefer not be more specific at this time.

                SHERLOCK
Anonymous client, anonymous victim – would it help if I investigated wearing a blindfold?

                JOHN
You can't tell us anything?

                MYCROFT
I can tell you, it's a young person. (Hesitates) A young female person.

                SHERLOCK
... John, you probably want to keep that cup in the saucer now.

John has had the cup frozen half-way to his mouth. He now delicately sets it down.

                THE EQUERRY
It is our opinion that should these photographs come to light, they would have a catastrophic effect on the establishment you see around you. Can you help us, Mr Holmes?

                SHERLOCK
How?

66 **INT. IRENE'S BEDROOM – DAY**   66

                KATE
What are you going to wear?

                IRENE ADLER
My battledress.

                KATE
Lucky boy.

We hear the doorbell ring.

                KATE
Is that him?

                IRENE ADLER
Got to be.

                KATE
Ringing the doorbell? Does he think we'll just let him in?

                IRENE ADLER
He must think he's got a way of persuading us. Go and see what it is.

From 'A Scandal in Bohemia'
by Sir Arthur Conan Doyle

'The facts are briefly these: Some five years ago, during a lengthy visit to Warsaw, I made the acquaintance of the well-known adventuress, Irene Adler. The name is no doubt familiar to you.'

[...] 'Let me see!' said Holmes. 'Hum! Born in New Jersey in the year 1858. Contralto – hum! La Scala, hum! Prima donna Imperial Opera of Warsaw – yes! Retired from operatic stage – ha! Living in London – quite so! Your Majesty, as I understand, became entangled with this young person, wrote her some compromising letters, and is now desirous of getting those letters back.'

'Precisely so. But how—'

'Was there a secret marriage?'

'None.'

'No legal papers or certificates?'

'None.'

'Then I fail to follow your Majesty. If this young person should produce her letters for blackmailing or other purposes, how is she to prove their authenticity?'

'There is the writing.'

'Pooh, pooh! Forgery.'

'My private note-paper.'

'Stolen.'

'My own seal.'

'Imitated.'

'My photograph.'

'Bought.'

'We were both in the photograph.'

'Oh, dear! That is very bad! Your Majesty has indeed committed an indiscretion.'

'I was mad – insane.'

'You have compromised yourself seriously.'

'I was only Crown Prince then. I was young. I am but thirty now.'

'It must be recovered.'

'We have tried and failed.'

'Your Majesty must pay. It must be bought.'

'She will not sell.'

From A Scandal in Belgravia
by Steven Moffat

THE EQUERRY
My employer has a... problem.

MYCROFT
A matter has come to light of an extremely delicate, and potentially criminal nature – and in this hour of need, dear brother, your name has arisen. [...]

He has taken an ENVELOPE from his CASE, now slides a PHOTOGRAPH from it. He passes it to Sherlock.

MYCROFT
What do you know about this woman?

On the photograph – a headshot of a stunningly beautiful woman. [...]

SHERLOCK
Nothing whatsoever. [...] Who is she? [...]

MYCROFT
Irene Adler. Professionally known as the Woman.

JOHN
Professionally?

MYCROFT
There are many names for what she does – she prefers dominatrix. [...] She provides, you might say, recreational scolding to those enjoy that sort of thing, and are prepared to pay for it.

[...] On Sherlock's face. He frowns in distaste, puts the sheets face down on the table.

SHERLOCK
I assume this Adler woman has some compromising photographs.

THE EQUERRY
You're very quick, Mr Holmes.

SHERLOCK
Hardly a difficult deduction. Photographs of whom?

THE EQUERRY
A person of significance to my employer. [...]

SHERLOCK
How many photographs?

MYCROFT
A considerable number, apparently.

SHERLOCK
Do Miss Adler and this young female person appear in the photographs together?

MYCROFT
Yes, they do.

SHERLOCK
I assume in a variety of compromising scenarios.

MYCROFT
An imaginative range, we're assured.

A silence. They digest. [...]

THE EQUERRY
It is our opinion that should these photographs come to light, they would have a catastrophic effect on the establishment you see around you. Can you help us, Mr. Holmes?

SHERLOCK
How?

THE EQUERRY
Will you take the case?

SHERLOCK
What case? Pay her. Now, and in full. As Miss Adler remarks on her masthead – know when you are beaten.

'MISS HOOPER BURSTS INTO TEARS AND RUNS OUT OF THE ROOM'

'When they wrote Irene Adler into the series, there were all sorts of arguments in the press about whether she should have been portrayed as she was – whether she should have had her bum out or whatever. I'm not really interested in any of that,' laughs Louise Brealey, *Sherlock*'s Molly Hooper. 'What was interesting for me was the idea of the contrast between The Woman and the other women in the show. Lara is a great beauty and she's ravishing in *Sherlock*. Irene Adler is a bit of a male fantasy: she's a slash of red lips, flawless skin, beautiful, symmetrical features, wonderful cat eyes... And little Molly, she's a mouse. She's your mate, watching *Sherlock* on the sofa with you. She's just ordinary, which is great!

'I think Molly was originally intended to just be a little, funny, sweet turn. I didn't know at the time but they intended her to be in the first episode only. And something worked on screen between Benedict and myself and between the viewer and Molly, so they decided that she would stay. I don't think the intention was to create a new regular character for *Sherlock*, but the character grew. So you can draw a line for Molly's growth through the series and how important she becomes in the second season. It feels that she grows in a really organic way.'

Sue Vertue confirms this. 'Molly was brought in on the first episode of the first series as a means for the lipstick joke, really, and wasn't supposed to stay at all. But we loved Loo Brealey and what she did with it, and Steven and Mark enjoy writing for her. And so she's the first regular that isn't in any of the original stories.

'There's a very important relationship between her and Sherlock. He trusts

From The Hound of the Baskervilles
by Sir Arthur Conan Doyle

'I must thank you,' said Sherlock Holmes, 'for calling my attention to a case which certainly presents some features of interest. I had observed some newspaper comment at the time, but I was exceedingly preoccupied by that little affair of the Vatican cameos, and in my anxiety to oblige the Pope I lost touch with several interesting English cases. This article, you say, contains all the public facts?'

```
                  From 'A Scandal in Belgravia'
                          by Steven Moffat

 - Sherlock, a frown, a flicker of thought, gets
it - now reaching for safe door -

                          SHERLOCK
                     Vatican cameos!

On John, hearing that, recognising the words -
what?
```

From 'The Adventure of the Greek Interpreter'
by Sir Arthur Conan Doyle

'… For many years I have been the chief Greek interpreter in London, and my name is very well known in the hotels.'

```
               From A Scandal in Belgravia
                      by Steven Moffat

John typing away at his computer, Sherlock
looking grumpily over his shoulder.

                      SHERLOCK
            The Geek Interpreter. What's that?
```

her, and she takes the time to try and understand him. She's obviously deeply in love with him but she moves on to a point across the three series. She realises they're not going to end up together, but she moves on with a boyfriend that looks pretty much identical to Sherlock. She's a very strong character now, though, and she's much stronger in Series Three than she was before.'

Louise thinks that Molly allows the audience to see a side of Sherlock that might not be seen without her. 'Series Two is very much about Sherlock's humanity – he is a good deal more recognisably human by the end, and Molly is important in that journey. The first time we ever hear him say "I'm sorry" is to Molly, to which Martin Freeman does a wonderful double take. Just as there is through John Watson, there is a way in for the audience through Molly. I think you get something of Sherlock through her.'

SHERLOCK

… the fact that she's seeing him tonight is evident from her **make-up** and **clothing**. She's obviously trying to compensate for the size of her mouth and breasts –

As he speaks he's picked up the parcel, taken a look –

– and now **freeze** in the closest he gets to **embarrassment**. The label says Sherlock. An aching silence. Everyone avoiding looking at anyone – cos everyone saw this **train crash** coming.

Finally: On Molly – so discomforted, almost **tearful**.

MOLLY

You always say such **horrible** things. Every time, you're just **so mean**, always, always…

Train crash now getting worse. No one can even look at Sherlock now. On Sherlock: and even he – perhaps for the first time ever – is **getting it**. He glances round to the others – no help there – and is about to step away… but no. **He can do better!** He almost has to brace himself, but …

SHERLOCK

I'm sorry. **Forgive me**.

John, Mrs Hudson, Lestrade – just staring. What? That's new, what??

Louise Brealey

Born 27 March 1979, Bozeat, Northamptonshire

SELECTED FILM ROLES

2013	Delicious	Stella
2011	The Best Exotic Marigold Hotel	Hairdresser
2010	Reuniting the Rubins	Miri Rubins

SELECTED TV ROLES

2014	Ripper Street	Dr Amelia Frayn
2013	Father Brown	Eleanor Knight
2012	The Charles Dickens Show	Nelly Trent / Scrooge / Tiny Tim
2011	Law & Order: UK	Joanne Vickery
2010–2014	Sherlock	Molly Hooper
2008	Hotel Babylon	Chloe McCourt
2007	Green	Abi
2006	Mayo	Scene-of-Crime Officer Harriet 'Anorak' Tate
2005	The English Harem	Suzy
	Bleak House	Judy Smallwood
2002–2004	Casualty	Roxanne Bird

SELECTED STAGE ROLES

2014	Miss Julie
2012	The Trojan Women
	Birthday
2011	Government Inspector
2008	Uncle Vanya
2007	Little Nell
2006	After the End
2005	Arcadia
2001	Sliding with Suzanne

'It's not necessarily the comedy of cruelty,' Louise goes on. 'although there is a little bit of that. My job in *A Study in Pink* was to tell the story of an ordinary girl who is in love with him but has no way of expressing it. She doesn't know how to be the woman that he might respond to. She does it her own little way and asks him for a coffee with her lipstick on. I can see how that might make people smile, because there is a sense in which it can be quite hard to ask somebody for anything if you feel like there is a lot at stake.

'Benedict is ridiculously talented at giving those two levels of machine and man. The first time I saw him playing Sherlock was at the read-through for the

pilot. He and Martin were at the head of the table, and they just started, there was no fanfare. And there was immediately something in the room because of their chemistry – everyone's eyes were wide, there was something really special happening. Benedict is wonderful to work with, and a lot of my scenes are just with him, and it's really nice working so intimately. He'll try different things on different takes, he's very bold. That's a confident actor – unconfident actors will do the same thing over and over with maybe a tiny adjustment because they're afraid of what might end up in the edit. Benedict does this whole shebang of different stuff, and then they find it in the edit.

'MRS HUDSON LEAVE BAKER STREET? ENGLAND WOULD FALL'

'In the original stories, of course, Sherlock Holmes and Dr Watson had a housekeeper who was also the landlady, who used to deliver muffins and moved in and out and never did very much but was just a sort of hugely put upon servant,' notes Steven Moffat. 'That sort of thing doesn't really exist now, so in *Sherlock* they have a landlady but – in keeping with the original – they treat her like a housekeeper. They just constantly expect her to turn up with food and look after them. So she is in a genuinely maternal role but she is also fond of pointing out from time to time that she's not actually their housekeeper, she's the owner of the flat they live in.'

Mrs Hudson pipes up from the kitchen.

MRS HUDSON
It's a **disgrace**, sending your little brother into danger like that. **Family's** all we have in the end, Mycroft Holmes!

MYCROFT
Oh, **shut up**, Mrs Hudson!

SHERLOCK	JOHN
(Outraged)	(Outraged)
Mycroft!	Oi!

Two indignant stares, and Mycroft realises he's **crossed a line**.

MYCROFT
(To Mrs Hudson)
Apologies.

MRS HUDSON
Thank you!

SHERLOCK
Though do, in fact, **shut up**.

'She's the most verbose Mrs Hudson there's ever been,' Sue thinks. 'She knows her own mind, she won't accept bad manners... And Sherlock and John obviously think the world of her. When they're talking about moving her out of 221B in *Scandal*, Sherlock isn't having

Una Stubbs Born 1 May 1937, Welwyn Garden City, Hertfordshire

SELECTED FILM ROLES

2007	Angel	Miss Dawson
1969	Till Death Us Do Part	Rita
1967	Mister Ten Per Cent	Lady Dorothea
1965	Three Hats for Lisa	Flora
1964	Wonderful Life	Barbara
	The Bargee	Bridesmaid
1963	Summer Holiday	Sandy

SELECTED TV ROLES

2013	The Tractate Middoth	Miss Chambers
	Starlings	Molly
	Coming Up	Cynthia
2012	National Theatre Live	Mrs Alexander
2011	The Bleak Old Shop of Stuff	Aunt Good Spelling
2010–2014	Sherlock	Mrs Hudson
2009	Ingenious	Gransha
	Benidorm	Diana Weedon
2007–2009	Mist: Sheepdog Tales	Fern
2006	Agatha Christie's Marple: Sleeping Murder	Edith Pagett
	EastEnders	Caroline Bishop
2005	The Catherine Tate Show	Carole-Ann and Ursula
2004	Von Trapped	Kath Moogan
2003	Born and Bred	Joy
2000	Casualty Joan	Bannville
1998–2000	The Worst Witch	Miss Bat
1998	Midsomer Murders	Selina Jennings
1996	Wings the Legacy	Fay
	Delta Wave	Gilly Pigeon
1995–1997	Heartbeat	Anthea Cowley
1995	Keeping Up Appearances	Mrs Moody
1989	Tricky Business	Mrs Breeze
	Morris Minor's Marvellous Motors	Mrs Plugg
1987–1989	Worzel Gummidge Down Under	Aunt Sally
1985-1986	In Sickness and in Health	Rita
1985	Happy Families	Mother Superior
1981	Till Death...	Rita
1979–1981	Worzel Gummidge	Aunt Sally
1979	Fawlty Towers	Alice
1971	The Rivals of Sherlock Holmes	Katie Harris
1966–1974	Till Death Us Do Part	Rita
1960	The Strange World of Gurney Slade	Girl in park

SELECTED STAGE ROLES

2012	Emil and the Detectives
	The Curious Incident of the Dog in the Night-Time
2005	Pillars of the Community
2004	Don Carlos
2001	Star Quality
1986	The Secret Life of Cartoons
1977	Oh Mr Porter
1972	Cowardy Custard

any of it. At all. They protect her fiercely. And she's a hugely important character to the show now.'

Lara Pulver is admiring of what Una Stubbs brings to the part. 'There's a couple of moments where Sherlock is just as rude to Mrs Hudson as he would be to a complete stranger, and you see the pain that it causes her because she cares so much about this man. I love the humour of her opening her fridge every day to find God knows what in there, and her acceptance that "that's Sherlock". So she's a character that helps us love a man who we should actually find really quite unlovable. There's a wonderfully *parental* relationship between Mrs Hudson and Sherlock.'

Sherlock has stepped forward to Mrs Hudson. Gently he pushes one of her sleeves up – **blotches** on her arm. Finger marks where she's been **tightly gripped**. Now his fingers go to where there's **a rip** in her blouse – he's almost tender. She's been **roughed up** – and now she's **shaking** like a leaf.

NEILSON
I've been asking this one – she doesn't seem to know anything. But you know what I'm asking for, don't you, Mr Holmes?

Sherlock's gaze slams on to Neilson – a stare like **cold blue lasers**.

SHERLOCK
I believe I do.

On Neilson – and now words start swirling round him. CAROTID ARTERY. RIBS. SKULL. LUNGS. EYES. THROAT. The word ARTERY appears over several areas on his body. Sherlock Holmes, choosing a **target**.

'I'M ON HOLIDAY WOULD YOU BELIEVE?'

'Sherlock regards Lestrade as an idiot,' Steven declares, 'but we see very quickly that Lestrade's a clever man and an extremely good copper. He's clever enough to know when someone is cleverer than him. There's a line in the original Sherlock Holmes stories where Watson observes that mediocrity recognises nothing higher than itself and talent recognises genius; Lestrade is the talent that recognises the genius and he's prepared to put up with being insulted and demeaned by Sherlock to get to the solution. When there's a crime that's beyond him, he is smart enough to know when he is out of his class, and very few people are that smart.'

'Lestrade's a good policeman,' says Sue Vertue. Even without Sherlock, he'd be a very good policeman. In a way, he becomes a sort of minder to Sherlock. He will always run to Sherlock when he's in trouble, but he will also turn up when Sherlock's in trouble. He's the one who understands Sherlock. And Rupert Graves puts the heart into Lestrade. During the Christmas scene in *A Scandal in Belgravia*, when Sherlock tells him that his wife's still seeing the PE teacher, Rupert shows everything in Lestrade's face. You watch him realising that she's still having an affair when he thought everything was fine – it's all there in his performance.

Mark agrees. 'We really wanted to get away from the idea of the police being stupid, which can be done an awful lot – in the old films, Inspector Lestrade has no brains at all! Our point is that Lestrade is the best Scotland Yard has to offer, but he's not Sherlock Holmes. In the original stories, Lestrade frequently says words to the effect of "It's a good job you're on the side of the angels, Mr Holmes"...'

Rupert Graves
Born 30 June 1963, Western-super-Mare, Somerset

AWARDS

Outer Critics Circle **Special Award** for *Closer* (1999)
Best Actor for *Intimate Relations* (Montreal World Film Festival, 1996)
Best Film for *Different for Girls* (Montreal World Film Festival, 1996)

SELECTED TV ROLES

2014	**Turks and Caicos / Salting the Battlefield** Stirling Rogers
	The White Queen Lord Stanley
	Secret State Felix Durrell
2012	**Doctor Who** Riddell
2011	**Death in Paradise** James Lavender
	Scott & Bailey Nick Savage
	Case Sensitive Mark Bretherick
2010-2014	**Sherlock** Lestrade
2010	**New Tricks** Adrian Levene
	Single Father Stuart
	Law and Order: UK John Smith
	Lewis Alec Pickman
	Wallander Alfred Harderberg
2009-2011	**Garrow's Law** Sir Arthur Hill
2009	**Marple: A Pocket Full of Rye** Lance Fortescue
2008	**God on Trial** Mordechai
	Midnight Man Daniel Cosgrave
	Waking the Dead Colonel John Garrett
	Ashes to Ashes Danny Moore
2007	**Death at a Funeral** Robert
2005	**A Waste of Shame** William Shakespeare
	Spooks William Sampson
2003	**Charles II: The Power and the Passion** George Villiers, Duke of Buckingham
	The Forsyte Saga: To Let Young Jolyon Forsyte
2002	**The Forsyte Saga** Young Jolyon Forsyte
2000	**Take a Girl Like You** Patrick Standish
1996	**The Tenant of Wildfell Hall** Arthur Huntingdon
1994	**Open Fire** David Martin
1987	**Fortunes of War** Simon Boulderstone

SELECTED FILM ROLES

2012	**Fast Girls** David Temple
2010	**Made in Dagenham** Peter Hopkins
2009	**The Good Times Are Killing Me** Lexy
2007	**The Waiting Room** George
	V for Vendetta Dominic
2002	**Extreme Ops** Jeffrey
2000	**Dreaming of Joseph Lees** Joseph Lees
1999	**Cleopatra** Octavius
1996	**Different for Girls** Paul Prentice
1996	**Intimate Relations** Harold Guppy
1996	**The Innocent Sleep** Alan Terry
1991	**Where Angels Fear to Tread** Philip Herriton
1988	**A Handful of Dust** John Beaver
1987	**Maurice** Alec Scudder
1985	**A Room with a View** Freddy Honeychurch

SELECTED STAGE ROLES

2006	**The Exonerated**
2004	**Dumb Show**
2003	**A Woman of No Importance**
2002	**The Elephant Man**
2001	**Speak Truth to Power: Voices from Beyond the Dark**
2000	**The Caretaker**
1999	**Closer**
1998	**The Iceman Cometh**

Another episode, another recce for the production team. Eaton Square, London supplied the exterior for Irene Adler's residence (above); Battersea Power Station, London supplied several locations for *A Scandal in Belgravia* (below).

The Buckingham Palace scenes were filmed in the drawing room of Goldsmith's Hall, London (above left); Mycroft's meeting with John in Speedy's was shot inside the café itself in North Gower Street (above right); Mycroft's home (below)

The interiors for Irene Adler's residence were shot in Newport. Part of the set was then reconstructed and taken into the Welsh countryside to film the scenes where Sherlock and Irene discuss the death of the hiker.

6

THE FEAR OF DOG

Hounds, visual effects and computer-generated imagery…

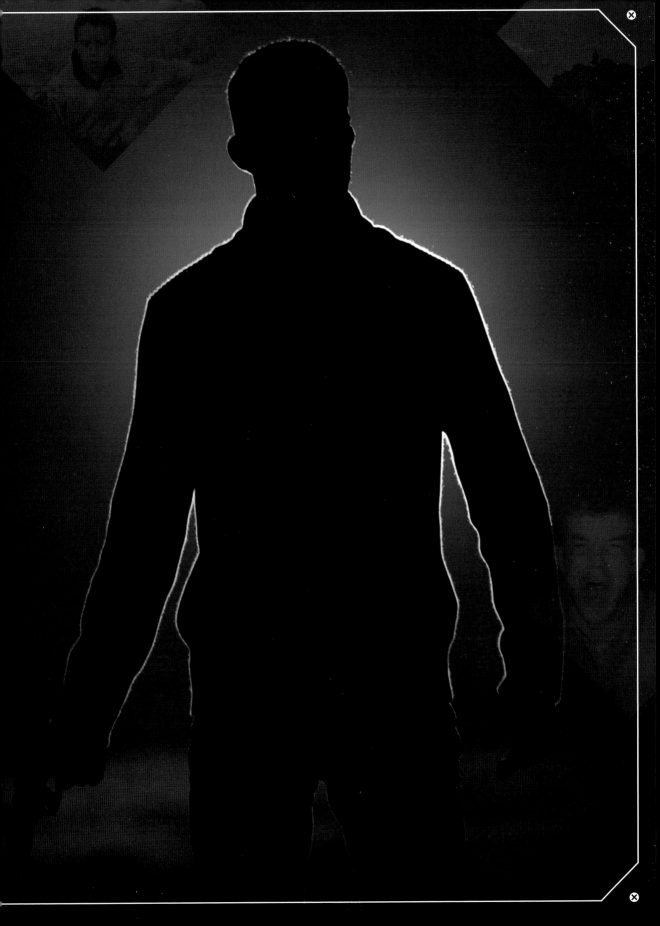

'FEAR. SHERLOCK HOLMES GOT SCARED'

'I t's a panic attack,' says Benedict. 'Of course, it's actually a psychotropic mist that screws with his perception and puts the fear of God into him, but to most people that would look like a full-blown panic attack.

'And it's not an internalised one; it's very verbalised, full of anger and rage. It's amusing as well at points, but it's pretty frightening.'

Mark Gatiss, writer of *The Hounds of Baskerville*, describes Sherlock's first sighting of the Hound as 'his crisis moment. It was an area we wanted to play with: confronting the arch-rationalist with something that appears to be impossible. In the aftermath of that, he needs to prove – to himself as well as to John – that he's still got it. It was Steven's idea for Sherlock to use a deduction as a weapon.'

SHERLOCK
(suddenly furious)
There is **nothing wrong**
with me! You understand?
You want me to **prove it**?
Do you?

He looks round wildly.

SHERLOCK (CONT'D)
We're looking for a dog,
yes? A **great big dog**!
That's your brilliant
theory. Cherchez le chien!
Excellent. Good. Yes!
Where shall we start?

He scans the room.
There's a MAN (40s, **scruffy**)
in a loud jumper eating
in silence with a **smartly**
dressed WOMAN (60s).

SHERLOCK (CONT'D)
How about them –

Text **explodes** around
them: Christmas. Scars.
Threadbare. Heels. Worn.
Starter. Pudding. Wedding
ring. Jewellery. Cheap.
Hairs. Knee high.

SHERLOCK (CONT'D)
– the **sentimental**
widow and her son the
unemployed fisherman?
The answer's yes.

EXT. GRIMPEN. HENRY'S HOUSE.
SHERLOCK make their way down an avenue of
trees to Henry's house.
SHERLOCK pocket.)

DELETED SCENES

Sherlock Series Two   The Hounds of Baskerville

22   INT. BASKERVILLE. SERVICE CORRIDOR. DAY.   22

A long, dimly lit corridor. Antiseptic in its starkness. LYONS appears, SHERLOCK and JOHN following close behind.

> JOHN
> Get out much, do you? From Baskerville, I mean?

> LYONS
> Not really, sir. It's a bit like doing a tour of duty on a sub. We rarely come up for air. There's a mess room where we're meant to unwind. But you can only watch 'The Lion King' so many times, you know.

They pass a door. Sherlock peers through the round glass panel inset in it.

Sherlock's POV: Another white-coated scientist is by a glass tank. He's wearing a surgical mask. The room is bleach-white. Microscopes, computer screens everywhere.

The golden tracery of numbers splits the screen into two, following the path of a phone line.

We stay with Sherlock, John and Lyons on one side of the screen. In the other, a WOMAN, seen only from behind, picks up a phone.

Sherlock Series Two   The Hounds of Baskerville

34   EXT. GRIMPEN. HENRY'S HOUSE. NIGHT.   34

SHERLOCK and JOHN make their way down an avenue of trees to Henry's house.

> SHERLOCK
> ('Racing Post' in his back pocket.) Did you see it? You can always draw information from people like that with the threat of a bet. If I'd offered him a grand he'd never have told us as much!

Henry's house is unexpectedly imposing. A very old, ramshackle conservatory with a very modern extension (patio doors, security lights). They pass through a ruined, overgrown conservatory to get to the front door. Sherlock rings the bell, then holds out his hand to John.

> JOHN
> No. I'm keeping that.

> SHERLOCK
> You can't. It wasn't a real bet.

> JOHN
> You owe me.

> SHERLOCK
> Do I?

> JOHN
> Oh yes.

The door opens and Henry is framed there.

> HENRY
> Hi. Come in, come in.

They pass through –

Sherlock Series Two   The Hounds of Baskerville

42   EXT. BASKERVILLE. CHECKPOINT. NIGHT.   42

In full running gear, CORPORAL LYONS jogs back towards the base. He nods to the MP on duty –

> MP
> 'Evening, sir.

– and swipes his ID card. Beep!

As he passes through into the compound, something catches his eye. Distantly, out on the moor, a light flashes. He frowns. Then goes inside.

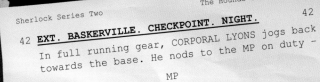

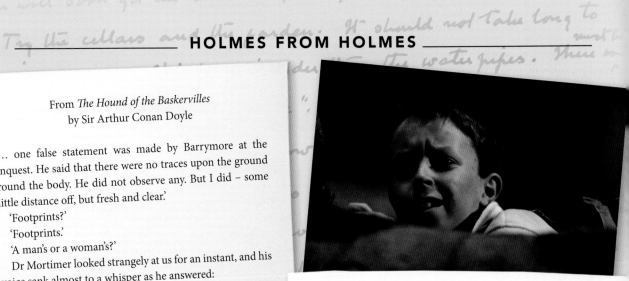

From *The Hound of the Baskervilles*
by Sir Arthur Conan Doyle

'... one false statement was made by Barrymore at the inquest. He said that there were no traces upon the ground round the body. He did not observe any. But I did – some little distance off, but fresh and clear.'

'Footprints?'

'Footprints.'

'A man's or a woman's?'

Dr Mortimer looked strangely at us for an instant, and his voice sank almost to a whisper as he answered:

'Mr Holmes, they were the footprints of a gigantic hound!'

I confess at these words a shudder passed through me. There was a thrill in the doctor's voice which showed that he was himself deeply moved by that which he told us. Holmes leaned forward in his excitement, and his eyes had the hard, dry glitter which shot from them when he was keenly interested.

'You saw this?'

'As clearly as I see you.'

'And you said nothing?'

'What was the use?'

'How was it that no one else saw it?'

'The marks were some twenty yards from the body, and no one gave them a thought. I don't suppose I should have done so had I not known this legend.'

'There are many sheepdogs on the moor?'

'No doubt, but this was no sheepdog.'

'You say it was large?'

'Enormous.'

From The Hounds of Baskerville
by Mark Gatiss

HENRY
But what about the footprints?

SHERLOCK
Paw-prints, I assume, Could be anything –
therefore nothing. Off to Devon with you –
have a cream tea on me.

Starts heading away again.

HENRY
Mr Holmes... they were the footprints
of a gigantic hound!

On the back of Sherlock's head as he jolts to
a halt. Now turns slowly. Now he's looking at
Henry, now he's interested.

SHERLOCK
Say that again.

HENRY
I found paw-prints - they were big, they were -

SHERLOCK
No, no. Your exact words. Repeat your exact words
from a moment ago, exactly as you said them.

On Henry. Puzzled, a little self-conscious.
Exchanges a look with an equally bewildered
John - who just nods. Do as he says.

HENRY
Mr Holmes... they were the footprints
of a gigantic hound.

On Sherlock: eyes gleaming, mind whirling.

SHERLOCK
... I'll take the case.

'That's actually Sherlock's way into the story,' Mark goes on. 'He can't have seen it but he *did* see it, so what is the explanation? We needed to avoid Sherlock's presence and his brilliance simply shutting down the story.'

'We needed to change the structure of the story,' agrees Steven Moffat. 'In Doyle's *Hound of the Baskervilles*, Holmes doesn't appear at Dartmoor until the very end. You can see why Doyle keeps him off stage for so long: he's going to end the fun. "You haven't seen a ghost dog, you've seen a man with a dog." In our version, his presence now ups the stakes, because the arch-rationalist *has* seen a ghost dog, and he's genuinely frightened. All bets are off.'

'In the book,' notes Martin Freeman, 'Watson leaves London and goes out to Dartmoor and, as far as he's aware, he's on his own for ages. Our version is more two-handed. Sherlock and John are both put through hell and scared half to death.'

FROM HOUND TO HOUNDS

◆ In the original novel, the potential victim is Sir Henry Baskerville. Russell Tovey's Henry Knight, the character's modern-day equivalent, has lost his title but retained reference to it in his surname.

◆ One of Holmes's most famous quotes is 'When you have eliminated the impossible, whatever remains, however improbable, must be the truth.' Originally uttered in the novel *A Sign of Four*, it finds its modern home here, slightly rephrased.

◆ In Doyle's novel, Barrymore is the butler at Baskerville Hall and he's caught by Watson signalling to his wife's brother with a lantern. The brother Henry Selden, was an escaped convict from Dartmoor prison. He was also a whopping red herring.

◆ Mark Gatiss retains the glimpsed flashing of a light on the moor, but the source is revealed as a selection of cars rocking in the darkness, with the breathless exclamation: 'Mr Selden, you've done it again.' Mr Selden is engaged in 'dogging'. 'That's a meta-joke if ever there was one!' notes Mark Gatiss.

'I DON'T KNOW HOW WE SLEEP AT NIGHT, DO YOU?'

'If I'm honest,' admits director Paul McGuigan, 'we went out of our comfort zone a little bit there. It's the only episode so far that doesn't happen in and around London, and I felt nervous about that. I was excited too, in the sense that it's *the* iconic Sherlock Holmes story, but I did feel a great pressure.'

On top of all that, *The Hounds of Baskerville* was the most effects-heavy episode the series has made. 'Normally,' says Paul, 'I don't rely on other people, but here I was relying on the computer-generated imagery. How the hell was I going to achieve this? By putting the fear of God up the visual effects team, for a start! But it was trial and error, really. Making movies, you have more time to pre-visualise, make initial drawings and conceptualise everything. Here, a lot of the key scenes were basically empty frames; we had storyboarded everything, but we didn't *really* know how it was going to look. So we were taking the show into a realm that felt slightly less familiar. That's not to say that it didn't work, but it was a difficult one. I still have nightmares about the hound. It was a great responsibility to come up with a visual way of doing this horror story.'

Art Department visuals for *The Hounds of Baskerville* (opposite). Clive Mantle donned a wig for the archive photos of Bob Frankland at Project H.O.U.N.D. (top), his disguise for the murder of Henry Knight's dad was another Art Department construction (above left). The art director's set and strike schedule (above right).

'ANY LONG-TERM EFFECTS?'

Among the people most crucial to Paul McGuigan's conception of 'a visual way of doing this horror story' were the team from The Mill, a London-based visual effects, animation and design studio. Alongside a mountain of acclaimed movie work, including the Oscar-winning *Gladiator*, The Mill had already established themselves in BBC drama, having contributed to *Doctor Who*, *Torchwood*, *The Sarah Jane Adventures*, *Merlin* and numerous other shows. Their work on the first two series of *Sherlock* culminated in the creation of *Baskerville*'s computer-generated hound.

The VFX crew on *The Hounds of Baskerville* comprised fifteen or twenty people, headed by visual effects supervisor Jean-Claude Deguara. 'We put all our resources into that episode,' Jean-Claude says. 'We had a modeller, a picture artist, a rigger, three animators, a lighting team, five or six compositors, and a tracking team to fit the creature into its environment – about twenty people in all.

'The first key thing was to get a concept. Paul McGuigan came in for a chat with the concept artist to discuss what his vision was, what he wanted to see. That process went through several stages. There was originally talk of the Hound being on fire, and we started off with a very demonic, ghostly-looking creature that Paul didn't really buy into. He wanted something that felt very real – your worst nightmare of a terrifying dog. We went for a really evil-looking muscular dog, and made it bigger and more menacing.'

Will Cohen, at that time managing director of Mill Film and TV, points out that 'in *Sherlock* you're allowing layers of discovery. If you saw a very real-looking dog, like a pit-bull, you might think this is a real thing, it's just a dog. The whole idea was that it was a hallucination, so we needed to convey a greater sense of abnormality and scale. It's very difficult conveying scale in a wood, and that was made harder because the Hound is always at some distance from the characters. When a tree is the only measurement of scale you have, you can't really tell how big something is.'

'That issue pushed us on to the next design,' Jean-Claude goes on. 'The idea that this hound might have come out of experimental laboratories led us down this Frankenstein route, where the Hound had been cut into slices. We put scars and cuts on it and made it look as gruesome as we could.'

'Internally, we were calling that "Frankenhound",' say Will.

The concept for the Hound's realisation on screen may have been developed in the very early stages of the episode's

creature movements as he makes his way through the scene – green because the VFX team's computers will later be programmed to ignore anything green and replace it with the CG effect. 'On *Hound*, our man walking through the scene wasn't there to show detailed movement, so we didn't need anyone in a green suit. But we did need to give an eye line for the actors and the cameras, so we had a little green light on his chest.'

Back in 2006, The Mill had created a werewolf for *Doctor Who*, one of the first full CG creatures they had produced. At that time, there were technical constraints on the amount of computer-generated hair or fur that could be achieved within budget and on schedule. Just five years later, they were making a creature with 300,000 hairs on it; a year after that, they could generate a creature with 3 million hairs on it. 'That was thanks to one piece of updated software which meant that 3 million hairs were rendering more quickly than 300,000 a year earlier,' Will reveals. 'Hair or fur adds another dimension, and that does mean it's going to cost a little bit more. But it's not something we're scared of any more. Two things are running side by side: our technological skill-base evolving at the same time as the advances that get made in technology. And we can get this lovely stretching of skin over muscles that's real and lifelike.'

'Nobody wanted a shaggy dog for *Hound*,' Jean-Claude adds, 'so we didn't put too much hair on that. They wanted something muscular and gruesome. But those technical advances have meant that when we build a creature, we can put a skeleton into it, and put muscle systems in where muscles would really be. We can put a layer of skin over the top with areas that represent fat and movement and muscle-bulging. There's so many extra bits that we can add in now. We try to make "under the bonnet" work just as well as the external look of a creature.'

production, but it would be quite a while before the CG effect itself would be created – during post-production several months later. On location, the filming crew were spending their days and nights shooting empty patches of woodland. Well, nearly empty...

'When you're going to have a CG creature, it's quite hard for the camera team to work out where it is, and its style of movement. The Hound was very slow and creepy, so we just had someone walking through the scene to show the cameraman the pacing. They'd do a pass at filming each scene where they followed that person walking through. After that, we took him out and we shot the real plate.'

A lot depends on the nature of the creature. On some shows, there'll be somebody in embarrassingly tight and embarrassingly green lycra, replicating

The initial concept for the Hound: a big, realistic, ferocious, muscular, pit-bull style creature. This was used throughout the shooting stage and then progressed into the modelling. During the edit, it became apparent that the Hound's distance from the actors was not helping give it its sense of scale. The redesign produced a Frankenstein-style, hacked-up and reassembled laboratory Hound with a supernatural demonic edge, which helped sell its size, scale and nightmarish qualities.

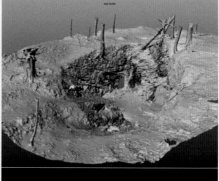

The animation process began with a tracked camera scene using data collected on-set and a LIDAR scan of the hollow created before shooting. This was used to capture the exact geometry, which is difficult to recreate 'by eye' in the studio due to the uneven organic environment.

The creature was rigged in Maya with custom tools and a plug-in was used to achieve muscle bulge, contraction and jiggle. The Hound was skinned and weighted using custom deformation tools to give it its fleshy look. The fine details were painted in Mudbox and the colour created in Mari – an essential tool for achieving the Hound's high-resolution and photorealistic skin textures.

Writer Mark Gatiss wanted to keep the Hound largely hidden for most of the episode, with viewers getting only momentary glimpses of it, so the team used smoke and trees to delay its reveal, giving its final dramatic appearance greater impact.

Three Bears Cave at Forest Fawr Country Park near Cardiff supplied the spooky setting for the scenes at Dewer's Hollow (above); Persuading the 'real' Hound to play dead (below)

Recce pictures showing the Bush Inn, St Hilary, Vale of Glamorgan, inside and out, as used for the Cross Keys gastro-pub (above left and below), and a continuity photo taken during the shoot (above right)

Dynevor Arms LNG Storage Facility, Merthyr Tydfil, setting for the Baskerville research lab exteriors (above); 'LNG' stands for 'Liquefied Natural Gas'. The interiors were filmed in Newport (below). 'That photo is of a genuine giant rat,' says Mark Gatiss. 'It's one of the specimens used in the lab sequence of *The Hounds of Baskerville*.'

Major Barrymore's office (top); Henry Knight's house at Grimpen (above left). A couple of days into shooting on The Hounds of Baskerville, Martin Freeman won Best Supporting Actor at the 2011 BAFTA awards (above right).

7

THE WATER-COOLER MOMENT

Confrontations, music, and heading for a fall...

SHERLOCK
HOLMES

'WE HAVE OUR BEST PEOPLE INVESTIGATING'

Detective Inspector Lestrade might think that Sherlock's on the side of the angels, but not all his colleagues agree. Throughout the first two series of *Sherlock*, the ranks below Lestrade are shown to be suspicious of the consulting detective, culminating in the destruction of Sherlock's reputation in *The Reichenbach Fall*.

'Sherlock patronises Lestrade, and everyone below Lestrade comes in for even shorter shrift,' Mark Gatiss points out. 'Over the years that Lestrade knows him, the police grow to resent Sherlock more and more, particularly Anderson and Donovan. Sally Donovan, of course, thinks that Sherlock is a borderline criminal himself.'

'Anderson thinks he's as brainy as Sherlock Holmes,' says actor Jonathan Aris, 'which is absurd. He clearly isn't. He's no dummy, though; he's a really skilled forensic officer, and Sherlock respects and recognises that more as the series progresses. But I think it's pretty humiliating for him, watching as Sherlock departs from forensic science and makes these incredible deductive leaps. It's totally magical, and it's way beyond Anderson's approach. Right from the start, we see Sherlock and Anderson both present at the crime scene. In *A Study in Pink*, the forensics team gets pulled out so Sherlock can work his magic – and for Anderson that's both irritating and embarrassing. He and his team are all in those paper suits and paper galoshes for Scene of Crime Officers, so they don't contaminate the scene with anything. Sherlock just wanders straight in, busting dust and germs everywhere, and, with no scientific equipment, he can deduce where the victim's come from, where's she going, that there is a suitcase missing…

'So in Series One we see Sherlock deliver a succession of crushing put-downs, while Anderson thinks *he's* really the Sherlock Holmes in the room. Anderson is totally unimpressed by Sherlock's deductive leaps and thinks there's actually something wrong with him. By the end of Series Two, Anderson and Donovan have become more and more suspicious of him, so that ultimately they are party responsible for pushing Sherlock over the edge…'

> ANDERSON
> (at the door) That's **the end** of it. We don't know where they went from here. Tells us **nothing**, after all.
>
> SHERLOCK
> Right, Anderson. Nothing at all. Except his **shoe size**, his **height**, his **gait**, his walking **pace**.

Vinette Robinson   Born 1981, Leeds, Yorkshire

SELECTED TV ROLES

2014	Death in Paradise Lauren Campese
2013	Vera Corinne Franks
	Assistance Jenny
2010–2014	Sherlock Sgt Sally Donovan
2009	Waterloo Road Helen Hopewell
	Hope Springs Josie Porritt
2008	The Passion Mina

2007	Doctor Who Abi Lerner
	Doctors Katie Waters
	Hustle Tina
	Party Animals Kerry
2004	Doctors Melanie
2005	Casualty Kirsty Evans
2004	Blue Murder Andrea
	Murphy's Law Aimie
2003	Between the Sheets Tracy Ellis
2000	Doctors Cath Bickerstaff

SELECTED FILM ROLES

2011	Powder Hannah
2006	Imagine Me & You Zina
2005	Vera Drake Jamaican Girl

SELECTED STAGE ROLES

2011	Hamlet
2011	Tender Napalm
2009	Darker Shores
2008	War and Peace

Jonathan Aris   Born 1971

SELECTED TV ROLES

2014	The Game Alan Montag
2013	Whitechapel Clerk
2012	Peep Show Ben Prenderghast
	Silk Dr Liam King
	Sightseers Ian
2011	New Tricks David Crawley
2010–2014	Sherlock Phillip Anderson
2010	The Little House Doctor McFadden
	Spooks Azis Aibek
	Being Human Newsreader
2009	Ideal Rich
2008	Wallander Albinsson
	Merlin Matthew
2008	Bonekickers Jeff Greenwood
	Margaret Thatcher: The Long Walk to Finchley Stanley Soward
2007	My Family Mr Channing

SELECTED FILM ROLES

2013	The World's End Group Leader
2010	Gulliver's Travels Lilliputian Scientist
2009	Bright Star Mr Hunt
2008	Flawless Boyle

SELECTED STAGE ROLES

2005	Death of a Salesman
1995	Fame: The Musical

'COME AND PLAY. TOWER HILL'

The job of pushing Sherlock over the edge fell to writer Steve Thompson and a director new to the show – Toby Haynes. Toby's directing debut came with the short film *Looking for Al Bowlly* in 2003, after which he worked on TV shows like *Coming up, Hollyoaks, MI High, Holby Blue, Spooks: Code 9, Being Human* and *Five Days*. In 2009, the *Doctor Who* team at BBC Wales invited him to direct Steven Moffat's two-part finale to Matt Smith's first series as the Eleventh Doctor. Toby went on to direct the 2010 Christmas special and the opening episodes of the next year's series.

'I was finishing off some *Doctor Who* episodes, just before Christmas 2010,' recalls Toby, 'when I got the call asking if I was interested in directing a *Sherlock* story. I was a bit reticent at first. I was excited and terrified at the thought of playing on the same level as Paul McGuigan. Paul's work on the first series had really kicked it out of the park in terms of what TV could do – it was phenomenal – so I was a bit nervous that I might be shown up by this Hollywood director. But it was actually quite a way off – about four months into the following year – so I took some time out to travel to Australia, and I was there when I made the decision to commit to *Sherlock* in late February. Doctor Who had been a character I'd always wanted

to do and had loved as a kid, and it was so exciting to be part of it as an adult. Sherlock Holmes was the other TV hero for me, I'd also obsessed about him as a kid – I'd read the books, and I was really into Jeremy Brett's Holmes on television and Clive Merrison's on the radio. I just really loved this straight-up hero, and in some ways it's a short leap from cosmic smartarse Doctor Who to Earthbound smartarse Sherlock Holmes. It was very easy to feel great about it once the decision had been made.

'Then I went to a comic book, science fiction and movie convention in San Francisco called WonderCon. I was on a panel with Neil Gaiman, and we were promoting the launch of the new series of *Doctor Who*. There were about 3,000 people in the audience, and, when I was asked what I'd be doing next and said I was doing this little show called *Sherlock*, they all went completely mad! When I saw that reaction, I realised this was really something special.

'Hartswood weren't specific at first about which story I was going to do, and I was very keen to do *Hound*. It's the quintessential Sherlock Holmes story, it has horror undertones, and I'm a big fan of horror. Plus I'd done *Doctor Who*, and I knew *Hound* would suit my sensibilities as a director. Then they told me I wouldn't be doing *Hound*, I'd be doing the series finale and it would be *The Reichenbach Fall*, and that was a no-brainer.

'The other factor was that it was a 90-minute feature-film format, and that would be my first for TV and was very attractive. It's very daunting to shoot a movie in four weeks, especially when you read the early drafts of the script and see how hugely ambitious it is – you see a car chase casually written into the third act and start to panic! In terms of budget and schedule, you have a TV approach, using the same section of corridor from every possible angle. The script was 112

From 'The Final Problem'
by Sir Arthur Conan Doyle

'I think that I may go so far as to say, Watson, that I have not lived wholly in vain,' he remarked. 'If my record were closed to-night I could still survey it with equanimity. The air of London is the sweeter for my presence. In over a thousand cases I am not aware that I have ever used my powers upon the wrong side. Of late I have been tempted to look into the problems furnished by nature rather than those more superficial ones for which our artificial state of society is responsible. Your memoirs will draw to an end, Watson, upon the day that I crown my career by the capture or extinction of the most dangerous and capable criminal in Europe.'

From 'The Final Problem'
by Sir Arthur Conan Doyle

'Well,' said I, as I came hurrying up, 'I trust that she is no worse?'

A look of surprise passed over his face, and at the first quiver of his eyebrows my heart turned to lead in my breast. 'You did not write this?' I said, pulling the letter from my pocket. 'There is no sick Englishwoman in the hotel?'

'Certainly not!' he cried. 'But it has the hotel mark upon it! Ha, it must have been written by that tall Englishman who came in after you had gone. He said—'

But I waited for none of the landlord's explanations. In a tingle of fear I was already running down the village street, and making for the path which I had so lately descended.

From 'The Adventure of the Priory School'
by Sir Arthur Conan Doyle

'Important!' Our visitor threw up his hands. 'Have you heard nothing of the abduction of the only son of the Duke of Holdernesse?'

'What! the late Cabinet Minister?'

'Exactly. We had tried to keep it out of the papers, but there was some rumour in the *Globe* last night. I thought it might have reached your ears.'

From 'The Reichenbach Fall'
by Steve Thompson

SHERLOCK
It's all true. Everything Kitty wrote about me.
I invented Moriarty. I'm a fake. Every case.
All those deductions. The newspapers were right.
Tell Lestrade. And Mrs Hudson. And Molly.
In fact tell everyone who will listen.
I created Moriarty for my own purposes.
No one could be that clever. I researched you.
Before we met. I discovered what I could to
impress you. It's a trick, John. Just a magic
trick. Don't. Don't move. Stay right where you
are. Keep your eyes fixed on me. I need you to do
this for me. This phone call. It's my note,
in a way. You have to write a note.

From 'The Reichenbach Fall'
by Steve Thompson

As he reaches the front door, MRS HUDSON appears in her own flat doorway with a WORKMAN in overalls.

MRS HUDSON
Oh, Dr Watson! You did make me jump.

JOHN
But –

MRS HUDSON
Is everything ok now? With the police?
Has Sherlock sorted it all out?

On John: cold, dawning horror.

JOHN
Oh my God.

He tears outside, leaving the door wide open.

From 'The Reichenbach Fall'
by Steve Thompson

SHERLOCK
Kidnapping.

LESTRADE
Rufus Bruhl. The Ambassador to the U.S.

JOHN
(Confused) Isn't he in Washington?

LESTRADE
Not him. His children.

JOHN
What?

LESTRADE
(Reading from notes) Max and Claudette. Seven and nine.

DONOVAN shows them a photo. Angelic children.

LESTRADE (CONT'D)
They're at St Aldate's.

DONOVAN
Posh boarding place down in Surrey.

pages long, and you usually reckon on one minute per page. But the scripts were building on the success of the first series, so there was a huge sense of trepidation about doing it. You read the script and think, "That's absolutely impossible," but it's the job of the director to look at those scripts and find a way to do these huge, elaborate things.

'It was a lot of fun making it. The edit was tough; it took seven weeks not the usual five. The focus of our edit was to make you think the problem was more unsolvable so the solution would be even more impressive. The editor, Tim Porter, did a fantastic job on that and really responded to the show. Charlie Phillips was the editor on Paul McGuigan's episodes, and in a way Charlie was the monkey on Tim's shoulder just as Paul was the one on mine – we were both trying to raise our game with those great mentors behind us. We wanted to do the sequence of spinning newspapers, and we all discussed that early on, but we thought there might be too many sequences. When we assembled the episode, though, that sequence really felt needed, so we generated it in the edit from the Art Department newspapers that had been made for the shoot.'

10p DAILY EXPRESS

How a tiny dose of aspirin can prevent cancer

FREE BEDDING PLANTS FOR EVERY READER

CRIME OF THE CENTURY?

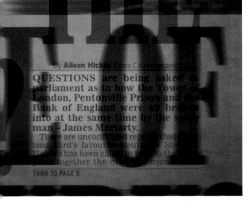

By Aileen Hickey Crime Correspondent

QUESTIONS are being asked in parliament as to how the Tower of London, Pentonville Prison and the Bank of England were all broken into at the same time by the same man – James Moriarty.

There are unconfirmed reports that Scotland Yard's favourite amateur, Sherlock Holmes has been called in to help them piece together the most suspicious...

TURN TO PAGE 5

JEWEL THIEF IN TRIAL AT BAILEY

By Aileen Hickey Crime Correspondent

CROWN Jewel thief is to be tried at the Old Bailey and Sherlock Holmes is named as

the guar...

...eur detective to be ...d as expert witness

DELETED SCENES

Sherlock Series Two   The Reichenbach Fall

2 **EXT. GALLERY/CAB. DAY**   2

Coming out of the Gallery, into the street –

> SHERLOCK
> High-functioning sociopath, remember,
> John? I don't do 'please' and 'thank
> you' and all those... slow bits.

> JOHN
> Sociopath, I get. Still waiting for
> the 'high-functioning'.

Chin-nods at the REPORTERS, leaving to file their stories.

> JOHN (CONT'D)
> Look at them all. Off to file their
> stories.

> SHERLOCK
> I know.

> JOHN
> About you.

> SHERLOCK
> So?

On John, troubled, watching them.

> JOHN
> Watch it. That's all, just watch it.

Sherlock Series Two   The Reichenbach Fall

24A **INT. JEWEL HOUSE. DAY**   24A

The smashed glass case, the floor glittering
with glass. Now TAPED OFF – a FORENSICS TEAM
picking their way through the evidence.
SHERLOCK, JOHN, LESTRADE on the other side
of the tape, just watching.

> LESTRADE
> Shouldn't have been possible. That
> glass, tougher than anything.

> SHERLOCK
> Perhaps.

His eyes flick down, as he zeroes in on
something.

Sherlock's POV. We zoom in on another piece
of glitter in among all the shattered glass
– Jim's diamond.

> SHERLOCK (CONT'D)
> (Rounds on Lestrade) Where is he, where
> did you take him? I want Moriarty!

> LESTRADE
> Well. It's mutual.

DELETED SCENES

36 INT. 221B BAKER STREET. NIGHT   36

Returning to Baker Street - cameras clicking.
Door slams. MRS HUDSON pokes her head out.
A new outfit and very bold make-up. Most glam
we've ever seen her.

              MRS HUDSON
    Saw you on the telly. John looked smart.

              SHERLOCK
    Lipstick?

              MRS HUDSON
    In case they catch me through a window.
    Don't want to do a Cherie.

JOHN and SHERLOCK whistle past her,
trudge upstairs.

---

49 INT. 221B BAKER STREET. DAY   49

              JIM
    Learn to. Because I owe you a fall,
    Sherlock Holmes. I. Owe. You.

Voices from outside. Sherlock looks out the
window. Sherlock's POV. LESTRADE climbing out
of his squad car. Running out. JOHN with him.
Turns. JIM's gone. The lamp in the kitchen
swinging - the door to the bedroom banging.
He's gone out the back, down the fire escape.

LESTRADE bursts in. JOHN behind.

              LESTRADE
    Moriarty…?

SHERLOCK shakes his head. Picks up the apple.
MORIARTY has carved three letters in it with
the knife: 'IOU'.

---

54 INT. DIOGENES CLUB. DAY   54

              JOHN
    Pinched all his Smurfs? Broke his action men?

              MYCROFT
    I know you want to protect him. From the
    'slings and arrows of outrageous fortune'.
    Is that the doctor in you, I wonder? Or
    something else. The soldier's weakness.
    Hero worship.

              JOHN
    Are we done?

Gets up to go.

              MYCROFT
    We both know what's coming, John. Moriarty is
    obsessed. He's sworn to destroy his only rival.

Steve Thompson was responsible for the script, and he says the ambition comes from a very collaborative process. 'Steven and Mark plot out the series, then invite me in. So they came to me and said we'd be doing "A Scandal in Bohemia", *The Hound of the Baskervilles* and "The Final Problem", and I would be writing the third one – a very big deal, with the centrepiece being the apparent death of Sherlock. You read the story then riff a little bit. We borrow constantly from all the books and other Sherlock Holmes versions.' Moriarty's trial scene in *The Reichenbach Fall* is a beat-by-beat homage to one important source: the second of Basil Rathbone's Holmes movies, *The Adventures of Sherlock Holmes*. The film opens with Moriarty being acquitted of murder before attempting to steal the Crown Jewels from the Tower of London.

Depicting Jim Moriarty's break-in at the Tower presented the *Sherlock* team with a fresh problem. 'The script was written,' Steve goes on, 'and then, two weeks before we were due to start filming, we were told we couldn't film in the Tower. Apparently, some sort of bylaw says you can't show the Queen's possessions being stolen.'

'The Tower of London people were going to cooperate,' confirms Toby. 'They were absolutely fine about it. Then we went there to do a recce. They were showing us around the Waterloo Barracks at the Tower, where the Crown Jewels are kept, and I said, "This is great, this is where he can steal the Crown Jewels." One of the officials said, "I beg your pardon?" "Oh, Moriarty will be breaking in to steal the Crown Jewels." "OH! I'm afraid you can't do that." Car chases through the grounds of the Tower – no problem. Stealing the Crown Jewels – out of the question. So the Tower of London was suddenly off limits, and we ended up shooting the scenes in Cardiff Castle.'

'A SPIDER AT THE CENTRE OF A WEB'

'It was a riveting first day's filming,' recalls Steve. 'Andrew Scott and Benedict Cumberbatch in 221B Baker Street, both actors finding their way into the script.'

Subject: The Woman in Green
From: Steven Moffat
To: Toby Haynes
Sent: 4 June 2011 08:52

This is the Rathbone/Moriarty meeting that we love so much, which we patterned our version after. Not to be slavishly followed, but this is the idea, and I rather love it. Just the approach on the stairs, and the violin. Though Rathbone and Henry Daniel (the prof) are good value if you want to be amused in an old-fashioned way.

Steven

Subject: Re: The Woman in Green
From: Toby Haynes
To: Steven Moffat
Sent: 4 June 2011 09:26

Cool. I'll catch up with this as soon as I get near some wifi. I love the stairs/violin bit in our ep and have it pretty worked out, I have this whole thing of making JM this faceless sinister presence… Just for moments, like here and at the Tower (boo hoo!).

But I hadn't realised we were paying homage!

Sent from my iPhone despite O2

Subject: Re: The Woman in Green
From: Steven Moffat
To: Toby Haynes
Sent: 4 June 2011 09:28

Not to so much homage, as nicking a good bit of storytelling.

'Mark and Steven had shown me various Sherlock Holmes films,' says Toby. 'There's this really nice sequence in *The Woman in Green* with Moriarty coming into the house at Baker Street. In story terms, they were echoing that scene in *The Reichenbach Fall*, so we needed to do it in filmmaking terms, too. The true echo

that we did was the shot of Moriarty's feet going up the stairs. I prepared my own set of mini-storyboards; I wanted to really ramp up the tension, with very close profiles, frame the subject very close to the edge, make it all feel awkward. It was a big scene – eight script pages – and we had another set of scenes scheduled to do that day. In television, a heavy day is six pages of script, a good day is three. This first day was epic: we had the eight-page confrontation, plus Sherlock and John looking at the newspapers and maybe the scene with the hanging dummy. But I knew I had to do a lot of shots for that scene with Moriarty. We

didn't actually complete everything that day. Paul McGuigan phoned me up and said, "Keep focused. If you need a shot, make sure you get it, don't move on until you've got it." Which was very kind of him, but actually made me even more anxious! Paul was the prime influence on me for that episode.

'Andrew Scott is a very interesting actor to work with. He does all sorts of things, he's very brave and he's always trying different stuff. So every take is very different. Some of the lines he was opera singing – it's really bonkers. He pushes himself into new places. I loved working with him but it required a lot of coverage.'

'I think it's very important that Moriarty is playful,' Andrew declares. 'Moriarty is funny, and there's enormous pleasure in it all for him as well as for the audience – they have to laugh along with him.' He cites Moriarty's street scenes in *A Scandal in Belgravia* as a good example. 'That scene is fun is because it incorporates London, you see Moriarty blowing a raspberry at Big Ben. Because we were in such a public place, that was the first day that I was really aware of people knowing who the character is and recognising us and recognising me. I realised how much the character had developed in people's minds. It was amazing to me how much of an impact he had in relatively little screen time, because Steven and Mark kept him in the background, they really spared him. The threat of something can seem much scarier than the actuality of it.'

Andrew is also fond of the Crown Jewels scenes. 'One of the great pleasures of doing *Sherlock* is that really serious things can be done that cause absolute havoc, but Moriarty doesn't have to take things seriously. It felt right to dance through that scene. I had no idea they were going to use *The Thieving Magpie* but, when they played that music in, it felt fantastic.'

'The music is a vital component,' Mark Gatiss notes. 'You'd really notice how important it is if it was absent, it's part of the whole package. When the music really delivers, it's fantastically satisfying – your emotions are rising at the same time as the score is taking you along the journey. For a thriller like *Sherlock*, we really wanted to give it an epic, filmic sound.'

'On set I often play in some music to help the actors during non-dialogue sequences and guide them to where things are about to build,' says Toby. 'We were thinking of using Rossini's *Thieving Magpie* for Moriarty's great robbery. I always start with a single image from the script, and that music seemed right for this great heist.'

DELETED SCENES

Sherlock Series Two   The Reichenbach Fall

56A   **EXT. BAKER STREET. DAY**   56A
      JOHN and SHERLOCK climbing into a police car.

                         SHERLOCK
            How was Mycroft?

      JOHN confused - how does he know? From the
      smell...

                         SHERLOCK (CONT'D)
            Leather polish. Stale whisky. (Gestures
            to the street) He was asking about our
            new neighbours.

                         JOHN
            You already know.

                         SHERLOCK
            I know that there are four sets of
            curtains that are closed in broad
            daylight. 'Who's behind them?' is the
            interesting question, though.

      JOHN looks up - sure enough, four sets of
      curtains are closed - four separate flats in
      the street. Closer on Sherlock as he looks up
      at them - and then frowns - something else!
      Some graffiti on a section of wall - woven
      into it, quite clearly if you look, three
      letters: I.O.U. On Sherlock - alive to this
      now, fascinated.

                         SHERLOCK (CONT'D)
            Here we go!

                         JOHN
            Sorry, what?

                         SHERLOCK
            Nothing. Nothing.

Sherlock Series Two   The Reichenbach Fall

83   **INT. SCOTLAND YARD, INCIDENT ROOM. NIGHT**   83
     Darkness. DONOVAN at a computer. She's playing
     the CCTV tape of CLAUDIE RUHL. In the movie
     SHERLOCK enters the room and she starts to
     scream. Scream scream scream. Freeze frame on
     her screaming face. And then a knock at the
     door. ANDERSON enters.

                         ANDERSON
            Got your text.

                         DONOVAN
            Something I need you to see.

Whenever *Sherlock*'s music is not by Rossini, Bach or The Bee Gees, it's the work of David Arnold and Michael Price, two award-winning composers with a huge track record of film and TV scores. Michael's credits include *Lightfields*, *Mr Stink*, *A Fantastic Fear of Everything* and *The Inbetweeners Movie*, while David is well known for his soundtracks for five James Bond movies, *Independence Day*, *Little Britain* and the Opening Ceremony of the 2012 Olympics in London.

'The first thing to do was to come up with a central theme and a character for it,' remembers David. 'Finding a way to score this that is relevant to the movie and the character they are making. So there were discussions with Steven and Sue and Mark and then Michael and I finding common ground on the defining sound of the show. What was our approach going to be – electronic, synthetic, classic orchestral, a band, jazz…? You need to find a palette of sound. So the initial stage involved finding an approach. We did the pilot episode together, and everything gelled.

'The central characters are very different. Sherlock is an enigma, a high-functioning sociopath or borderline psychopath, with an element of heroism to him in his utter genius. He enjoys figuring things out in the midst of the macabre and the serious. He gets off on it to a certain extent. So we wanted to deliver something musically for Sherlock that would allow the audience to enjoy his determination and his skill but also to enjoy it in a cinematic sense. It needs to feel like what's going on is grand and important and dangerous yet beautiful and ridiculous at the same time.

'In a way, it's far more difficult to get access to John Watson. His status as an army medic returned from Afghanistan has a certain resonance, and he's more

than just a cypher for Sherlock to throw his theories at. He has his own history and a life, and he has doubts and emotions. So we felt, right from the beginning with his flashbacks to his wartime experiences, that we wanted to create something that had resonance in reality.

'The directors and producers like to hear demos of the music before we record it so we can make any changes before we get to the recording stage. So we pre-record a lot of the music, either with people playing it or using synthesizers and samplers. That ends up as our background track, over which we record the real instruments and the orchestral aspects. The musicians have a matching click track in their headphones to give them the right tempo for the scene, so we can make sure the music fits the picture – if, say, Sherlock walks from one side of the screen to the other and looks around, we'll know how many seconds and frames that is. The musicians then play along at the right speed.'

Michael Price points out that the preparations for those live recording sessions can be quite arduous and complex. 'To say the least. We're writing very, very fast because we're working on three 90-minute episodes, and they each need a certain amount of music. That's a substantial quantity of dots to get on paper for everybody to play! It really is a team effort; the commitment and contribution from everybody in the composers' teams is huge. David and I both work

Composer David Arnold

with assistants, programmers, orchestrators and arrangers – lots of people who all work really, really hard to make sure that when we come here for the sessions everything is absolutely flawless before we even involve the musicians. Then we can just fly through things, and create a real buzz in the studio as well, because you're going quickly but you're doing amazing work. I'm conducting, and my headphones have the click track and whatever instruments we have on our backing track, plus I'm hearing the voices of everyone in the control room telling me what to do. That's always entertaining. We don't usually show any musicians the filmed footage at that point, although I always have it in front of me, and I've got various other technical information as well.'

'Once you add in those real musicians,' David says, 'the music starts to come to life and has a real personality. And that can make so much difference to the way the music sounds and to the

way the audience perceives the programme.'

Mark agrees. 'It makes a huge difference. The strings bring something very special, particularly because we always associate Sherlock Holmes with the violin. David and Michael have written some fantastic, very driving themes for the show.'

'I always use a lot of music in my work,' says Toby. 'My job as director is to take these high-concept ideas and help reveal the human element in there. Understanding where the character is and complementing it with a very subtle camera move – you're after emotional impact without being sentimental. And the music is a vital element in that. The director Stephen Frears was my tutor at the National Film and Television School, and one of the most important things he taught me was not to get in the way of other talented people doing their jobs. You've got to have a good ego, but be flexible enough not to get in the way of others.'

DELETED SCENES

Sherlock Series Two   The Reichenbach Fall

100 INT. FLAT. NIGHT   100

                    JIM (CONT'D)
        Don't you hit me. Don't you
        dare lay a finger on me!!

                    SHERLOCK
        Enough of this. Stop it, stop it right
        now!

Jim, staring at him, appalled but fascinated.

                    JIM
        Jesus, look at you. It's like you think
        it's all real. Just how mad are you?

                    KITTY
        Mad enough to invent his own super-
        villain, so he could look good. (to
        John) Dr Watson, please just think about
        it. An arch-enemy? A master criminal?
        How real does any of this seem to you?
        Who's the one man who could make this
        stuff up?

On John - almost like he's rocked for a
moment. Then - Jim is bolting for it, racing
down the hall, slamming into the bathroom.
Sherlock, racing after him. Door's locked!
Kicks it once, twice. The door slams open.
Jim is gone. John leaps towards the
window, Sherlock holds him back.

                    SHERLOCK
        He'll have back-up.

Kitty is behind them in the hallway.

                    KITTY
        You know what, Sherlock Holmes -
        I look at you now and I can
        read you. And - You. Repel. Me.

Sherlock, striding past her now!

Sherlock Series Two   The Reichenbach Fall

107E EXT. BART'S ROOFTOP. DAY.   107E

                    SHERLOCK
        You're too obvious. Getting John out of
        the way.

                    JIM
        You realised?

                    SHERLOCK
        Please!

                    JIM
        Well... I just wanted us to be alone.
        No gooseberries. (smiles) You did it
        to yourself, you know? All I did was
        pull one tiny little thread. All that
        resentment, you created that - I just
        had to pull it down on top of you.

                    SHERLOCK
        You haven't won yet.

                    JIM
        No?

                    SHERLOCK
        No. I can still prove my innocence.
        Prove you made up a whole false
        identity...

                    JIM
        Killing yourself would really
        be a lot less effort.

'COME AND PLAY. BART'S HOSPITAL ROOFTOP'

'Where and when is the water-cooler moment? That is one thing that we're always looking for when we discuss the stories,' Steve Thompson notes. 'What's everyone going to be talking about at work on Monday morning? Sherlock's "death" was our ultimate water-cooler moment, really. We knew it would have a massive impact, but we never guessed quite how massive. For months afterwards, I'd be visiting schools and the first question, always, was "How did Sherlock come back to life?" And I couldn't believe that web pages were being set up by *The Times* and *The Guardian* with everyone trying to work out how he'd done it. Some of those online discussions came close, and one or two had extra little ideas which were so clever we later added them into the mix to embroider what we already had.'

What they already had came from discussions with the illusionist Derren Brown and his team, in a meeting set up by Mark Gatiss. 'Sue, Toby, Mark and I sat with these experts in illusion and got them to tell us how they thought we could do it.'

'When I read it,' recalls Toby, 'I said, "He's dead. There's no way out." We needed to have the solution in order to work out how to film it, so the film becomes an integral part of the stunt that Sherlock is pulling – I'm making the audience believe it, just as Sherlock is making John believe it. Derren Brown and his team showed us a stunt for somebody surviving jumping off a building. It was very simple: across the tower was a banner, just big enough to hide a slide. So we knew that the key thing was to obscure part of the relevant building.'

And in the earliest outlines for the script, the relevant building was going to be very

different. 'For a while, the episode was
going to end with Sherlock being in the
Shard as it was being built, and jumping
off it to his apparent death. He was going
to fall into some scaffolding on the side
of the Shard and then a body would be
dropped from the scaffolding – but there
is no scaffolding on a building that size.
Access would have been a problem: we
knew what it was like trying to get into
half-constructed buildings, the health
and safety issues around getting film
crews in. Also, if we'd got a stuntman to
do this, he's dead – there's no way I could
even fake that without an awful lot of
computer-generated imagery, at the level
of say the *Avengers* movie. Our feeling
was that we didn't want CGI getting in
the way of the impact of Sherlock's death.
And we were going to be shooting in
daylight, which would have exposed the
CGI massively. So... did it have to be the
Shard?

'Around the same time, we went to St
Bart's hospital, because we had some
scenes set there during the episode,
and I thought it was actually as good
as anywhere for the Fall. Not only was
it high enough, but the roof was very
good for filming: there were platforms
that made it accessible. We could do the
stunt of someone jumping off the roof
to just six feet below because there were
layers to the roof. And I was squinting
up at the top of the building, picturing
Sherlock standing on the edge, when
I nearly got run over by this double-
decker bus that was swinging round.
The location guy pulled me out of
the way, and I watched the bus as it
disappeared completely. In the middle
of the parking area is this ambulance
station, a very low building, only about
the height of a garden shed, which
created a roundabout for the buses to
go round. Because of the angle that I
was watching from and the size of the
building, when the bus swung round the

DIRECTION

Director Toby Haynes's preparations for the Series Two climax included recce shots of the Bart's location and extensive storyboards.

fig.1) *This photo shows Bart's exterior with the Ambulance station outside. Note: the ambulance station is only one story high and yet it covers one and a half floors of Bart's...*

fig.2) *...which is tall enough to hide a double-decker bus - these photos were taken concurrently.*

roundabout and parked by the bus stop it was completely obscured by this low building. It was like an optical illusion. I realised that this shed was big enough to hide a double-decker bus, and as soon as I realised that I knew that we had a chance in hell of making our own magic trick occur.

'So I pitched the notion of using Bart's to Sue, Steven, Mark and Steve. I put together a big package to sell the idea – and then everyone was much more open to it than I thought they were going to be, and I didn't really need the big pitch!'

A few weeks later, Toby and the team converged on Bart's for the recording. 'We were supposed to do the stunt in the morning and then go and do the eight-page conversation between Sherlock and Moriarty in the afternoon. In the end, we had to drop the whole roof conversation from the scheduled day of filming, because it was raining.'

'The weather was so incredibly bad,' Andrew Scott remembers, 'that we just couldn't film it, but we did manage to shoot some rehearsal footage. That meant that Benedict and I were able to take advantage of the fact that we had to do it again, to recalibrate how that scene should go. It's the final showdown, which is based on the famous waterfall scene in the Doyle story, and it goes through lots of different elements. There's the thriller factor to it, of course, and the mystery of how Sherlock pulls it off, but I think there's also a real sense of forgiveness. I really liked the moment where we shake hands – the light was falling beautifully that second time we shot it. It's the most beautiful bit of writing there too, you know.'

BOFFIN SHERLOCK SOLVES COLD CASE

Amateur sleuth Sherlock Holmes – famous for his amazing powers of deduction – has done it again!

By Luke Rumbelow

Amateur sleuth Sherlock Holmes – famous for his amazing powers of deduction – has done it again!

Boffin Sherlock has solved a case that has Metropolitan police baffled for nearly thirty years. The case concerning dangerous madman Peter Ricoletti – top of Scotland Yard's 'Most wanted' list – a killer who has remained at large despite an investigation spanning two continents...

SUPER-SLEUTH IS DEAD

SUICIDE OF FAKE GENIUS

Fraudulent detective takes his own life

From Luke Rumbelow

SUPER-SLEUTH Sherlock Holmes, who has recently been exposed as a fraud has decided to end his life. Was the theatre too much to bare? Or was this his plan all along? The Sun Endeavours to find out the truth.

Out-of-work actor Richard Brook revealed exclusively to THE SUN that he was hired by Holmes in an elaborate deception to fool the British public into believing Holmes had above-average 'detective skills'.

"He had the whole 'Moriarty' cover cooked up from the beginning, and invented all the crimes," said Brook. "All I had to do was learn my lines."

SHERLOCK: THE SHOCKING TRUTH

(Close Friend Richard Brook Tells All)

EXCLUSIVE

Exclusive From Kitty Riley

SUPER-SLEUTH Sherlock Holmes has today been exposed as a fraud in a revelation that will shock his new found base of adoring fans.

Out-of-work actor Richard Brook revealed exclusively to THE SUN that he was hired by Holmes in an elaborate deception to fool the British public into believing Holmes had

above-average 'detective skills'.

Brook, who has known Holmes for decades and until recently considered him to be a close friend, said he was at first desperate for the money, but later found he had no

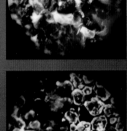

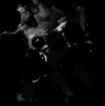

For *The Reichenbach Fall*, the Art Department created everything from a Turner masterpiece to newspapers and microscope slides, as well as helping transform location footage into computer-screen CCTV displays, and faking the documentary evidence for the existence of Moriarty's alter ego, Richard Brook.

St Bart's Hospital, London: the crucial ambulance station (top) and the rooftop (above);
applying blood... (below left); Benedict Cumberbatch and Andrew Scott discuss the final scene (below right).

Mark Gatiss with Douglas Wilmer, a former Sherlock Homes, in the Diogenes Club (above right);
Benedict Cumberbatch and director Toby Haynes on location at St Woolos Cemetery in Newport (below left).

8

I BELIEVE IN SHERLOCK HOLMES

Fandom, visual effects, and happy returns…

'BACK TO BAKER STREET, SHERLOCK HOLMES'

'**E**very series has a cliffhanger, which is probably really annoying for Benedict Cumberbatch,' admits Sue Vertue.

'Every time Benedict thinks he can have his hair cut, we have a cliffhanger to pick up from, and everything has to start from exactly where it was two years earlier.'

'It did become something of a national water-cooler moment,' smiles Benedict. 'It was quite enthralling to be part of a piece of "event television". It's a testament to the power of the writers that the denouement of a three-part series could keep people hooked for almost two years. I had two years of people asking "How did you survive?" Well, apart from one interviewer who asked how the series would work now that Sherlock was dead – would it be going into the spirit realm? So perhaps not quite everybody got it!

'We'd done the "big three" stories for Series Two,' says Mark Gatiss, 'so it wasn't so obvious a process for the third series. It all fell into place, not as easily as the second series, but quite swiftly. As ever, we just got very excited about the ideas. We'd been discussing "The Adventure of Charles Augustus Milverton" for a long time – it's one of our favourite stories – and it had always seemed to us that Milverton was a very translatable modern character. The idea of the master blackmailer has never really gone away – they're definitely still out there, however they're disguising themselves these days. So we thought that we would build towards Milverton as the climax to the third series, and we would sprinkle references to him in the first two episodes. Steven had always had a hankering to do Milverton, so once we knew we were going to do it as the third one, I said, "Oh god, I'll have to do the opener!"

'And the first, obvious thing was we had to bring Sherlock back from the dead. Everyone agrees that Doyle's story, "The Empty House", is really just an excuse to bring Sherlock Holmes back, and in a way that's what happened to us as well, with the added complication that we knew we had an awful lot of explaining to do. We'd had no idea that Sherlock's fall from the hospital rooftop was going to become this international

DELETED SCENES

23 **INT. RESTAURANT. NIGHT.** 23

                    JOHN
        Two years! Two years! I thought... I
        thought... (chokes up) You were dead!
        And you've let me grieve. How? How could
        you do that?? How??

Sherlock spots a pile of food through the service
hatch and grabs some.

                    SHERLOCK
        You must be starving. Chip? Have a chip!

John smashes the food away.

                    SHERLOCK
        No chips?

John tightens his grip.

                    SHERLOCK (CONT'D)
        Wait! Wait! Before you do anything
        you'll regret - one question! Let me ask
        you one question!

8 **EXT. MOUNTAINSIDE. DAY.** 8

        A breathtaking, snowy peak. Nestled into a rock
        wall - a monastery. Prayer flags ripple in the
        wind.

Caption: Tibet.

                                CUT TO:

9 **INT. MONASTERY. DAY.** 9

        A row of shaven-headed BUDDHIST MONKS in red
        robes are praying. The atmosphere is serene,
        heavy with incense.

                                CUT TO:

        CLOSE on bare feet as the ABBOT enters the
        room, moving slowly through the shadows. The
        robed newcomer walks in front of the Monks, who
        bow their heads low in supplication.

        The Abbot's hand comes into shot, gently
        blessing each Monk's head. The hand reaches the
        last Monk in the line and -

        WHAM!

        - smacks the Monk's head off the marble floor!
        The Monk howls in pain, looks up - and pulls a
        massive Magnum.44 out of his robes! But with
        lethal accuracy, the Abbot kicks him in the
        face, sending him flying over the flagstones.

Note: This scene from an early draft of *The Empty Hearse* was
subsequently adapted to appear in the prequel to Series Three,
Many Happy Returns, released online on Christmas Eve in 2013.

talking point and there'd be all these amazing theories – there were video lectures on YouTube and things like that – and we were all taken aback. We'd known it would have an impact, but we had no idea it would become this phenomenon. So what became clear was that we couldn't just say in the first two minutes how he got out of it. Unlike the previous cliffhanger, which was sorted out by a joke, we just couldn't do that. Then we had the idea of doing a fake opening and making it as outrageous as possible, so that you could almost hear people's jaws dropping at how stupid it was, just in time to pull the rug out and discover that it was just Anderson

theorising. And then, of course, having had that idea, we realised we could do it several times.

'I had a great time creating all those fake openings, and trying to work out how long to keep them apart, and how long we could let John brood, when everybody wants them to get back together. There's a lovely tension there, because you know what everybody wants but, at the same time, if you don't give it to them, they keep wanting to watch because they're being denied the thing that they crave.

'I was thinking of the Giant Rat of Sumatra, which is the most famous of the "untold stories" in the Doyle canon, and I thought it would be interesting to find a way of doing that without it actually being a giant rat. So that led to the idea of the terrorist markers that Sherlock identifies, people who would desert the city if something big was coming. And I'm obsessed with the tube and I'd always wanted to do a story about the tube...

'So the plot of *The Empty Hearse* is really a McGuffin to bring Sherlock back, but also to deal with things that Steven and I felt very strongly about, particularly that Dr Watson, in the original story, accepted Holmes's return rather too easily. We always thought that maybe he was disguising the truth as he wrote about – that he actually fainted and Holmes had to revive him!'

'As a viewer, you are so pulled in by the real emotion of a man grieving for his best friend,' says Benedict. 'It's one of the best bits of screen acting I've ever seen. Martin Freeman in that graveyard is extraordinary, he gives a master-class in the suppressed emotion of a man struggling to come to terms with being on his own.'

Public interest in *Sherlock* had reached astonishing levels by the time Series Three began shooting. 'There was so much written about it on the internet,' notes Jonathan Aris. 'When we were filming the exteriors of the house in Baker Street, I walked onto the Gower Street location, and there were crash barriers, and crowds – a dozen deep, hundreds and hundreds of people – watching us. It was a bit frightening, in a way.'

'Gower Street can be quite daunting,' agrees Amanda Abbington, partner to Martin Freeman, on and off screen. 'There are always hordes of fans

waiting and watching, lots of young girls. I used to visit when they were filming Series Two, and couldn't quite believe it; being part of that for Series Three was overwhelming. It's a bit like Beatlemania. There was an element of that sort of hysteria when Benedict and Martin were on location. I can understand that – I remember growing up and being in love with certain pop stars and just crying if I didn't meet them.'

Amanda Abbington
Born February 1974, North London

SELECTED TV ROLES

Year	Show	Role
2014	Sherlock	Mary Morstan
2013	Mr Selfridge	Miss Mardle
2012	Being Human	Golda
2011–2013	Case Histories	DC Louise Munroe
2010	Married Single Other	Babs
2009	Psychoville	Caroline
2008	Harley Street	Susie Linn
	Agatha Christie's Poirot	Miss Blake
	Coming Up	Daughter
2007	Sold	Zoe
2007	Doc Martin	Isobel
	The Bill	Rachel Inns
2007–2008	After You've Gone	Siobhan Casey
2006	The Booze Cruise III	Leonie
2005	The Booze Cruise II	Leonie
	Derailed	Kerry Hodder
	The Robinsons	Polly
2005–2007	Man Stroke Woman	various roles
2004	Teachers	Sarah
	Bernard's Watch	Sonia

SELECTED STAGE ROLES

2004	Love Me Tonight
2002	The Safari Party
2002	Something Blue

'There is a group of core fans who are absolutely in *love* with John and Sherlock,' says Amanda Abbington, who plays Mary Morstan throughout Series Three. 'They are very, very protective of *Sherlock*, and of John and Sherlock. So you have to tread very carefully because they want Sherlock and John to be together. Mary is a character who doesn't come between John and Sherlock at all, but does become an integral part of their relationship.

'Mary is not in the books for very long; she dies quite quickly. And she's quite a mild-mannered, loyal wife to Dr Watson. Mary in the show is just as loyal to John, and she loves him, but she's more ballsy, she's more independent, and she's a very strong character. In terms of restoring John and Sherlock's relationship at the start of Series Three, she's a catalyst – she can see John's in pain and that he wants to be friends with Sherlock again and pick up where they left off, but he's very stubborn.'

Sue Vertue and Mark Gatiss had both worked with Amanda a few times before, as Martin Freeman recalls. 'When they were talking to me during Series Two about who might be good casting for Mary Morstan and I mentioned Amanda, Mark said, "Oh good, that's exactly what we were thinking." That relationship between John and Sherlock is obviously very important to the show, and we form a very tight unit, so we needed to bring someone in who wouldn't unbalance that. It's not creating a new gang, it's introducing somebody who complements what's already there and has their own identity. The combination of the writing and Amanda's performance achieves all that.

'I think Amanda was quite nervous joining such an established show, but she was also excited because she was a huge fan. It was a little bit nerve-wracking for her, and it was slightly odd for me because I hadn't worked with her for years. And also because the dynamic between Benedict, Amanda and me was different. But I think she slotted into it very well.'

The disused Aldwych tube station in London provided the setting for the scenes set in Sumatra Road, although Sherlock and John's access to the fictional station was filmed at Westminster and Charing Cross underground stations. The set for the tube train itself was built in the studios at Upper Boat in Cardiff.

HOLMES FROM HOLMES

From 'The Reigate Squires'
by Sir Arthur Conan Doyle

It was some time before the health of my friend, Mr Sherlock Holmes, recovered from the strain caused by his immense exertions in the spring of '87. The whole history of the Netherland-Sumatra Company and of the colossal schemes of Baron Maupertius are too recent in the minds of the public, and are too intimately concerned with politics and finance, to be a fitting subject for this series of sketches.

From 'The Empty Hearse'
by Mark Gatiss

        MYCROFT
You have been busy.

        SHERLOCK
(shrugs) Moriarty's organization. Took me
two years to dismantle it.

        MYCROFT
And you're confident you have?

        SHERLOCK
The Serbian side was the last piece of
the puzzle.

        MYCROFT
Yes. You got yourself in deep there with
Baron Maupertius. Quite a scheme.

        SHERLOCK
Colossal.

        MYCROFT
Anyway. You're safe now.

And it wasn't just North Gower Street that was invaded by the watching fans. This time around, everybody knew that picking up from that cliffhanger would involve the team returning to the scene of Sherlock's 'death'. 'St Bart's is a very well-known location,' Benedict points out. 'There's a lot of traffic every day, even at the weekend, there are bars and restaurants nearby, so there are lots of people around all the time, before you add in our very big "live audience". That was... interesting, and probably a big problem for Steven, Sue and Mark to manage. That street theatre is now a regular part of our working day on *Sherlock*. But we do try to be respectful to the fans; they are there to see something being made that they enjoyed watching on television.'

'When we went back to Bart's to prepare for filming,' reveals Sue, 'we really appreciated the impact of that Series Two cliffhanger. There were stickers on phone boxes and graffiti saying "Sherlock Lives!" and "I believe in Sherlock!" Which meant we had to clear it all up to restore the location to how it had been when we were filming *The Reichenbach Fall* two years earlier.'

Revisiting the magic trick of Sherlock's apparent suicide also required some post-production trickery. For Series Three, this was handled by Milk, a newly established visual effects company founded by many of the same team that had worked on the first two series. 'When they shot Sherlock's jump for the end of Series Two,' recalls Jean-Claude Deguara, 'all we did was a bit of painting out wires. Two years later, Sue rang up and asked how much would it cost to place a bungee cord into the same shot. And I was thinking to myself, "That is *awful*!" We watched it back in the screening room and people saw this bungee cord and you could see the disappointment in their faces – it was such a brilliant red herring.'

The bungee-cord 'solution' provided one of Louise Brealey's favourite moments in the series: 'Benedict flew through the window and then landed a great big smacker on my lips. We had a film-star-kiss moment in slow-motion, which was *dreadful*. We had to do it a few times, and I hated every minute of it,' laughs Louise.

EXT. BART'S HOSPITAL.
DAY.
SHERLOCK falls
towards the pavement –
a blur of **windmilling arms**
– but then he's **jerked
back** up by a bungee
rope attached to his waist!
John is still sprawled,
disorientated on
the road.

CUT TO:
INT. BART'S HOSPITAL.
DAY.
SMASH!! SHERLOCK
crashes through a window,
still attached to the
bungee. MOLLY HOOPER
is waiting for him
on the other side. With
Bond-like **nonchalance**,
he disconnects his harness,
kisses her on the mouth
and **saunters off** into the
corridor beyond.

From 'The Empty House'
by Sir Arthur Conan Doyle

[…] I had not been in my study five minutes when the maid entered to say that a person desired to see me. To my astonishment, it was none other than my strange old book-collector, his sharp, wizened face peering out from a frame of white hair, and his precious volumes, a dozen of them at least, wedged under his arm.

'You're surprised to see me, sir,' said he, in a strange, croaking voice.

I acknowledged that I was.

[…] 'I am a neighbour of yours, for you'll find my little bookshop at the corner of Church Street, and very happy to see you, I am sure. Maybe you collect yourself, sir; here's *British Birds*, and Catullus and *The Holy War* – a bargain every one of them. With five volumes you could just fill that gap on that second shelf. It looks untidy, does it not, sir?'

I moved my head to look at the cabinet behind me. When I turned again Sherlock Holmes was standing smiling at me across my study table.

From 'The Empty Hearse'
by Mark Gatiss

JOHN holds up a specimen jar.

            JOHN
    Nothing to worry about. Take your...
    (suspicious) ... take your time.

An old man, MR SZIKORA sits opposite him. He has a woolly hat, big bushy, white beard, dark glasses and a thick foreign accent.

            JOHN
    Infection of some sort, by the sound of
    it. Dr Verner's your usual GP, yes?

            MR SZIKORA
    Yeah. Looked after me man and boy.
    I run a little shop just on the corner
    of Church Street. Magazines. DVDs.
    Got a few little beauties here might
    interest you?

John looks sidelong at the old man. The dark glasses, the beard...

Mr Szikora rummages through his mucky carrier bags.

            MR SZIKORA (CONT'D)
    'Tree Worshippers', that's a corker.
    Very saucy. 'British Birds' – same
    sort of thing.

            JOHN
    (wary) No, I'm good, thanks.

            MR SZIKORA
    'The Holy War'? Sounds a bit dry,
    I know but it isn't. There's a nun
    with all these holes in her habit –

Suddenly, John launches himself at Mr Szikora, pulling off his woolly hat.

            JOHN
    You bastard!

            MR SZIKORA
    Eh?

            JOHN
    What do you want? Have you just come to
    torment me?

He tugs at the old man's beard.

            MR SZIKORA
    Ow! What are you talking about? Help!

Tugs again.

            JOHN
    Stick a stupid beard on and you
    think you can get away with it?

He drags the dark glasses off the old man.

            MR SZIKORA
    (shouts) Help me! This man is crazy!

            JOHN
    And you know what? It's not even a good
    disguise! Where'd you get it? A bloody...

John looks into the old man's eyes. His face falls.

            JOHN (CONT'D)
    ... joke... shop.

Oh dear.

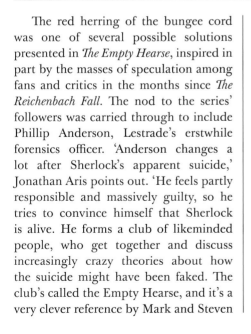

The red herring of the bungee cord was one of several possible solutions presented in *The Empty Hearse*, inspired in part by the masses of speculation among fans and critics in the months since *The Reichenbach Fall*. The nod to the series' followers was carried through to include Phillip Anderson, Lestrade's erstwhile forensics officer. 'Anderson changes a lot after Sherlock's apparent suicide,' Jonathan Aris points out. 'He feels partly responsible and massively guilty, so he tries to convince himself that Sherlock is alive. He forms a club of likeminded people, who get together and discuss increasingly crazy theories about how the suicide might have been faked. The club's called the Empty Hearse, and it's a very clever reference by Mark and Steven to the enormous public response. The internet was full of theories about how the suicide might have been faked, and it was great fun to show a little subset of people discussing exactly that.'

'IT'S LIKE A SHRINE'

The level and intensity of interest from fans, press and public prompted Hartswood and the BBC to explore some innovative strategies to promote the series' return. The broadcast date for *The Empty Hearse* was revealed when a hearse was driven around London on Friday 29 November 2013, the flowers on the coffin arranged to spell out "Sherlock 01 01 14", alongside a car decal bearing the official hashtag

HOLMES FROM HOLMES

From 'The Empty House'
by Sir Arthur Conan Doyle

'… We tottered together upon the brink of the fall. I have some knowledge, however, of *baritsu*, or the Japanese system of wrestling, which has more than once been very useful to me. I slipped through his grip …'

From The Empty Hearse
by Mark Gatiss

SHERLOCK (V.O.)
I calculated that there were thirteen possibilities once I'd invited Moriarty onto the roof. I wanted to avoid dying if at all possible. The first scenario involved hurling myself into a parked hospital van filled with washing bags. Impossible. The angle was too steep. Secondly, a system of Japanese wrestling...

From 'The Adventure of the Gloria Scott'
by Sir Arthur Conan Doyle

'… Then in an instant the key of the riddle was in my hands, and I saw that every third word, beginning with the first, would give a message which might well drive old Trevor to despair.'

From 'The Empty Hearse'
by Mark Gatiss

MARY
Someone sent me this. I thought it was just some Bible thing. Spam. But it's not. It's a skip code.

On Sherlock: just the briefest beat of surprise. He looks at the phone.

SHERLOCK
(nods) Every third word. Starting with the first.

From 'The Adventure of the Sussex Vampire'
by Sir Arthur Conan Doyle

'Matilda Briggs was not the name of a young woman, Watson,' said Holmes in a reminiscent voice. 'It was a ship which is associated with the giant rat of Sumatra, a story for which the world is not yet prepared.'

From 'The Empty Hearse'
by Mark Gatiss

HOWARD
Sumatra Road, Mr Holmes! You mentioned Sumatra Road. There is something! I knew it rang a bell.

From 'The Final Problem'
by Sir Arthur Conan Doyle

… if I have now been compelled to make a clear statement of his career, it is due to those injudicious champions who have endeavoured to clear his memory by attacks upon him whom I shall ever regard as the best and the wisest man whom I have ever known.

From 'The Empty Hearse'
by Mark Gatiss

JOHN
But I couldn't have asked for a better friend. You were the best. The best and the... wisest man I've ever known.

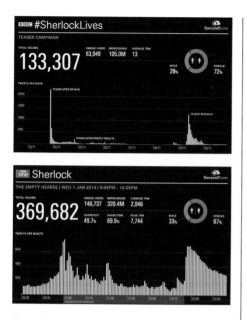

for the returning series: *#SherlockLives*. The hashtag had been announced the previous Saturday, in a teaser trailer shown immediately after *Doctor Who*'s 50th anniversary special. Already a formidable presence online, *Sherlock* was about to take Twitter by storm...

The evening of Saturday 23 November saw *#SherlockLives* mentioned in 31,898 tweets, and there were another 18,867 the next day. That surged again on 29 November, with 58,989 times during the day and a single tweet from Mark Gatiss being retweeted 6,099 times. BBC One got in on the act, changing the channel's Twitter name to #SherlockLives throughout that Friday.

During the New Year's Day broadcast itself, *#SherlockLives*, was used 98,533 times, but that was just one small part of the story. *The Empty Hearse*'s 86-minute transmission saw 369,682 tweets about the show, peaking at 7,744 tweets per minute as the episode was starting, and averaging 2,046 tweets a minute. Social media analysts SecondSync recorded that *Sherlock* was provoking a huge response, way beyond anything it had achieved previously:

Mark Gatiss ✔
@Markgatiss

🔽 Follow

Sherlock Holmes, consulting detective. Much missed by friends & family. In *living* memory. Jan 1st 2014! #SherlockLives

9:44 AM - 29 Nov 2013

6,875 RETWEETS 3,735 FAVORITES

'Comparing the Twitter statistics from the first episode of series three to that of the first episode of series two proves just how far *Sherlock* has come in its two year hiatus. The first episode of series three generated a total volume that is almost six times the amount generated by the first episode of series two. *A Scandal in Belgravia* saw a total volume of 61,948 Tweets, peaking at a 1,347 Tweets per minute as the episode began. The episode also only managed an average of 370tpm, a substantial amount less in comparison to *The Empty Hearse*'s 2,046tpm.'

Mark Gatiss's script for 'The Empty Hearse' called for a couple of showcase visual effects...

'We'll get a script and break down what we think are visual effects shots,' explains Jean-Claude Deguara from Milk, 'and then we sit down with the producer and director and go into much more detail about the types of things they want, work out all the FX shots through the episodes, and cost it all up.'

'There's an inevitable rationalisation that happens at that point,' continues Milk's CEO, Will Cohen. 'Sue will put aside a certain sum of money for the series, but it's a live situation and it can be quite fluid. Producers are great at moving money around, and money saved on one thing can be spent on another. The director, the director of photography and the production designer will identify what's essential to the story and what's a luxury. We might simplify some things, or cut others. A budget is agreed before the shoot, but then things might develop differently during the shoot, or there might be more streamlining during the edit. Then the director and editor come round and go through the assembled episode with us and brief us on exactly what's wanted. We try to wait as late as we can for a locked cut to work out exactly how many shots there should be, so we don't do work that ends up being cut. Though in truth a cut is never locked until everyone's seen it and everyone's happy.'

Having defined what Milk will be working on, Jean-Claude will visit locations and studio sets when the relevant sequences are being filmed. 'I usually go up on my own,' he says. 'I'll only get one or two shots a day, so there's a lot of hanging around. I get all the information we need so we can replicate the scene in a digital environment. If for instance there's a bullet travelling through shot, we need to know where that bullet starts, where it leaves the gun, where it impacts and so on.

'When they were filming *The Empty Hearse*, they had this replica tube carriage, and I think they wanted to sell it on after the shoot. But the special effects supervisor Danny Hargreaves and I were adamant that we wanted to blow up this carriage in slow motion and have a big, realistic fireball running through the carriage. We kept pestering Sue, and we told her we wouldn't damage it, though it might get a little bit singed in places... She agreed to it, and we sent ten or twenty fireballs down that carriage. We didn't break anything, but that carriage was *black*!'

For Will Cohen, the visual effects on *Sherlock* play a supporting role. 'A lot of what we do is just about helping *Sherlock* tell the story – the matte paintings, the little bits of graphics on mobile phones, all these tiny details. We're working with directors who are pushing the boundaries of storytelling narrative on a TV show, and being associated with that and being part of the team is something we're all really proud of. It is one of the most sophisticated TV dramas going in the UK.'

Jean-Claude agrees. 'There are no restraints on *Sherlock* when it comes to filmmaking. The new techniques that they'll throw in, some of the slow-motion shots, the types of lenses they use – it's just brilliant.'

'The experimentation goes on, even in the way it's edited,' Will concludes. 'The brilliantly clever scripts and the wonderful performances make it special, but all this other little stuff makes it feel really different to everything else on television. If I wasn't doing it, I'd be really jealous of whoever was. Can you get that bit to Sue in time for Series Four?'

For special effects supervisor Danny Hargreaves, the tube-train sequence was a great opportunity to do something special. 'Arwel Jones had built this wonderful tube train interior, and we shot the whole sequence with the actors in place. We then took a plate shot – a shot of Sherlock sat on the left-hand side of the train. We locked the camera, which means we left it in position, rigged, and with everything measured. The next day, I came in with my team and a fire crew, with a high-performance camera called a Phantom running at 750 frames per second. When you shoot any fire at high speed, it looks stunning. We used a pressure vessel called a propane woofer, which is a compressor cylinder with a quick-actuating valve at the end – a valve that's controlled with air. A button on my firing box opens the valve at the speed I want and fires propane onto a naked flame – a firelighter placed on the floor of the tube train. Releasing an expansion of gas at a pre-tested pressure creates this wonderful orange fireball. We did that a number of times, moving the vessel down a few metres at a time, doing the same effect each time, and generated a big fireball that travelled down the tube train. It could have been computer-generated, but I was keen to do it because we got the fireball reacting with the environment that we put it in. It went up the seats, up the windows, it span around, we blew some paper around and shot it in slow-mo – you can't replicate that with CGI! So we created a fireball that rolled down the train, and then they stitched it all together in the edit and tied it in with the CG effect of the fireball travelling up the ventilation chimney to blow up the Houses of Parliament so you see the two effects coming together to create one big effect.'

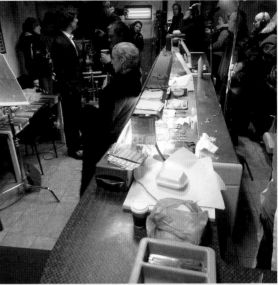

Sherlock surprises John in a 'dark, swanky, expensive' restaurant, the Reunion. Its exterior was shot at London's Marylebone Road, near Baker Street, but the interior filming took place at the Daffodil in Cheltenham.

The Art Department supplied a range of sets and props, including an actual tube carriage,
while Make-Up created a mask of Benedict Cumberbatch's face...

MANY HAPPY RETURNS

T*he Empty Hearse* was preceded by a 7-minute mini-episode, *Many Happy Returns*, written by Steven and Mark, released online on Christmas Eve 2013. At the same time, 'The personal blog of Dr John H. Watson', started on the orders of his therapist in *A Study in Pink*, sprang back into life.

The blog, mentioned and glimpsed in several episodes, including *The Great Game* and *A Scandal in Belgravia*, was made available at www.johnwatsonblog.co.uk, its entries written by Joseph Lidster. 'I was called to a meeting with Sue Vertue, Steven Moffat and Mark Gatiss when the series was first getting going,' Joe remembers. 'At that point it was still going to be lots of different episodes by lots of different writers, and they knew that I'd written for *Torchwood* and *The*

THE PERSONAL BLOG OF

Dr. John H. Watson

5th October

Many Happy Returns

So, Greg came around the other day. He had a load of stuff that had belonged to Sherlock. Just tat really. Nothing that even gets close to showing who or what he was. Stuff can't do that. Not physical stuff anyway. We've all got belongings and photos and furniture and books and... they're not who we are. They're just things we've accumulated over the years. They mean nothing.

But then there was this DVD. It was a video of Sherlock recording a message for my birthday dinner. A bunch of us went to this restaurant in Soho. It was great, actually. Everyone was there. Mike, Harry, Greg, Mrs Hudson, the usual suspects. Except Sherlock. He didn't come because he was 'busy'. He wasn't busy, he just... sometimes he struggled to fit in. He couldn't switch off, couldn't relax. He just struggled with people, I think. Yet the video... it showed the other side to him. He was rude, yeah. Arrogant. Apparently lacking in anything resembling empathy. But I'd forgotten just how funny he could be. He was so charming. So... human. It's bizarre because most people would say he was the most inhuman person they'd ever met. But he wasn't. He was everything a good person should be. He'd just often say what he was thinking rather than lying to protect our feelings. Maybe we should all be more like that? Maybe we should all be more honest? Although maybe it was a good thing he didn't come to that birthday dinner...

And now it's time for me to be honest. I'm meant to be keeping this blog to remind me of the good times. I know it's meant to be healthy but what's the point? I need to properly move on. I need to put it all behind me and move on.

And I'm so tired of deleting comments from people who don't believe me. Who think all this is a lie. I know it was real. There are so many people out there who know that all this was real. They believed in Sherlock.

And I've found someone. So I should concentrate on that.

So this'll be my last blog.

Sherlock, you bastard, wherever you are. Cheers.

John.

💬 **Comments disabled**

DELETED SCENES

Sherlock Series Three   The Empty Hearse

22 **INT. GYM. NIGHT.**   22

    CLOSE on feet in trainers, pounding away
    on a running machine. We pull up to see:
    MYCROFT! As we've never seen him before,
    in a grey jogging outfit; red-faced and
    exhausted.

    He's in an expensive-looking gym, totally
    empty apart from him. On a TV, the news
    is on. The strap-line reads: 'Terrorist
    threat level red.'

    Mycroft gives the machine one last sprint
    and then lets it wind down, panting with
    exertion. He steps off the treadmill and wipes
    his face with a towel. Then, surreptitiously,
    he lifts his sweatshirt and pats his stomach,
    checking his waistline. He looks pleased.
    Someone clears their throat. Mycroft looks
    round - a guilty thing surprised. ANTHEA is
    standing there, holding a manila file. She
    glances towards the TV.

                    MYCROFT
    No choice. The PM insisted we go to
    code red. Have there been any more?

                    ANTHEA
    Just the same message, sir.

                    MYCROFT
    'Remember, remember'.

    He broods.

                    MYCROFT
    And the... other matter?

                    ANTHEA
    I'm afraid it's no good, sir.

    She hands him the file. It's stamped
    'For Your Eyes Only'. He opens it.

                    ANTHEA
    Nothing can stop them now.

    Mycroft reads.

                    MYCROFT
    Oh God.

Note: This scene from an early draft of *The Empty Hearse*
was subsequently rewritten for the second episode
of Series Three, *The Sign of Three*.

Sarah Jane Adventures. They also knew that I was into Sherlock Holmes and that I'd written fictional websites for *Doctor Who* and *Torchwood*, and they asked me to do the same thing for *Sherlock*.

'We wanted to create an addition to the series – you can watch the series and then go and read John's blog. But we've also developed them so they do a bit more than that, because as a creative writer the one thing I didn't want to do was just reiterate what was in the episodes. So that's why you get lots of extra blog posts, and little ongoing storylines in the comments, like whether John's sister Harry is drinking or not. They add to the series; they're not something you need to read to understand the series but they add to it and give it extra colour.

> **SHERLOCK**
> So people **actually read** that blog.
>
> **JOHN**
> Where do you think our **clients** come from?
>
> **SHERLOCK**
> I have a website…

'There's Sherlock's *Science of Deduction* site and Molly Hooper's diary, and I did one for Connie Prince, the murdered TV personality in *The Great Game*. That was a one-off, just me having lots of fun. From Series Two, we decided that we should jsut focus on John's blog because it was better to send people to a single website. In the fiction of it, John's blog was making them famous so it made sense to follow that through. Sherlock's site is now only updated when it has to be to tie in with what's happening in the TV series.

'I get early drafts of the scripts, and chat through them with Jo Pearce, the BBC's interactive fiction producer, and with Sue and occasionally Steven. We talk about what we can do – how can we follow on from cliffhangers, how can we do it without giving away what's coming up...? In the lead-up to Series Three, we did lots of extra cases – John saying that although Sherlock was dead there were still lots of cases he'd never had the chance to write up. We also started incorporating videos: news reports, BBC Breakfast, things like that which will work within the fiction.

'We plan it out, get the order right, which can be tricky – with all the cases that were talked about at the wedding, for example, we didn't want to spoil it for people who were going to watch the episode, but those cases needed to go up in some form before the wedding. There's a scene where John is writing his blog so we had to reflect that. We have to work our way round how it's featured in the series.

'Once we have an approved plan, I'll write first drafts and send them through in batches, for feedback from the BBC and Hartswood, with notes from Sue, Steven and Mark. I usually do two or three drafts, then I just hand it over and clever people put it online. I can use Facebook and Twitter and that's about it, so I just write the words and sometimes specify some of the pictures, especially where there's lots of text going up at once. Sometimes I try to find pictures to put with it: for the murder in the Orient Express restaurant entry, you see Sherlock's evidence collection, which is something I put together. It's basically photos of my sister's 18th birthday – a few of the pictures I think I'm in – some receipts, things like that. There's also one where there's a dead body in a bath, and that's actually me.

'I mostly write original short stories. At first, I'd find a Sherlock Holmes story and adapt it, but you never know what'll end up being used in the series and

17th June

Murder at 'The Orient Express'

Sherlock worked it out by breaking it down to the simplest facts.

7th November

The Empty Hearse

Well.

So yes.

You'll have seen the news.

Where do I even begin?

As the trending hashtag says: #sherlocklives

there were a few times where they said no to one of my suggestions on the basis that they might want to use that for an episode in the future. In fact, there was one blog post that we dropped because its case ended up being incorporated into *The Sign of Three*...'

CHANGES

Writing speeches, making up, and dressing up...

'HARDEST THING
I'VE EVER DONE'

'*The Sign of Three* is an odd one,' declares Steve Thompson. 'Because of the structure of each series, with just three episodes, we always start with a bang, and end with an even bigger finale, so the trickiest thing in some ways is to find what goes in the middle.

'Steven and Mark said what can we do that's genuinely surprising, and we talked through all sorts of loopy ideas, eventually settling on the wedding and deciding to bring in much more overt comedy. It all seemed quite wild, and our big concern for a while was whether anybody else was going to laugh. Steven and Mark had a lot of input on Sherlock's best man's speech. We had one particularly silly lunch, talking about the stag night and the speech...'

'We decided to bring in Mrs Watson at an early stage,' recalls Mark Gatiss. 'We all think that Doyle slightly mistimed it: he married Watson in the second story and then had to set most of the adventures in some imagined bachelordom beforehand. So we thought that the third series of our show was the perfect time for John to get married because he's got over – as far as he can – the death of his best friend, and he's just about to move on, and that's the perfect time for Sherlock to come and mess things up again. So having decided that John's about to get married, and all that that would imply, the obvious thing to do with the second episode was make it the wedding.

'It really came from a casual conversation. Steven Moffat said that when he was little and first read about Dr Watson getting married, it occurred to him that Holmes must have been the best man, and that surely that was the strangest best man's speech in history. And we laughed about it, then thought actually this was what it should be. The idea of using it as a spine for the whole episode – and that the amusing bachelor

MOLLY
Greg... he'll make a **speech**!
A silence.
MOLLY (CONT'D)
In front of people. There
will be **actual people** there,
actually **listening**.

John and Sherlock's London pub crawl was shot entirely in Cardiff, beginning at Kitty Flyn's in St Mary Street, then moving to Mill Lane for recording at Kanu. The last two venues were also in Mill Lane: SodaBar and, finally, its next-door neighbour, The Attic.

stories would turn out to be unsolved cases which were then solved at the end – seemed very original, very exciting.

'We asked Steve Thompson to do the second episode but we ended up writing it between the three of us, because it became rather more complicated than we had anticipated. We had to keep the narrative going and not let it become too indulgent. We've always said that the important thing with our series is that there is development: you can't keep having John being amazed by Sherlock's deductions – he still finds them amazing but he wouldn't tell Sherlock that because he just looks like an idiot – so you have to find new ways of presenting it.

'Equally, you have to find new ways of progressing Sherlock himself. He's a bit like Pinocchio: he is creeping towards becoming more human. He'll never make it, but he has to change, otherwise you just set the whole thing in aspic and there's no point in doing that. We wanted to show that in his own slightly clumsy,

high-functioning way he is trying to reach out and say how much he cares but he just doesn't know how to do it. So he does it by making the most insulting and upsetting best man's speech ever, but then rather brilliantly turns it round to say, "I don't know why I'm your best friend – in fact, I'm not any more, because look what you've found." We knew this was a slightly high-risk thing, but we wanted to make people think that he'd gone a bit soft, precisely because the events of the third episode were going to be so cataclysmic.'

For Benedict Cumberbatch, filming that speech felt like doing a one-man show – for five days. 'Well, it felt like five days. We did take quite a lot of time filming it, but that was actually only a couple of days. I think it's the biggest deduction we've ever done, and it's endless – I had the most amazing audience to help me out with it, and they were all having fun while I was cramming in another twelve pages of dialogue. It was a glorious episode to make, really good fun.'

JOHN
Sherlock, mate, I've smelled eighteen different **perfumes**. I've sampled nine different slices of **cake** that all tasted identical. I like the Bridesmaids in **purple**.

SHERLOCK
Lilac.

SHERLOCK
Oh, Mike Stamford you mean?
fella, not sure he'd handle all the -
JOHN
friend.

DELETED SCENES

Sherlock Series Three   The Sign of Three

20   INT. 221B BAKER STREET. DAY.   20

>   SHERLOCK
> Oh, Mike Stamford you mean? Nice fella,
> not sure he'd handle all the -
>
>   JOHN
> Mike's great, he's not my best friend.
>
>   SHERLOCK
> ... your Mum?
>
>   JOHN
> Is dead, and a woman.
>
>   SHERLOCK
> Dead? I was talking to someone's
> Mum, wasn't that yours?
>
>   JOHN
> Sherlock, this is the biggest
> and most important day of my life.

Sherlock Series Three   The Sign of Three

50   EXT. PARK. DAY   50

>   JOHN
> Which I don't.
>
>   SHERLOCK
> Of course you don't. You think highly of
> him. He was your previous best friend...
> ex-best friend. Whatever he was, why
> don't you keep in touch?
>
>   JOHN
> He doesn't. Long story - he had a bad
> time out there.
>
>   SHERLOCK
> Decorated, wasn't he? He's a war hero.

Sherlock Series Three   The Sign of Three

64   INT. BAR. NIGHT   64

> SHERLOCK, completely blotto, in the middle
> of a bar fight with a pissed up THUG. He's
> pointing at the THUG'S hoodie and yelling.
>
>   SHERLOCK
> Listen, I'm telling you - on your...
> hoodie. That's ash from a Marlboro light!
>
>   THUG
> I never smoke lights. Girls' fags!
>
>   SHERLOCK
> (Yelling) I know ash! Don't tell me I
> don't!

HOLMES FROM HOLMES

From 'The Adventure of Charles Augustus Milverton'
by Sir Arthur Conan Doyle

We had been out for one of our evening rambles, Holmes and I, and had returned about six o'clock on a cold, frosty winter's evening. As Holmes turned up the lamp the light fell upon a card on the table. He glanced at it, and then, with an ejaculation of disgust, threw it on the floor. I picked it up and read:

CHARLES AUGUSTUS MILVERTON,

Appledore Towers,

Hampstead.

Agent.

'Who is he?' I asked.

'The worst man in London,' Holmes answered, as he sat down and stretched his legs before the fire. 'Is anything on the back of the card?'

I turned it over.

'Will call at 6:30 – C.A.M.,' I read.

From 'The Sign of Three'
by Steve Thompson, Mark Gatiss & Steven Moffat

SHERLOCK has a bunch of telegrams - reading
them with no apparent feeling or warmth -
a rather agonising task for him -

    SHERLOCK (CONT'D)
'To John and Mary. All good wishes for
your special day. With love and... (Do I
really have to say this?) ... many big
squishy cuddles from Stella and Ted'.

John and Mary enjoy this.

    SHERLOCK (CONT'D)
(Takes another) 'So sorry I'm unable
to be with you... Mike Stamford...'
(another) 'Lots of love...'

    And he falters.

        JOHN
Yes?

    SHERLOCK
(Finds this word almost impossible)
'... poppet. Oodles of love and heaps
of good wishes from Cam. Wish your
family could've have seen this'.

A beat on Mary as she turns away, moved.
John squeezes her hand.

'That episode was a lot of fun to film,' agrees Amanda Abbington. 'Sherlock's this mad sociopath, and he has to get involved in planning the wedding, so he decides to do it all, in every tiny detail. Then that best man's speech starts beautifully, but that unsolved case is still ticking away in his head, so the speech is peppered with his thoughts about it and it ends up in a huge climax as he works out who is going to die. And at the end of the speech, Sherlock and John dash into action and, rather than sit there passively, Mary follows them – which helps set up what's revealed about her in the next story.'

'WELL, THEN. INTO BATTLE!'

Part of the fun making *The Sign of Three* was kitting out and making up a larger than normal supporting cast, along with all the regulars, for a wedding reception that lasted days not hours. 'Making that episode was like *Groundhog Day*,' laughs Claire Pritchard-Jones, make-up and hair designer on *Sherlock*. 'It was shot over several days, and all the guest and main artists had to look identical each day. And we had to remember to plaster on the sun screen to prevent anyone burning and changing colour through the scene!'

Claire came to *Sherlock* for the pilot version of *A Study in Pink*, after work on series like *Being Human*, *Doctor Who*, *Getting on* and *Torchwood*. 'Working on those sorts of shows, that circle of producers and scriptwriters gets to know you and gets to know your work. Just by chance I found out that *Sherlock* was happening, and I phoned up to say I was interested. It was their last afternoon of interviews in Cardiff, but they invited me to go in and see them, and then they called me back that same evening and said they'd love to have me on board. I did the pilot and Series One; I was booked for something else when they did Series Two, but I went back for Series Three.'

The process begins, as always, with an early draft of each script. 'Identifying what's needed for each character always starts with the script and conversations with Sue Vertue and the director. We get the first draft, and I plot out the characters, trying to find the back story for each of them and making a note of how I think they would look. It's important when developing a character to think about their lifestyle and the environment they live in. I then attend the tone meeting, where every department fleshes out their ideas. Of course, everyone's imagination works differently – all those people sitting round the table talking it through might have several different ideas. Then you meet the cast, and they'll have their own ideas, so you build on all of that.

'It's important to work with the costume department to establish a complete image. The hair and make-up and costume need to complement each other, not fight each other to make a character believable. So after the tone meeting stage, we'll hold a separate meeting for the director, the costume designer and myself, and we'll do a page-turn of the script, to highlight all of the characters and make sure we're all aiming for the same thing. Of course, until you meet the cast members, you don't know what you'll need to change or add to their appearance in terms of complexion, tattoos, wigs, hair colour... When Benedict Cumberbatch was cast, for example, he had short auburn hair, so we had to do something about that. They wanted him to look Byronesque – Mark and Steven were very definite about that poetic image – and Mark also said that Sherlock was very much a "creature of the night", stalking the city in the dark, so he wanted that pale complexion and dark hair. In fact, he was much paler in the pilot than he was in Series One.'

Photos recording the recce at the Bank of England during pre-production for *The Sign of Three*'s pre-titles bank job, plus a continuity photograph taken during the location shoot for the bank job

More continuity photos, this time for the scene of Sherlock's attempt to clue for looks in one of the Mayfly Man's ghost residences.

The Wellington Barracks interiors were shot at the Glamorgan Building in Cathays Park, Cardiff. The showers and the blood were provided by the practical effects team.

Wellington Barracks on Westminster's Birdcage Walk appeared as itself for the episode. Production designer
Arwel Wyn Jones was on location, taking photos of Benedict's turn as a Footguard, to the bemusement of the assembled paparazzi.
The bench on Birdcage Walk, opposite the Barracks, was an addition by the production team.

HOLMES FROM HOLMES

From 'The Sign of Four'
by Sir Arthur Conan Doyle

'Well, and there is the end of our little drama,' I remarked after we had sat some time smoking in silence. 'I fear that it may be the last investigation in which I shall have the chance of studying your methods. Miss Morstan has done me the honour to accept me as a husband in prospective.'

He gave a most dismal groan.

'I feared as much,' said he. 'I really cannot congratulate you.'

I was a little hurt.

'Have you any reason to be dissatisfied with my choice?' I asked.

'Not at all. I think she is one of the most charming young ladies I ever met and might have been most useful in such work as we have been doing. She had a decided genius that way; witness the way in which she preserved that Agra plan from all the other papers of her father. But love is an emotional thing, and whatever is emotional is opposed to that true cold reason which I place above all things. I should never marry myself, lest I bias my judgment.'

'I trust,' said I, laughing, 'that my judgment may survive the ordeal.'

From 'The Sign of Three'
by Steve Thompson, Mark Gatiss & Steven Moffat

SHERLOCK
I'm afraid, John, I can't congratulate
you. All emotion, and love in particular,
stand opposed to that pure, cold reason
that I hold above all things. A wedding
is, in my considered opinion, nothing
short of a celebration of all that is
false and specious and irrational and
sentimental in this ailing and morally
compromised world.

'*Sherlock* really pushes you to your limits, and then goes a bit further,' Claire continues. 'You put your ideas forward, but the directors will always ask you to show them something more and explore every option. In *A Study in Pink*, for example, Paul McGuigan wanted some extreme close-ups of the victim's hand where she'd been scratching "Rache" into the floorboard. So we gave her false nails, with little splinters of wood under the nails, knowing that the audience were going to see all those tiny extra details.

'There are three of us on the main team – I look after Benedict, Sarah Astley-Hughes looks after Martin, and Amy Riley looks after Amanda Abbington. We share the guest artists between us, according to scheduling requirements. Luckily we also had a trainee on each block of Series Three, which helped enormously. Every episode is quite intensive. Even a two-hander can leave you on the edge of your seat. In *A Study in Pink*, for instance, there was that seven-page scene with Benedict and Phil Davis, playing the taxi driver, which was shot over two days. They were incredibly hot, so we had to constantly make sure their hair was in the right place to match continuity and make everything easier in the final edit. The last episode of Series Three, *His Last Vow*, involved many different looks for Benedict when Sherlock was shot, so I had to work with him to nail all the different stages of his health and death!

'We're normally on location or in studio up to an hour and a half before the cameras start to record, so generally an hour or so is allowed for costume and make-up. It's usually a twelve-hour day from there through to a fifteen-minute clean-off session with a pampering hot towel for each artist at the end of the day. Sometimes, though, you'll need a bit longer. In *The Sign of Three*, we had to deal with Major Sholto's burns and scars. It was mentioned in the script that

there was a scar down the side of this face but when we started filming, we thought maybe he'd have more injuries, lots of little scars joining together. Alistair Petrie, playing Major Sholto, was in for seven consecutive days, so we had to replicate that make-up multiple times. We used silicon moulds to put the scars on in the same place and in the same way each time. That took about an hour and a half to apply each day of the shoot. Major Sholto featured in the main reception scene, but there were also his scenes

From 'A Case of Identity'
by Sir Arthur Conan Doyle

He had risen from his chair, and was standing between the parted blinds, gazing down into the dull, neutral-tinted London street. Looking over his shoulder, I saw that on the pavement opposite there stood a large woman with a heavy fur boa round her neck, and a large curling red feather in a broad-brimmed hat which was tilted in a coquettish Duchess-of-Devonshire fashion over her ear.

From under this great panoply she peeped up in a nervous, hesitating fashion at our windows, while her body oscillated backward and forward, and her fingers fidgeted with her glove buttons. Suddenly, with a plunge, as of the swimmer who leaves the bank, she hurried across the road, and we heard the sharp clang of the bell.

'I have seen those symptoms before,' said Holmes, throwing his cigarette into the fire. 'Oscillation upon the pavement always means an *affaire de cœur*. She would like advice, but is not sure that the matter is not too delicate for communication. And yet even here we may discriminate. When a woman has been seriously wronged by a man, she no longer oscillates, and the usual symptom is a broken bell wire. Here we may take it that there is a love matter, but that the maiden is not so much angry as perplexed or grieved. But here she comes in person to resolve our doubts.'

From 'The Sign of Three'
by Steve Thompson, Mark Gatiss & Steven Moffat

Sherlock is in his chair. John at the window, looking down into the street.

JOHN
She's nearly ringing the doorbell. Nope, she's changed her mind. She's going to ring it, she's leaving, she's leaving, she's coming back –

SHERLOCK
She's a client and she's boring. Seen those symptoms before.

JOHN
Hmm?

SHERLOCK
Oscillation on the pavement always means a love affair.

in his hotel room and at his home, and that all requires attention to continuity because you go from scene to scene and those scars all have to look the same.'

The episode also features flashback scenes to several different days and nights leading up to the wedding, and for those the challenge is different – everyone has to look slightly different. 'You might have three weeks between adjacent scenes,' Claire explains. 'Once we get a shooting script, we do a continuity breakdown for each character: pull out every actor's scenes and mark up make-up and hair references for all of it – what stage their make-up is at. The day before each filming day we have a call sheet and we add to that the relevant notes on each scene for each actor. Most of those days on *The Sign of Three* needed seven additional hair and make-up artists working with the basic team.'

> SHERLOCK
> And John's great, haven't said that enough. I've barely **scratched the surface**. I could go on all night about the **depth** and the **complexity** of his... jumpers.

Steven Moffat thinks it would be a mistake to think of Sherlock Holmes in terms of 'costume'. 'He doesn't wear a costume; he wears clothes like anybody else. If you look in the original stories he very rarely, even in most of the films, actually goes around in an Inverness cape and deerstalker. For the most part he just wears smart clothes of the period. There is a little bit of vanity in Sherlock, so he tends to be quite smartly dressed – he knows what he's doing in that regard. He is anxious to come over as a professional, so he wears a smart suit, and he's vain

enough that he knows how to look good. So we just dress him smartly for the modern day and we give him a little bit of the hero look, with the big coat and the scarf. So he becomes the alpha male in the room.'

Costume designer Sarah Arthur agrees. 'Sherlock is not supposed to be about clothing – he's just about the work, and so what he wears has to fit into the character, and his look hasn't really changed across the three series.'

Sarah began working in costume for TV in 1990, and her extensive list of costume design credits runs from *The Cops* and *Bad Girls* in the late 1990s, via *Footballers' Wives*, *Mistresses* and *Holby Blue*, to *Hunted*, *Love & Marriage* and, most recently *24: Live Another Day*. 'When *Sherlock* was commissioned for a series,

they asked about my availability. I used to live in Cardiff, and they were looking for a Welsh crew. I went and met Sue Vertue, and I was offered the job. Sue is very involved, as are Mark Gatiss and Steven: they're very hands on, they're always around, they're always on set. I get the script then I have a meeting with them and with the director, and I formulate some ideas. Then I meet the main actors, and they obviously have an input as well. It's a massive collaboration of really committed people.

'I have a costume supervisor, an assistant and a trainee, so it's quite a small team. I do every single costume, including guest artists and extras. We have already fitted the main cast by the time we get to recording, so I can focus on the crowd – we're fitting them on the

day, so we have no idea until then who we're getting or what they'll look like. I carry a lot of stock with me so I can be sure of covering myself from all angles – supporting artists are asked to wear something appropriate but that doesn't always work out.

'One of the hardest things was picking up from the end of Series Two for the start of Series Three at St Bart's, and dealing with a crowd of extras in their own clothes – two years later. That was quite tough. Generally, though, as long as you know what's coming, it'll be OK. I organise things up to a week before and set it all up the day before filming, so I have time to deal with any problems. Every single item is labelled with scene numbers and all the changes needed.

'I'm there an hour before filming, sometimes earlier. The assistant directors work all the schedules out. I don't want actors sitting in their costumes for an hour's make-up, so they have their make-up done before I have to get them into costumes. It's busy but it's all about organisation – it's fine if you're organised. I carry quite an extensive stock, and I use a lot of it and change it and alter it where

I need to. Not so much for Benedict and Martin, but for a lot of the other cast. Benedict's tramp clothes came out of my stock. We've had certain items made: the odd tie, hankie, waistcoat, slippers, and I made quite a few things for Irene Adler – some of her full outfits and some of the sexier stuff. But mainly the clothes are bought in.

'I inherited Sherlock's long coat from Ray Holman, who was the costume designer on the pilot, but that was the only thing I kept. We did attempt to make a new coat, but as a work in progress it wasn't quite what we wanted. We have three of those coats to cover damage and the need for stunt doubles. It is a lovely coat.

'I wanted very clean lines for Benedict, because his shape warrants that, so everything was chosen to contribute to the overall silhouette. The very first suit that we tried on Benedict worked – he thought so and I thought so. We did a fitting and everybody else loved it immediately too. It was one of those processes that worked out fairly simply. We use Spencer Hart suits and Dolce & Gabbana shirts because we needed something to match his stature and build, and they are sleek, straight and perfectly cut and the shirts suit his slim frame. Those suits were actually the very first thing he tried on for the role. He insists on doing his own stunts, so a lot of his suits get wrecked. We buy three complete plus an additional jacket for each different suit.

'The original pair of shoes was Yves Saint Laurent, then we used Poste then a pair from TK Maxx. I had them resoled with a thicker sole, because he does so much running around London. We also wanted a very small heel on them, because Benedict is quite a lot taller than Martin.

'For Martin, John is ex-military but he's moved on a bit, so we were looking at a slightly more casual contrast to Sherlock. He generally wears classic

Loake boots, with check shirts, Uniqlo jeans, which were actually Martin's suggestion, and cable-knit jumpers. We looked at knitwear with a little bit of a difference – not high street, not fashionable, but something with a texture or a stripe in it or a little trim... I wanted to make him look old school and slightly homely, but not old fashioned.'

On John: **defeated**. Slowly, he lets Jim go and steps aside. The laser light moves back onto John's body. Jim **straightens** his suit.

JIM
Tsk. **Prada**.

Mark Gatiss's script for Moriarty's appearance at the climax of *The Great Game* specified that his suit would be Prada, but Sarah went for Vivienne Westwood instead. 'The cut suited Andrew perfectly, and we thought the colour was very unusual. Putting that with a Spencer Hart shirt with a rounded collar and an Alexander McQueen tie created this great menacing look for him.

'When Amanda Abbington came into it for Series Three, we knew the character had a mysterious past, and I needed to reflect that in her costume. I made her look like a "mum at home", so to speak, rather than anything devious. When it came to Mary's wedding dress, I felt that Amanda has such a period quality about her, and I wanted something to reflect that without going over the top. So we looked at period options and antique lace.'

With the wedding and reception scenes shot over several days, that wedding dress brought its own set of challenges. 'Now, anyone who's got married and has spent a whole day in their wedding dress knows

Only in television-making would the throwing of small pieces of coloured paper become an exercise in special effects deployment. The confetti for John and Sarah's wedding appeared courtesy of Danny Hargreaves and Real SFX.

what it looks like the following day! But there was no budget for a second one. So you can imagine – she was in that dress for about nine days, and it was antique lace and incredibly delicate. There was all sorts of action, she was dancing, she was running up stairs... After every day's filming I had to stitch it back together, and then every morning I had to stitch Amanda back into it. I knew that it was a tall order to expect it to hold up for twelve hours a day, for nine days non-stop – but it did. I had to invisibly mend it constantly, but I was able to get away with it because there was so much lace.'

Continuity photographs are a vital part of the process, just as they are for the make-up team. 'We not only had all those guest artists and extras to deal with over all those recording days,' Sarah points out. 'There were also loads of flashback scenes throughout the episode, with the boys having to change for every scene. It was fine, though, because I keep all the existing costumes in stock so they can be reused. Benedict and Martin also needed morning dress for the wedding, of course. At one stage, we were going to do Martin in military dress but we were told that couldn't happen because John Watson's retired from the army. So we decided to go the safe route and put him in morning dress.'

Sarah reckons *The Sign of Three* was her best episode of *Sherlock* – 'I get lots of questions about the costumes on Twitter, wanting to know all about the dress and so on' – but the next episode brought her even more attention: in 2014 Sarah and costume supervisor Ceri Walford were nominated for a Creative Emmy Award for Outstanding Costumes for a Miniseries, Movie or a Special for *His Last Vow*. 'We had Magnussen, a very strong character in very sleek, expensive suits, and Sherlock dressed as a tramp, and John being married now and having moved on...'

WEDDING ALBUM

John & Mary

10

A DRAGON'S DEN

Making effects work, and putting texts on screen...

'ISS ME?

'IT'S NOT LIKE IT IS IN THE MOVIES'

'The wedding episode had been a fairly light one for us. The guardsman gets stabbed in the showers, but they weren't real showers so the water, the steam and the bleeding rig – all of that was us. We provided the confetti...

'We made the false eyeball that pops up out of the mug of tea... Then we did the Series Three finale, and that was massive.'

'We' is the practical effects company Real SFX, based in Cardiff and Manchester and headed by Danny Hargreaves, veteran special effects designer for *The Sarah Jane Adventures*, *Wizards vs. Aliens*, *Da Vinci's Demons*, *Doctor Who* and many other shows. 'I got involved on *Sherlock* off the back of my work on *Doctor Who*. It coincided with the conception of my own company, and the production designers Edward Thomas and Arwel Wyn Jones asked us to come in and work on the *Sherlock* pilot. I then came back for Series One, working with Arwel and developing a really strong working relationship with him. So I was there from those early days, helping to work out how the series was going to look.

'As you know, each department receives an early draft of the script – and we're all desperate to read them to find out what happens. Even we didn't know how he survived the end of Series Two, so it's always really exciting to get those scripts. We go through the scripts and highlight any practical effects: bullet hits, fires, rain effects, anything that requires a practical edge, and then we go to the tone meeting. All the heads of departments, sit round a table over a few hours with Steven and Mark and Sue, who put us on the right track for making those ideas in the scripts

The Real SFX team building the rig for Sherlock's shooting

Oh, I see! You give me the big dark ey...
and the deep, deep voice, and I'm
supposed to lie for you..
...e just slaps him hard across the face. And
...not reacting.

21 **INT. BARTS LAB - DAWN** 21

MOLLY
Clean?

She rounds on Sherlock.

MOLLY
What do you want me to tell them?

He fixes her with a look.

SHERLOCK
Whatever you feel you ought to tell them.

MOLLY
Oh, I see! You give me the big dark eyes,
and the deep, deep voice, and I'm
supposed to lie for you.

She just slaps him hard across the face. And
again. And again. He stands there, not reacting.

MOLLY
How dare you throw away the beautiful
gifts you were born with, and how dare
you betray the love of your friends. Say
you're sorry.

21 **INT. BARTS LAB - DAWN** 21

WIGGINS
Is it his shirt?

Sherlock looks quickly back to Wiggins.

SHERLOCK
... I'm sorry?

WIGGINS
Is that how you know about the cycling.
Sorry, should have let you do it.

SHERLOCK
Do what?

WIGGINS
The showing off.

SHERLOCK
(Amused now) The showing off??

WIGGINS
Cos I know who you are - I knew the
first day you came. I've always read
that blog. Not been much on it lately,
I thought you'd retired.

SHERLOCK
The band split up. Tell me about the
shirt?

WIGGINS
Well it's the creases, isn't it? The
two creases down the front. It's been
recently folded, but it's not new. (To
John) You must have dressed in a hurry
tonight, so all your shirts must be kept
like that. But why? Maybe cos you cycle
to work every morning, shower when you
get there, and then dress in the clothes
you brought with you. You keep your
shirts folded, ready to pack.

come to life. There's a sort of friendly rivalry at that stage, with Milk wanting to make a computer-generated effect and me wanting to make it practical. But there's certain things I can't do and certain things they can't do. We work closely together, we won a BAFTA together. I always fight for effects. Producers and production managers can be quite scared because they know it's going to hold them up. But I'll fight tooth and nail.

'We usually start filming about three weeks after the tone meeting, so it's very quick and you don't get a lot of time to get your head around it and make it happen, and that gets even quicker when you hit mid-series. For me, that works well because I don't have time to worry about it. Having said that, I do have plenty of time to experiment and nail an effect before we get on set. *Sherlock* isn't a massively effects-heavy show, but there's a lot of elements – atmospherics, fires, things that make it all come to life – that viewers might not realise are special

Danny Hargreaves at work on location

effects. Those are the textures that Milk and I put in to make the show what it is. It's not all about explosions but it is all about putting in things that aren't real but look as though they are.

'Quite often, for example, I'll have rain or snow falling outside the windows of the 221B interior studio set in Wales, things passing the window through the back of the shot which help sell the set as a real location. We'll put falling snow outside the window in the studio so that when they cut to an exterior where the snow has fallen it looks real and links together. Or you'll see something steaming or bubbling or cooking away in Sherlock's kitchen laboratory that helps make it all look like it's real.'

Danny had a taste of what was in store for him in *His Last Vow* during the Series Three opener, *The Empty Hearse*. 'Martin Freeman stuck in a bonfire... We had to create the exterior part of the fire – which didn't contain Martin but did have Benedict Cumberbatch ripping it apart to get in there. That was done on location. Then we had to put Martin inside the bonfire, and we did that in studio. Benedict and Martin are both very keen to do their own stunts, much to the dismay of producers – and myself, because I'm responsible for doing it and for their safety.

'One effect we did with Benedict back in Series Two was the bed that flips up behind him and cuts to him lying in it in Baker Street, during *A Scandal in Belgravia*. There's a recurrence of that effect in *His Last Vow* when Sherlock is shot. We had Benedict on another rig that he falls back on, so that it echoes what had happened in *Scandal*. It was a really tricky sequence.

Without hesitation, without a flicker on her face, **Mary fires**. A tiny sneeze of noise from the silenced gun – and now a dreadful **ringing silence**. Sherlock, comes to a halt again, now just standing there. **Frowns**, as if a thought had occurred to him – a look of the **mildest surprise**. Cocks his head, as if trying to figure something out.

MARY
I'm sorry, Sherlock.
I truly am.

Sherlock, now looking down at his shirtfront. A **bloodstain** flowering on his chest.

26 **INT. 221B BAKER STREET – MORNING** 26

ANDERSON
Sorry, Sherlock, it's for your own good.

BENJI
(To Anderson) Oh, that's him, isn't it?
You said he'd be taller. (To Sherlock)
He's a big fan.

SHERLOCK
Who are these people? What are they
doing in my flat? Do I know these ones?

BENJI
You said he had a photographic memory.

SHERLOCK
I make deletions.

BENJI
Do you? That's clever.

SHERLOCK
I'm glad you think so,
I'll be making one shortly.

Mycroft now entering, John behind him.

MYCROFT
Some members of your little fan
club. Do be polite, they're entirely
trustworthy and even willing to search
the toxic waste dump you are pleased
to call your flat. You're a celebrity
these days, Sherlock, you can't afford
a drug habit.

27 **INT. 221B BAKER STREET – DAY** 27

SHERLOCK
It is the greatest repository of
sensitive and dangerous information
anywhere in the world. The Alexandra
Library of secrets and scandals. And
none of it is on a computer. He's
smart, computers can be hacked. It's
all on hard copy, in vaults, underneath
that house. And as long as it's there
the personal freedom of anyone you've
ever met is a fantasy.

JOHN
And this is the guy we're going to go
and see?

SHERLOCK
I have an appointment at his office
in two hours. What do you think?

JOHN
I think it's strange you chose to go
back on drugs first.

SHERLOCK
Surely it's obvious why.

A tap at the door, Mrs Hudson popping her
head round.

MRS HUDSON
That was the doorbell. Didn't you hear it?

29 **INT. 221B BAKER STREET – DAY** 29

MAGNUSSEN
Anyway. They're funny.

He's heading for the door.

SHERLOCK
If you had no intention of negotiating
with me, why are you here?

MAGNUSSEN
You're Sherlock Holmes, you're famous.
I'm interested.

SHERLOCK
In what?

MAGNUSSEN
In you. I've never had a detective
before.

And out he goes. His men follow. On John –
a world of disgust and barely suppressed rage.

JOHN
Jesus!

37 **INT. CAM TOWER/ENTRANCE LOBBY – NIGHT** 37

SHERLOCK
I'll tell her our entire relationship
was a ruse so I could break into her
boss's office. I imagine she'll want to
stop seeing me at that point, but you're
the expert on women.

JOHN
She'll be bloody heart-broken.

SHERLOCK
Well we're splitting up, that's a
perfectly normal reaction.

JOHN
Sherlock!

SHERLOCK
Stop worrying – once I'm out of the
picture, I'll be the last thing on her
mind. Magnussen is definitely going to
sack her for this.

The lift chimes, and Sherlock strides happily
out of the lift. An appalled John follows a
beat later –

The drug den was filmed in Cardiff's Bute Street (opposite), the location for Magnussen's London offices (above)

'The first challenge was that the director, Nick Hurran, wanted a very precise bullet hole, punched out of the shirt but with no blood, for that moment of disbelief that he's been shot. The audience would be thinking he must be wearing a bullet-proof vest, he's still alive, he's still standing. And then the blood comes, which we provided, although I think Milk painted in a couple of millimetres of blood around the top edge of the bullet hole.

MOLLY
Plus, on your back,
gravity is working for us.
Fall now.

The whole room starts to **lean**. Sherlock's knees start to **buckle** – in agonising **slow motion** he starts to fall backwards.

'Nick then wanted Benedict to fall back onto a rig that pivoted and had to be safe for him to use. I was originally going to build a rig that went inside his suit but you can imagine – every time he wanted to get out of it he would have had to take the whole suit. So it was low profile hidden in his jacket. Benedict's very hard to get hold of because of his schedule, so my time with him is very brief: I had to walk into his trailer, measure him, follow the contours of his back, mirror that in a rig – and even then it wasn't right! I had to adapt it quickly on the day. I always like to create something manual rather than machine-operated, to keep that element of human control. We fitted the rig into the floor, attached to some bungee that went to a piece of scaffold on the other side of the set, and then we had a visual on the position of the rig and Benedict. We were under a lot of pressure not to drop him; he's a big star now, worth millions! We did the whole sequence a couple of times. That was probably the hardest effect I've ever done, to be honest, and it's a great sequence. I'm very proud to be a part of that.'

'THAT'S NOT LADY SMALLWOOD, MR HOLMES

Sherlock's assailant is, of course, Mary Watson, John's wife. 'She's an assassin,' says Amanda Abbington, 'who's worked for the CIA and many other questionable organisations. She's killed people for money, and she's killed people not for pleasure but because she was really good at it. She's been hiding that from John, and she's got a new identity and thought her secret was buried.'

For Benedict Cumberbatch, what's interesting is how consistently Sherlock supports Mary. 'He can see how good she is for John and that she has a love for him that goes well beyond the darkest episodes and chapters in her past. Sherlock can see that everything she does to conceal her identity is to save her love for John. So Sherlock can see the sacrifice, where John can only see the betrayal. John has a hell of a lot to take in during Series Three: his best friend comes back from the dead and then he marries an assassin. It's quite a journey he goes on through that series.'

John Watson isn't the only regular character whose development has reached a new level by the end of *His Last Vow*. Louise Brealey thinks that Molly surprised viewers over the three series. 'When we first meet her, she is so timid and so willing to please, and loving someone who hasn't loved her back. But she has other qualities that are also strengths: she's gentle, she's kind, she's steadfast, she's loyal, she's quietly perceptive. I think her confidence has built through the three series, so by the end of Series Three she's behaving in quite surprising ways.'

Sherlock Series Three   His Last Vow

82   **INT. SHERLOCK'S PRIVATE WARD – NIGHT**   82

JOHN
Christ knows – try and find Sherlock in London, bloody hell.

Now with Lestrade and the medical team.

DOCTOR
He took the morphine.

LESTRADE
Yeah, he does that.

John and Mary.

JOHN
So he was lying then.

MARY
Lying?

JOHN
He said he didn't know who shot him, but he does.

MARY
Why?

JOHN
Because Sherlock Holmes only ever goes out for one reason. He's hunting.

On Mary's face. So chilled. He's after her.

Sherlock Series Three   His Last Vow

97   **INT. 221B BAKER STREET – NIGHT**   97

MARY
Why would you help me?

SHERLOCK
Because you saved my life.

JOHN
... what? Sorry, what?

SHERLOCK
(Coughs, wheezes) So far, at any rate.

The doorbell rings.

SHERLOCK
(Calls) Mrs Hudson, stop listening and answer the door.

Mrs Hudson pops her head round the doorway.

MRS. HUDSON
Why can't you answer it yourself?

SHERLOCK
Because I'm dying of internal injuries compounded by inappropriate exertion and two packets of cigarettes.

MRS HUDSON
Well aren't you always!

She flounces off.

SHERLOCK
When I happened on you and Magnussen, you had a problem.

The most surprising, perhaps, being her response to John's discovery of Sherlock in the drug den.

'There are certain camera angles where you can fake a slap,' smiles Louise, 'and certain angles where you have to do it for real. On this one, I did make contact with Benedict's face a couple of times, which was a little alarming, although I must have done it about twenty times, so it wasn't too bad. It's nice to do a little stunt.'

'I'M IN AGONY'

His Last Vow is also something of a Holmes family affair, with more of Sherlock's background revealed than ever before. 'The relationship between Mycroft and Sherlock is interesting,' says Sue Vertue. 'There's the sibling rivalry, with each of them always saying they're cleverer than the other. A lot of the time they can't stand each other, but then Mycroft is incredibly caring about him deep down. We see the lengths that Mycroft goes to, to look after this troublesome brother. Series Three begins with Mycroft going undercover in Serbia to rescue Sherlock, and it ends with him bringing Sherlock straight back to England. In *His Last Vow*, he even admits that it would break his heart if Sherlock died.'

Sherlock's **Mother** pokes her head out the door.

SHERLOCK'S MOTHER
Are you two **smoking**?

They have instantly **hidden** their cigarettes.

MYCROFT   SHERLOCK
No!   It was Mycroft.

From 'The Man with the Twisted Lip'
by Sir Arthur Conan Doyle

[...] At the farther end was a small brazier of burning charcoal, beside which on a three-legged wooden stool there sat a tall, thin old man, with his jaw resting upon his two fists, and his elbows upon his knees, staring into the fire.

As I entered, a sallow Malay attendant had hurried up with a pipe for me and a supply of the drug, beckoning me to an empty berth.

'Thank you. I have not come to stay,' said I. 'There is a friend of mine here, Mr. Isa Whitney, and I wish to speak with him.'

There was a movement and an exclamation from my right, and peering through the gloom I saw Whitney, pale, haggard, and unkempt, staring out at me.

'My God! It's Watson,' said he.

[...] I walked down the narrow passage between the double row of sleepers, holding my breath to keep out the vile, stupefying fumes of the drug, and looking about for the manager. As I passed the tall man who sat by the brazier I felt a sudden pluck at my skirt, and a low voice whispered, 'Walk past me, and then look back at me.' The words fell quite distinctly upon my ear. I glanced down. They could only have come from the old man at my side, and yet he sat now as absorbed as ever, very thin, very wrinkled, bent with age, an opium pipe dangling down from between his knees, as though it had dropped in sheer lassitude from his fingers. I took two steps forward and looked back. It took all my self-control to prevent me from breaking out into a cry of astonishment. He had turned his back so that none could see him but I. His form had filled out, his wrinkles were gone, the dull eyes had regained their fire, and there, sitting by the fire and grinning at my surprise, was none other than Sherlock Holmes. He made a slight motion to me to approach him, and instantly, as he turned his face half round to the company once more, subsided into a doddering, loose-lipped senility.

From 'His Last Vow'
by Steven Moffat

INT. RUINED HOUSE - UPSTAIRS LANDING - DAWN
On the upstairs landing, John looking about in the various rooms, calling loudly.

                    JOHN
          Isaac? Isaac Whitney?

He looks round the various slumped figures, in the dim, reeking rooms. One of them is struggling to sit up...

                    JOHN
          Isaac?

John goes to him. Isaac is in his late teens - looks wasted and utterly wretched.

                    ISAAC
          Hello?

John hunkers down at him.

                    JOHN
          Hello, Isaac.

                    ISAAC
          Dr Watson? Where am I?

                    JOHN
          Arse end of the universe with
          the scum of the earth.

                    ISAAC
          Have you come for me?

                    JOHN
          Do you think I know a lot of people
          here?

A lying figure just behind Isaac, stirs and sits up. It's Sherlock Holmes. He looks blearily at John.

                    SHERLOCK
          Oh, hello John. Wasn't expecting you.

John just stares - wha-?????

                    SHERLOCK
          Have you come for me too?

From 'The Sign of Four'
by Sir Arthur Conan Doyle

He smiled at my vehemence. 'Perhaps you are right, Watson,' he said. 'I suppose that its influence is physically a bad one. I find it, however, so transcendently stimulating and clarifying to the mind that its secondary action is a matter of small moment.'

'But consider!' I said earnestly. 'Count the cost! Your brain may, as you say, be roused and excited, but it is a pathological and morbid process which involves increased tissue-change and may at least leave a permanent weakness. You know, too, what a black reaction comes upon you. Surely the game is hardly worth the candle. Why should you, for a mere passing pleasure, risk the loss of those great powers with which you have been endowed? Remember that I speak not only as one comrade to another but as a medical man to one for whose constitution he is to some extent answerable.'

From 'The Adventure of Charles Augustus Milverton'
by Sir Arthur Conan Doyle

'Do you feel a creeping, shrinking sensation, Watson, when you stand before the serpents in the Zoo, and see the slithery, gliding, venomous creatures, with their deadly eyes and wicked, flattened faces? Well, that's how Milverton impresses me. I've had to do with fifty murderers in my career, but the worst of them never gave me the repulsion which I have for this fellow. And yet I can't get out of doing business with him – indeed, he is here at my invitation.'

From 'His Last Vow'
by Steven Moffat

JOHN
Well? Is he clean?

Sherlock is lounging against the wall, quiet, watching.

MOLLY
Clean?

She rounds on Sherlock. She just slaps him hard across the face. And again. And again. He stands there, not reacting.

MOLLY
How dare you throw away the beautiful gifts you were born with, and how dare you betray the love of your friends. Say you're sorry.

From 'His Last Vow'
by Steven Moffat

SHERLOCK
Okay, Magnussen then. Magnussen is a shark. Only way I can describe him. Ever been to the shark tank at the London Aquarium, John – stood right at the glass? Those flat, gliding faces. Those dead eyes. That's what he is. I've dealt with murderers, psychopaths. Terrorists, serial killers. None of them can turn my stomach like Charles Augustus Magnussen.

From 'The Adventure of Charles Augustus Milverton'
by Sir Arthur Conan Doyle

'You would not call me a marrying man, Watson?'

'No, indeed!'

'You'll be interested to hear that I'm engaged.'

'My dear fellow! I congrat—'

'To Milverton's housemaid.'

'Good heavens, Holmes!'

'I wanted information, Watson.'

'Surely you have gone too far?'

'It was a most necessary step. I am a plumber with a rising business, Escott, by name. I have walked out with her each evening, and I have talked with her. Good heavens, those talks! However, I have got all I wanted. I know Milverton's house as I know the palm of my hand.'

'But the girl, Holmes?'

He shrugged his shoulders.

'You can't help it, my dear Watson. You must play your cards as best you can when such a stake is on the table. However, I rejoice to say that I have a hated rival, who will certainly cut me out the instant that my back is turned.'

From 'His Last Vow'
by Steven Moffat

JOHN
... Did you just get engaged to break into a bloody office?

SHERLOCK
Yeah. Stroke of luck, meeting her at your wedding - so you can take some of the credit.

JOHN
Jesus, Sherlock, she loves you!

SHERLOCK
Yeah, like I said - human error. He hits the button, the lift doors roll shut.

As they ascend:

JOHN
But it's Janine. What are you going to do?

SHERLOCK
Well, not actually marry her, obviously. There's only so far you can go.

JOHN
But what will you tell her??

SHERLOCK
I'll tell her our entire relationship was a ruse so I could break into her boss's office. I imagine she'll want to stop seeing me at that point, but you're the expert on women.

JOHN
She'll be bloody heart-broken.

SHERLOCK
Well we're splitting up, that's a perfectly normal reaction.

JOHN
Sherlock!

SHERLOCK
Stop worrying - once I'm out of the picture, I'll be the last thing on her mind. Magnussen is definitely going to sack her for this.

From 'The Second Stain"
by Sir Arthur Conan Doyle

So long as he was in actual professional practice the records of his successes were of some practical value to him; but since he has definitely retired from London and betaken himself to study and bee-farming on the Sussex Downs, notoriety has become hateful to him, and he has peremptorily requested that his wishes in this matter should be strictly observed.

From 'His Last Bow'
by Sir Arthur Conan Doyle

'… As to you, Watson, you are joining up with your old service, as I understand, so London won't be out of your way. Stand with me here upon the terrace for it may be the last quiet talk that we shall ever have.'

The two friends chatted in intimate converse for a few minutes, recalling once again the days of the past whilst their prisoner vainly wriggled to undo the bonds that held him. As they turned to the car, Holmes pointed back to the moonlit sea, and shook a thoughtful head.

'There's an east wind coming, Watson.'

'I think not, Holmes. It is very warm.'

'Good old Watson! You are the one fixed point in a changing age. There's an east wind coming all the same, such a wind as never blew on England yet. It will be cold and bitter, Watson, and a good many of us may wither before its blast. But it's God's own wind none the less, and a cleaner, better, stronger land will lie in the sunshine when the storm has cleared. Start her up, Watson, for it's time that we were on our way. I have a cheque for five hundred pounds which should be cashed early, for the drawer is quite capable of stopping it, if he can.'

From 'His Last Vow'
by Steven Moffat

SHERLOCK
Of course. Where did you buy the cottage?

JANINE
Sussex Downs.

SHERLOCK
Nice.

JANINE
View of the sea, gorgeous. There's beehives but I'm getting rid of those.

From 'His Last Vow'
by Steven Moffat

JOHN
The game is over.

SHERLOCK
The game is never over, John. But there will be some new players, now. That's okay. The East Wind takes us all in the end.

JOHN
The what?

SHERLOCK
A story my brother used to tell me, when I was a kid. The East Wind, a terrible force that lays waste to all in its path. It seeks out the unworthy and plucks them from the Earth. That was generally me.

[...] MARY
So how can [Moriarty] be back?

A noise has been building in the background – an aircraft is approaching. John looks up. And starts to smile.

JOHN
Well if he is, he better wrap up warm.

Mary looks at him – what? Now following his look. And there it is! Sherlock's plane is returning.

JOHN
There's an East Wind coming.

Now on John and Mary watching, as the plane comes in to land...

'My mum and dad play my mum and dad, which is great,' says Benedict, 'but it's not just some sort of in-joke. They are really good, and they know how to place themselves as fictional characters as my parents. It's a very family-orientated show. Martin's other half is Amanda and she is playing his other half. And then there's Sue and Steven's son Louis as the younger Sherlock; he was superb. This show is, I hope, always a family thing, the kind of programme that whole families can sit and watch together. It speaks to the technically adept younger viewers, and it has that huge internet presence and following, at the same time as being a thrill for parents and grandparents to see this beloved character brought back to television and done with reverence and love. And that all works itself into the nature of our working day on the show. So to have people who are that familiar because they are family working with you is a really nice synchronicity.'

'HERE BE DRAGONS'

Series Three introduces one of *Sherlock*'s most terrifying original villains, Charles Augustus Magnussen, first glimpsed in *The Empty Hearse* and dominating the screen from the first moments of *His Last Vow*. Actor Lars Mikkelsen thinks his character is an intellectual sociopath to match Sherlock. 'He's very sinister, emotionless, he has no weak points. He's a horrible human being. He's the kind of villain you wouldn't want to oppose, because he has so much power behind him.

Proof? What would I need proof for? I'm in news, you **moron**. I don't have to prove it – I just have to **print** it.

Benedict Cumberbatch with his mum and dad, Martin Freeman with his partner Amanda, and Sue Vertue and Steven Moffat's son Louis as the young Sherlock.

The striking Gloucestershire setting for Magnussen's Appledore, inside and outside.

Magnussen's Mind Palace was constructed and dressed in the studio, every element bought in or specially created.

Lars Mikkelsen
Born 6 May 1964, Gladsaxe, Denmark

SELECTED FILM ROLES

2014	When Animals Dream Thor
	Nordic Factory Daniel
	Töchter Rauch
2012	Max Pinlig 3 – på Roskilde Henning
	A Caretaker's Tale Per
	What Richard Did Peter Karlsen
2011	Those Who Kill – Shadow of the Past
	Magnus Bisgaard
2010	Lost in Africa Victor
2009	Headhunter Martin Vinge
	The Escape Thomas Jargil
2008	Flame and Citron Frode 'Ravnen' Jacobsen
	What No One Knows Marc Deleuran
2007	Cecilie Lasse N. Damgaard
	Island of Lost Souls Necromancer

SELECTED TV ROLES

2014	Sherlock Charles Augustus Magnussen
2013	Borgen Søren Ravn
2011	Unter anderen Umständen Erik Nielsen
	Those Who Kill Magnus Bisgaard
2007	The Killing Troels Hartmann
2004-2007	Better Times Jens Otto Krag

'Magnussen is a major media mogul, and you learn through the episode that he has the power of knowledge, knowing what people are about. He enjoys watching people and identifying their weak points. He knows everything about everyone and, supposedly, has some sort of archive of all his files in a vault in his house. The house that they found for Appledore was just unbelievable – it was a real Bond Villain sort of house! It would have been nice to have had a few more days there to take it all in. But actually he has a mind palace equivalent to Sherlock's. Which of course makes him even more similar to Sherlock.

'So I've chosen to play him as *non-threatening*, because the threat he poses is always there, always present, it's talked about a lot – and a man like that wouldn't have to actually use his power. He's so powerful that he doesn't even have to raise his voice. He just tells people that he knows what they are about and what their little secrets are. And that's it. So I tried to play him very calmly – sometimes too calmly and we had to do it again to get the pace up! It was quite a hard role for me because it was one of the first times I had acted in English. And I was working with top-quality actors on top-quality scripts so I didn't want to mess it up.

'I've never seen a script like that one before. That script was so clever, and so good at misleading the audience. Right from the start, during the enquiry, you see Magnussen wearing his glasses, and in the glasses you see all the information coming up about his opponents in the room. So everyone – the audience and Sherlock – is misled into believing that Magnussen has some kind of computer or gadget. And that's the beauty of it and makes it impossible for Sherlock to get to him.

'I was finishing a film in east London, when Sue Vertue contacted my agent to ask if I would meet her to talk about

doing *Sherlock*. I hadn't seen any of the series and I was a bit pressed for time, so I said, "No, I can't meet her, she'll have to come to me," which is not how these things are done! But she did, and we sat around talking and then they sent me some scripts and some episodes. And I was just flabbergasted – it was so good, and I really wanted to be in it.

> Magnussen's POV.
> The round, glittering lenses raise up – now looking through them:
> A heads-up display.
> **Text streaming** across Magnussen's view – like Sherlock's text-vision, but apparently electronically originated. A 3D projection, with the lenses.
> **Cursors quiver** around Garvie's face – facial recognition software. Now his name **flickers** into position next to his face.

> JOHN GARVIE
> MP ROCKWELL SOUTH
> **ADULTERER** (SEE FILE)
> REFORMED ALCOHOLIC
> PORN PREFERENCE:
> NORMAL
> FINANCES: 41% DEBT
> (SEE FILE)
> STATUS: **UNIMPORTANT**.
> In red letters below this (so that it stands out.)
> PRESSURE POINT:
> **DISABLED DAUGHTER**
> (SEE FILE)

'Magnussen is in the real world, his power is based on real people, and on the tragedies of real people. He's not the same sort of super-villain as Moriarty, in the sense that he works in the shadows and cannot be a presence in real life, he's hiding all the time. Apart from that they are both super-villains. You have to be, I guess, if you are to go against Sherlock Holmes.'

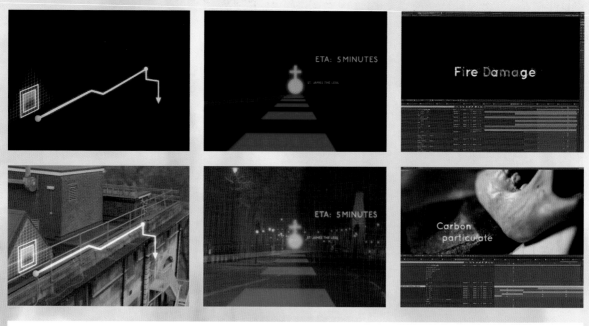

The graphics have been a hugely important part of the style of *Sherlock*. 'They do seem to have reinvented how, for instance, text messages are shown in pretty much any other programme now!' notes Sue Vertue. 'When Paul McGuigan was shooting *The Great Game*, he said that he didn't want to shoot a whole load of close-ups of phones because that was boring and that he was going to put it on screen somehow. I remember Steven saying at the time that he thought that sounded awful but he was passing the cutting room and Paul and Charlie Phillips were playing with the text – putting it on the back wall for instance and letting it reduce in size when we moved forward, having other lettering that moved as the phone moved, etc – and Steven thought it looked brilliant. At that point, he was still

writing *A Study in Pink* so was able to write the 'pink lady' scene with all the graphics detailed in the script. So in that first series, lots of the graphics were initially done by Charlie on his Avid and then we had to recreate them or embellish them at the online stage. That's where Peter Anderson came in.'

Peter Anderson Studio is the graphic design company commissioned by BBC Wales and Hartswood to provide a lot of the on-screen text for the series. Sue initially contacted Peter about the series' title sequence, 'and then very casually mentioned there would be some in-show graphics – "if you don't mind doing that as well…" – which of course turned out to be much more than that!

'With the titles we wanted to give the viewer thirty seconds of being inside Sherlock's head, so you as a viewer at the start of

the programme are invited to *be* Sherlock. He's looking at people almost as if they're tiny insects, and then suddenly you jump to the tiniest detail that he notices and nobody else does – it might be the hair on a jacket or a spot of blood but it leads to a conclusion that's macroscopic. It's a different way of seeing: the programme begins by saying, "Sherlock sees the world differently and you're invited to be part of this."

'The typeface is Underground P22, which is the font designed for the London Underground in 1916. It's an understated font with a history in London, and that's why that was chosen. The font itself, though, is actually a code based on an old-fashioned typewriter where you take the head off the typewriter and each of the letters makes a different mark, and that mark is a vocabulary within which

you can encode secrets… We haven't used it in that way all that much, but it is there in its creation.

'When it came to the graphics, they showed us the scripts and asked, "Can you look at these scenes and think of some way to bring this to life?" We worked out how it would look, what the typeface was… taking that lead we came up with some other stuff that could happen. In *The Blind Banker*, Sherlock's thinking about Chinese symbols at one point, and we had a conversation with the director, Euros Lyn, about how the graphics for that could follow on from the previous episode. So Sherlock's turning his head, thinking, and the 3D symbols on the wall are moving with him. By that stage, we'd got into the philosophy that graphics could be one of the story elements.

'When you reach the third series, there's a whole sequence of words when Sherlock first meets Mary, where the word 'Liar' is hidden within layers of words throughout his appraisal of her, and that comes out in the collage of words around her in *His Last Vow*. It's a lovely moment where one episode comes together with another – the writers had been hinting at the idea of her being a 'liar' and that was hidden amongst a whole other set of deductions, concluding in that third episode when he discovers that his deduction was absolutely right… a really simple but nice case of thinking things through.

'There were lots of moments in Series Three where we pushed what the typography was doing, using elements of dust and heat to take it a step forward in terms of it being even more concrete in what it was doing: the letters formed in dust, so it took on an extra figurative layer, and that was more illustrative than before.

'We're given the scenes, ungraded, without effects, quite raw – a low-res mp4, just emailed over. From that, we'll create a "this is how it'll look" animation and send a series of tests to the director. Once everyone's happy, we'll send the text on its own, which is then uploaded into the online edit and composited. We give them the layer exactly as it should be and they just drop it on.

'I think that *Sherlock*'s been a game-changer and a landmark in TV history. We had the creative freedom to set up and bring to life what we thought would work with the script. The combination of the writers', directors' and editors' vision started the whole thing off, and we were privileged to be part of that thought process.'

_ 'GHOST OF A SMILE' _

nd so a series that has seen Sherlock, inch by inch, becoming more human, climaxes as he becomes a murderer. 'That was the big thing,' says Mark Gatiss. 'We had a lot of discussion about this because no one, I think, has ever actually criminalised Holmes. He's come very close, he's done a lot of things, he's let a lot of people go, he decides when he is above the law.'

Sherlock's shooting of Magnussen parallels the end of "The Adventure of Charles Augustus Milverton", where Holmes lets Milverton's murderer go free. 'That ending is really brutal,' Mark notes. 'She grinds her shoe into Milverton's face. In the case of Magnussen, I think that Sherlock is exterminating a pest rather than murdering anybody. But I think Magnussen is one of the only people he truly hates – he hates everything he stands for. And that's how the world is run. I think the most chilling bit in the whole episode comes when Magnussen calls the UK a petri dish and says if it works here he tries it on a real country.'

His Last Vow provoked another Twitter storm with its closing moments, as the hashtags *#didyoumissme* and *#MoriartyLives* began to trend. The shock reappearance generated 74,447 mentions of Moriarty and actor Andrew Scott. So how is Moriarty's return possible?

'I don't know,' insists Andrew. 'I do like the idea that Moriarty is always there, whether or not he's on screen, whether he's dead or alive, he's always there. But I'm telling you the truth: I don't know.'

Mark Gatiss knows. 'We're shooting a special episode in January 2015, and then another three-episode series. Steven and I are writing the special together, and we reconvened at the end of August 2014 to see where we are. It was another of our exotic meetings – in Los Angeles this time! (We've wearied of Monte Carlo.) It's a very special special – that's all I can say.'

In the past, Steven and Mark have offered clues to future series' content with three-word teases. For Series Two, these were 'Woman', 'Hound' and 'Fall'. Series Three's were 'pipe', 'slippers' and 'bed' (according to a tweet from Mark) or 'Rat', 'Wedding' and 'Vow' (said Steven, speaking at the 2012 Edinburgh International Television Festival). So... time to revive the tradition for the next four adventures?

'I can certainly give you one word,' smiles Mark. 'Ghosts...'

MIND PALACE

Stuff that's useful

A STUDY IN PINK (Original version)

Shoot dates: 12 January –1 February 2009
Not broadcast (DVD release: 30 August 2010)
Duration: 55 minutes 14 seconds

Writer.....................................STEVEN MOFFAT
Producer .... SUE VERTUE
Director................................COKY GIEDROYC
Executive Producers ....BERYL VERTUE,
STEVEN MOFFAT,
MARK GATISS

CAST
Sherlock Holmes... BENEDICT CUMBERBATCH
Dr John Watson ....MARTIN FREEMAN
Inspector Lestrade.................RUPERT GRAVES
Mrs Hudson .... UNA STUBBS
Dr Anderson ....JONATHAN ARIS
Molly Hooper............................ LOO BREALEY
Sally Donovan ....ZAWE ASHTON
Angelo.......................................JOSEPH LONG
Mike Stamford ....DAVID NELLIST
Ella...TANYA MOODIE
Cabbie.....................................JAMES HARPER
and
The Taxi Driver................................PHIL DAVIS

CREW
BBC Production Executive.......... JULIE SCOTT
Line Producer .... KATHY NETTLESHIP

Director of Photography .... MATT GRAY
Production Designer.......... EDWARD THOMAS
Series Designer...............ARWEL WYN JONES
Editor..NICK ARTHURS
Casting Director... KATE RHODES JAMES CDG
Costume Designer.....................RAY HOLMAN
Make-up Designer ....
CLAIRE PRITCHARD-JONES
Sound Recordist ....BRIAN MILLIKEN
Music ....DAVID ARNOLD,
MICHAEL PRICE
1st Assistant Director.................PAUL JUDGES
2nd Assistant Director...................LISA MARSH
3rd Assistant Director ....DAVID CHALSTREY
Floor Runners ....LOWRI DENMAN,
RUSSELL TURNER
Location Managers .... PAUL DAVIES,
GARETH SKELDING,
RUSSELL TURNER
Production Co-ordinator...... KATE THORNTON
Production Secretary ....KEVIN PROCTOR
Production Runner................... HARRY BUNCH
Production Accountant..........JENNINE BAKER
Continuity ....NON ELERI HUGHES
Focus Puller ....MARTIN PAYNE

Clapper Loader........................ RACHEL CLARK
Grip ....DAN INMAN
Boom Operator ....BRADLEY KENDRICK
Gaffer... PAUL JARVIS
Best Boy... LLYR EVANS
Standby Art Director....... CIARAN THOMPSON
Standby Props .... JOHN JONES,
JULIA CHALLIS
Standby Carpenter ....PAUL JONES
Property Master ....MATTHEW IRELAND
Properties ....JAYNE DAVIES,
IAN DAVIES
Set Decorator .... JOELLE RUMBELOW
Construction Manager... MATT HYWEL DAVIES
Costume Supervisor ... CHARLOTTE MITCHELL
Costume Assistant...................SARA MORGAN
Make-up Artist...........SARAH ASTLEY-HUGHES
Online Editor ....SIMON O'CONNOR
Colourist ....KEVIN HORSEWOOD
Supervising Sound FX Editor STEVE GRIFFITHS
Dialogue Editor ....PETE GATES
ADR Editor...........................KALLIS SHAMARIS
Recording Mixer .... HOWARD BARGROFF
VFX Supervisor ....CHRIS MORTIMER
Titles .... PETER ANDERSON STUDIO

SERIES ONE

John Watson, army doctor, invalided home from Afghanistan, alone and friendless. Sherlock Holmes, the most brilliant intellect of his generation, alone and friendless. London 2010 – the best and longest friendship in all of fiction is about to begin anew. The most famous detective, the most baffling mysteries, the most thrilling adventures and the deadliest foes, are coming in out of the fog. Sherlock Holmes was always a modern man – it was the world that got old. Now he's back as he should be – edgy, contemporary, difficult, dangerous. Inspector Lestrade is the best Scotland Yard has got, but he knows he's not as good as a strange young man called Sherlock.

Shoot dates: 11 January–18 April 2010   Additional days: 19–23 April 2010

SHERLOCK SERIES ONE AWARDS

BAFTA TELEVISION AWARDS
Drama Series
Supporting Actor (Martin Freeman)

BAFTA TELEVISION CRAFT AWARDS
Editing: Fiction (Charlie Phillips)

BAFTA CYMRU AWARDS
Director: Fiction (Euros Lyn)
Director of Photography: Fiction (Steve Lawes)
Production Design (Arwel Wyn Jones)
Make Up and Hair (Claire Pritchard-Jones)
Television Drama

BANFF WORLD TELEVISION AWARDS
Continuing Series Program
Best in Series

BROADCAST AWARDS
Best Drama Series or Serial

BROADCASTING PRESS AWARDS
Best Actor (Benedict Cumberbatch)

CRIME THRILLER AWARDS
Best Actor (Benedict Cumberbatch)
TV Dagger

**MGEITF CHANNEL OF
THE YEAR AWARDS**
Best Terrestrial Programme

PEABODY AWARDS
Entertainment

PRIX EUROPA
Best Episode of a Television Fiction
Series or Serial of the Year
(A Study In Pink)

**ROYAL TELEVISION SOCIETY
PROGRAMME AWARDS**
Best Drama Series

**ROYAL TELEVISION SOCIETY
CRAFT AND DESIGN AWARDS**
Original Title Music
(David Arnold and Michael Price)
Tape and Film Editing (Charlie Phillips)
Effects: Picture Enhancement
(Kevin Horsewood)

SATELLITE AWARDS
Best Miniseries

**TELEVISION CRITICS ASSOCIATION
AWARDS**
Outstanding Achievement in Movies,
Miniseries and Specials

TELEVISUAL BULLDOG AWARDS
Best Drama Series
Best Editing (Charlie Phillips and Mali Evans)

TV CHOICE AWARDS
Best New Drama

A STUDY IN PINK

Duration: 88 minutes 6 seconds
First broadcast on BBC One   9.00 –10.30pm   Sunday 25 July 2010
Audience: 9.23 million

Writer......................................STEVEN MOFFAT
Producer .... SUE VERTUE
Director................................. PAUL McGUIGAN
Executive Producers ....BERYL VERTUE,
STEVEN MOFFAT,
MARK GATISS
Executive Producer for Masterpiece..................
REBECCA EATON
Executive Producer for BBC.... BETHAN JONES

CAST

Sherlock Holmes... BENEDICT CUMBERBATCH
Dr John Watson .... MARTIN FREEMAN
DI Lestrade ....RUPERT GRAVES
Mrs Hudson .... UNA STUBBS
Molly Hooper........................LOUISE BREALEY
Sgt Sally Donovan............VINETTE ROBINSON
Ella................................TANYA MOODIE
Helen ....SIOBHÁN HEWLETT
Sir Jeffrey Patterson ....
WILLIAM SCOTT-MASSON
Margaret Patterson................VICTORIA WICKS
Gary ....SEAN YOUNG
Jimmy ....JAMES DUNCAN
Political Aides .... RUTH EVERETT,
SYRUS LOWE
Beth Davenport ....KATY MAW
Reporters ....BEN GREEN,
PRADEEP JAY,
IMOGEN SLAUGHTER
Mike Stamford ....DAVID NELLIST
Jennifer Wilson ....
LOUISE BRECKON-RICHARDS
Anderson ....JONATHAN ARIS
Anthea ....LISA McALLISTER
Angelo ....STANLEY TOWNSEND
Taxi Passenger ....PETER BROOKE
and
Jeff...PHIL DAVIS

CREW

Line Producer .... KATHY NETTLESHIP
Editor.................................... CHARLIE PHILLIPS
Production Designer........ ARWEL WYN JONES
Director of Photography.............STEVE LAWES
Music .... DAVID ARNOLD, MICHAEL PRICE
Casting Director... KATE RHODES JAMES CDG

Costume Designer...................SARAH ARTHUR
Make-up Designer ....
CLAIRE PRITCHARD-JONES
Sound Recordist ....RICHARD DYER
1st Assistant Director ....TOBY FORD
2nd Assistant Director................ PAUL MORRIS
3rd Assistant Director ....BARRY PHILLIPS
Location Managers .... IWAN ROBERTS,
PETER TULLO
Script Supervisor..............LLINOS WYN JONES
Production Co-ordinator.............CERI HUGHES
Production Secretary ....JANINE H JONES
Production Runner ....HARRY BUNCH
Production Accountant.....ELIZABETH WALKER
Stunt Co-ordinator.....................LEE SHEWARD
Stunts....................................JAMES EMBREE,
MARCUS SHAKESHEFF, PAUL HEASMAN
Focus Puller ....JAMES SCOTT
Clapper Loader.................... CHRIS WILLIAMS
Camera Assistant...................CLARE CONNOR
Grip ....DAN INMAN
Assistant Grip ....STEVE SMITH
Gaffer.. LLYR EVANS
Best Boy.................................JOHN TRUCKLE
Electricians...........................GAWAIN NASH,
BEN PURCELL, CLIVE JOHNSON
Boom Operator .... JOHN HAGENSTEDE
Sound Assistant.........................GLYN HAMER
Assistant Editor...........................LEE BHOGAL
Art Director.......................DAFYDD SHURMER
Standby Art Director...............NICK WILLIAMS
Special Effects Supervisor...............................
DANNY HARGREAVES
Production Buyer ....LIZZI WILSON
Property Master ....NICK THOMAS
Properties ....DEWI THOMAS,
JULIA CHALLIS
Costume Supervisor ....CERI WALFORD
Wardrobe Assistant................. LOUISE MARTIN
Make-up Artists ....SARAH ASTLEY-HUGHES,
EMMA COWEN
Post-Production Supervisor ...... SAM LUCAS
Dubbing Mixer.......................ALAN SNELLING
Sound Effects Editor.................JEREMY CHILD
Supervising Sound Editor ....DOUG SINCLAIR
Colourist ....KEVIN HORSEWOOD
Online Editor ....SCOTT HINCHCLIFFE

VFX Supervisor .... JAMES ETHERINGTON
Titles and Graphic Design...................................
PETER ANDERSON STUDIO

ADDITIONAL CREW

Assistant Co-ordinator.......................JO HEALY
Rushes Runners............. WAYNE HUMPHREYS,
DELMI THOMAS
Casting Associate ....JANE ANDERSON
Floor Runners .... JENNY MORGAN,
LLOYD GLANVILLE
Assistant Accountant .... TORI KEAST
Set Decorator ....JOELLE RUMBELOW
Storyboard Artist ....JAMES ILES
Standby Chippie..........................PAUL JONES
Construction Chargehand ....MARK PAINTER
Trainee Carpenter.................JOSEPH PAINTER
Chargehand............................CHARLIE MALIK
Dressing Properties ....MATT IRELAND,
RHYS JONES, JAYNE DAVIES
2nd Camera Operator ......MARK MILSOME
2nd Camera Focus Puller...........JAMES SCOTT
2nd Camera Clapper Loader .... LYDIA HALL,
ELLIOT HALE,
JESSICA GREENE
Costume Trainee .... SHERALEE HAMER
Post-Production ....PEPPER POST
Post-Production Sound.....................................
BANG POST PRODUCTION
Rigger .... BRYAN GRIFFITHS
Genny Operators........................SHAUN PRICE
Unit Managers ....BECCY JONES,
TOM STOURTON
VFX ....THE MILL
VFX Co-ordinator.................... KAMILA OSTRA
BBC Publicity .... GERALDINE JEFFERS
BBC Picture Publicity ....ROB FULLER
Hartswood Publicity..................ANYA NOAKES
Photographer ....COLIN HUTTON
Unit Drivers ...... COLIN KIDDELL, ROB DAVIES,
ROB McKENNA
Minibus Drivers....................NIGEL VENABLES,
RAY ROBINSON
Health and Safety Adviser ....JASON CURTIS
Unit Nurses .... RUTH GIBBS, JOHN GIBBS
Facilities....................ANDY DIXON FACILITIES
Caterers .... CELTIC FILM CATERERS

THE BLIND BANKER

Duration: 88 minutes 27 seconds
First broadcast on BBC One   9.00–10.30pm   Sunday 1 August 2010
Audience: 8.07 million

Writer..................................STEVE THOMPSON
Producer ....SUE VERTUE
Director...EUROS LYN
Executive Producers ....BERYL VERTUE,
....STEVEN MOFFAT,
.... MARK GATISS
Executive Producer for Masterpiece.................
REBECCA EATON
Executive Producer for BBC.... BETHAN JONES

CAST

Sherlock Holmes... BENEDICT CUMBERBATCH
Dr John Watson ....MARTIN FREEMAN
Mrs Hudson .... UNA STUBBS
Sarah....................................... ZOE TELFORD
Molly Hooper......................LOUISE BREALEY
Soo Lin Yao ....GEMMA CHAN
Andy Galbraith ....AL WEAVER
Seb Wilkes .... BERTIE CARVEL
Eddie Van Coon......................DAN PERCIVAL
DI Dimmock............................PAUL CHEQUER
Brian Lukis .... HOWARD COGGINS
Museum Director.................JANICE ACQUAH
Raz .... JACK BENCE
Community Officer ....JOHN MACMILLAN
Amanda .... OLIVIA POULET
Shopkeeper ....JACQUI CHAN
Opera Singer .... SARAH LAM
Surgery Receptionist...................GILLIAN ELISA
Box Office Manager.................. STEFAN PEJIC
German Tourist .... PHILIP BENJAMIN

CREW

Line Producer .... KATHY NETTLESHIP
Editor... MALI EVANS
Production Designer........ ARWEL WYN JONES
Director of Photography............STEVE LAWES
Music .... DAVID ARNOLD, MICHAEL PRICE
Casting Director... KATE RHODES JAMES CDG
Costume Designer..................SARAH ARTHUR
Make-up Designer ....
CLAIRE PRITCHARD-JONES
Sound Recordist ....RICHARD DYER
1st Assistant Director .... NIGE WATSON
2nd Assistant Director...............BEN HOWARD
3rd Assistant Director ....BARRY PHILLIPS
Location Managers .... PETER TULLO,

NICKY JAMES
Script Supervisor..............LLINOS WYN JONES
Production Co-ordinator............CERI HUGHES
Production Secretary ....JANINE H JONES
Production Runner...................HARRY BUNCH
Production Accountant.....ELIZABETH WALKER
Stunt Co-ordinators .... LEE SHEWARD,
MARC CASS,
ANDREAS PETRIDES
Stunts......................................JAMES EMBREE,
MARCUS SHAKESHEFF,
NRINDER DHUDWAR,
WILLIE RAMSAY,
MARK ARCHER
Camera Operator ....MARK MILSOME
Focus Pullers.....................MARTIN SCANLAN,
JAMES SCOTT
Clapper Loaders .... EMMA FRIEND,
CHRIS WILLIAMS
Camera Assistant..................CLARE CONNOR
Grip .... DAN INMAN
Assistant Grip ....STEVE SMITH
Gaffer.. LLYR EVANS
Best Boy............................. PAUL JARVIS
Electricians.............................GAWAIN NASH,
BEN PURCELL
.... CLIVE JOHNSON
Boom Operator .... JOHN HAGENSTEDE
Sound Assistant ....GLYN HAMER
Assistant Editor........................... LEE BHOGAL
Art Director......................DAFYDD SHURMER
Standby Art Director.................. TOM PEARCE
Special Effects Supervisor.................................
DANNY HARGREAVES
Production Buyer .... SUE JACKSON POTTER
Property Master ....NICK THOMAS
Properties ....DEWI THOMAS,
JULIA CHALLIS
Costume Supervisor ....CERI WALFORD
Wardrobe Assistant................ LOUISE MARTIN
Make-up Artists ....SARAH ASTLEY-HUGHES,
AMY RILEY
Post-Production Supervisor .... SAM LUCAS
Dubbing Mixer.......................ALAN SNELLING
Sound Effects Editor .... JEREMY CHILD
Colourist ....KEVIN HORSEWOOD
Online Editor ....SCOTT HINCHCLIFFE

Titles and Graphic Design ....
PETER ANDERSON STUDIO

ADDITIONAL CREW

Assistant Co-ordinator......................JO HEALY
Rushes Runners.............. WAYNE HUMPHREYS,
DELMI THOMAS
Casting Associate .... JANE ANDERSON
Floor Runners .... JENNY MORGAN,
LLOYD GLANVILLE
Assistant Accountant .... TORI KEAST
Set Decorator .... JOELLE RUMBELOW
Storyboard Artist ....JAMES ILES
Standby Chippie ....PAUL JONES
Construction Chargehand ....MARK PAINTER
Trainee Carpenter................ JOSEPH PAINTER
Chargehand............................CHARLIE MALIK
Dressing Properties ....MATT IRELAND,
RHYS JONES,
JAYNE DAVIES
2nd Camera Focus Puller...........JAMES SCOTT
2nd Camera Clapper Loader ....LYDIA HALL
Costume Trainee .... SHERALEE HAMER
Post-Production .... PEPPER POST
Post-Production Sound....................................
BANG POST PRODUCTION
Supervising Sound Editor ....DOUG SINCLAIR
Rigger .... BRYAN GRIFFITHS
Genny Operators.......................... SHAUN PRICE
Unit Managers ....BECCY JONES,
TOM STOURTON
VFX ....THE MILL
VFX Supervisor .... JAMES ETHERINGTON
VFX Co-ordinator.................... KAMILA OSTRA
BBC Publicity .... GERALDINE JEFFERS
BBC Picture Publicity .... ROB FULLER
Hartswood Publicity.................ANYA NOAKES
Photographer .... COLIN HUTTON
Unit Drivers ...... COLIN KIDDELL, ROB DAVIES,
ROB McKENNA
Minibus Drivers....................NIGEL VENABLES,
RAY ROBINSON
Health and Safety Adviser .... JASON CURTIS
Unit Nurses ....RUTH GIBBS,
JOHN GIBBS
Facilities....................ANDY DIXON FACILITIES
Caterers .... CELTIC FILM CATERERS

THE GREAT GAME

Duration: 89 minutes 20 seconds
First broadcast on BBC One   9.00–10.30pm   Sunday 8 August 2010
Audience: 9.18 million

Writer.. MARK GATISS
Producer .... SUE VERTUE
Director............................... PAUL McGUIGAN
Executive Producers ....BERYL VERTUE,
STEVEN MOFFAT,
MARK GATISS
Executive Producer for Masterpiece.................
REBECCA EATON
Executive Producer for BBC.... BETHAN JONES

CAST

Sherlock Holmes... BENEDICT CUMBERBATCH
Dr John Watson ....MARTIN FREEMAN
DI Lestrade ....RUPERT GRAVES
Mrs Hudson .... UNA STUBBS
Sarah... ZOE TELFORD
Molly Hooper.......................LOUISE BREALEY
Jim...ANDREW SCOTT
Sgt Sally Donovan...........VINETTE ROBINSON
Bezza ....MATTHEW NEEDHAM
Tube Guard........................KEMAL SYLVESTER
Alan West .... SAN SHELLA
Crying Woman.................. DEBORAH MOORE
Lucy ....LAUREN CRACE
Scared Man.......................... NICHOLAS GADD
Mrs Monkford ....CAROLINE TROWBRIDGE
Mr Ewart ....PAUL ALBERTSON
Blind Lady.....................................RITA DAVIES
Connie Prince ....DI BOTCHER
Kenny Prince.........................JOHN SESSIONS
Raoul................................STEFANO BRASCHI
Homeless Girl .... JEANY SPARK
Julie .... ALISON LINTOTT
Miss Wenceslas....................HAYDN GWYNNE
Joe..DOUG ALLEN
Golem..JOHN LEBAR
Professor Cairns..................... LYNN FARLEIGH

CREW

Line Producer .... KATHY NETTLESHIP
Editor.................................... CHARLIE PHILLIPS
Production Designer........ ARWEL WYN JONES
Director of Photography ....STEVE LAWES
Music ....DAVID ARNOLD, MICHAEL PRICE
Casting Director... KATE RHODES JAMES CDG
Costume Designer...................SARAH ARTHUR
Make-up Designer...

CLAIRE PRITCHARD-JONES
Sound Recordist ....RICHARD DYER
1st Assistant Director .... TOBY FORD
2nd Assistant Director...............BEN HOWARD
3rd Assistant Director .... BARRY PHILLIPS
Location Managers .... PAUL DAVIES,
PETER TULLO
Script Supervisor..............LLINOS WYN JONES
Production Co-ordinator............CERI HUGHES
Assistant Co-ordinator......................JO HEALY
Production Runner................... HARRY BUNCH
Production Accountant.....ELIZABETH WALKER
Stunt Co-ordinator....................LEE SHEWARD
Stunts..................................JASON HUNJAN,
JAMES EMBREE,
MARCUS SHAKESHEFF
Focus Puller ....MARTIN SCANLAN
Clapper Loader......................... EMMA FRIEND
Camera Assistant...................CLARE CONNOR
Grip ....DAN INMAN
Assistant Grip ....STEVE SMITH
Gaffer...LLYR EVANS
Electricians..........................GAWAIN NASH,
BEN PURCELL, CLIVE JOHNSON
Boom Operator .... JOHN HAGENSTEDE
Sound Assistant ....GLYN HAMER
Assistant Editor............................ LEE BHOGAL
Art Director.....................DAFYDD SHURMER
Standby Art Director ...... NICK WILLIAMS
Special Effects Supervisor....................................
DANNY HARGREAVES
Production Buyer .... SUE JACKSON POTTER
Property Master .... NICK THOMAS
Properties ....DEWI THOMAS,
JULIA CHALLIS
Costume Supervisor .... CERI WALFORD
Wardrobe Assistant................ LOUISE MARTIN
Make-up Artists ....SARAH ASTLEY-HUGHES,
AMY RILEY
Post-Production Supervisor .... SAM LUCAS
Dubbing Mixer.......................ALAN SNELLING
Sound Effects Editor .... JEREMY CHILD
Supervising Sound Editor ....DOUG SINCLAIR
Colourist ....KEVIN HORSEWOOD
VFX Supervisor .... JAMES ETHERINGTON
Titles and Graphic Design ....
PETER ANDERSON STUDIO

ADDITIONAL CREW

Rushes Runners............. WAYNE HUMPHREYS,
DELMI THOMAS
Casting Associate ....JANE ANDERSON
Floor Runners .... JENNY MORGAN,
LLOYD GLANVILLE
Assistant Accountant .... TORI KEAST
Set Decorator .... JOELLE RUMBELOW
Storyboard Artist ....JAMES ILES
Standby Chippie..........................PAUL JONES
Construction Chargehand ....MARK PAINTER
Trainee Carpenter.................JOSEPH PAINTER
Chargehand............................CHARLIE MALIK
Dressing Properties ....MATT IRELAND,
RHYS JONES,
JAYNE DAVIES
2nd Camera Operator ....MARK MILSOME
2nd Camera Focus Puller...........JAMES SCOTT
2nd Camera Clapper Loader ....LYDIA HALL,
ELLIOT HALE,
JESSICA GREENE
Costume Trainee .... SHERALEE HAMER
Post-Production .... PEPPER POST
Post-Production Sound.....................................
BANG POST PRODUCTION
Best Boys ....JOHN TRUCKLE,
PAUL JARVIS, SAM KITE,
CHRIS DAVIES
Rigger .... BRYAN GRIFFITHS
Genny Operator ....SHAUN PRICE
Unit Managers ....BECCY JONES,
TOM STOURTON
VFX ....THE MILL
VFX Co-ordinator.................... KAMILA OSTRA
Online Editor ....SCOTT HINCHCLIFFE
BBC Publicity .... GERALDINE JEFFERS
BBC Picture Publicity .... ROB FULLER
Hartswood Publicity..................ANYA NOAKES
Photographer ....COLIN HUTTON
Unit Drivers ....COLIN KIDDELL,
ROB DAVIES, ROB McKENNA
Minibus Drivers....................NIGEL VENABLES,
RAY ROBINSON
Health and Safety Adviser ....JASON CURTIS
Unit Nurses .... RUTH GIBBS, JOHN GIBBS
Facilities....................ANDY DIXON FACILITIES
Caterers .... CELTIC FILM CATERERS

SERIES TWO

Hartswood Films' multi-award-winning *Sherlock*, starring Benedict Cumberbatch and Martin Freeman, returns to the BBC for an eagerly awaited second series of three 90-minute films: *A Scandal In Belgravia*, *The Hounds of Baskerville* and *The Reichenbach Fall*. The first episode aired on BBC One on New Year's Day 2012.

Shoot dates: 16 May–19 August 2011 Additional days: 22–24 August 2011

SHERLOCK SERIES TWO AWARDS

BAFTA CYMRU AWARDS
Make-up and Hair (Meinir Jones-Lewis)
Production Design (Arwel Wyn Jones)

BAFTA TELEVISION AWARDS
Supporting Actor (Andrew Scott)
Special Award (Steven Moffat)

BAFTA TELEVISION CRAFT AWARDS
Editing: Fiction (Charlie Phillips)
Sound: Fiction (Howard Bargroff, Jeremy Child,
John Mooney, Doug Sinclair)
Writer (Steven Moffat)

BRITISH FANTASY AWARDS
Best Television

BROADCASTING PRESS GUILD AWARDS
Best Actor (Benedict Cumberbatch)

CRIME THRILLER AWARDS
The TV Dagger
Best Actor Dagger (Benedict Cumberbatch)
Best Supporting Actor Dagger (Martin Freeman)

CRITICS' CHOICE TELEVISION AWARDS
Best Movie or Miniseries
Best Actor (Benedict Cumberbatch)

EDGAR AWARDS
Best Television Episode Teleplay
(Steven Moffat)

FESTIVAL POLAR DE COGNAC AWARDS
Polar Prize for Best International Series

FREESAT AWARDS
Entertainment Show of the Year

GOLD DERBY TV AWARDS
Best Movie/Miniseries Actor
(Benedict Cumberbatch)
Best Movie/Miniseries Supporting Actor
(Martin Freeman)

**IRISH FILM AND TELEVISION
ACADEMY AWARDS**
Actor in a Supporting Role: Television
(Andrew Scott)

MGEITF CHANNEL OF THE YEAR AWARDS
Terrestrial Programme of the Year
The Network and Ones to Watch Programme
Choice Award

**NATIONAL TELEVISION
AWARDS**
Best TV Detective (Benedict Cumberbatch)

PAAFTJ AWARDS
Best Miniseries or TV Movie
Best Cast in a Miniseries or TV Movie
Best Writing for a Miniseries or TV Movie
(Steven Moffat, Steve Thompson, Mark Gatiss)

**ROYAL TELEVISION SOCIETY PROGRAMME
AWARDS**
Best Drama Series
Best Writer – Drama (Steven Moffat)

SATELLITE AWARDS
Best Actor in a Miniseries/Motion Picture Made
For Television (Benedict Cumberbatch)

SEOUL DRAMA AWARDS
Best Miniseries – Silver Bird Prize

SOUTH BANK SKY ARTS AWARDS
Best TV Drama

TELEVISUAL BULLDOG AWARDS
Drama Series
Music

TOTAL FILM HOTLIST AWARDS
Hottest TV Show

TV.COM AWARDS
Best Drama Series
Best Dramatic Actor (Benedict Cumberbatch)

VIRGIN MEDIA AWARDS
TV Moment of the Year
Best TV Actor (Benedict Cumberbatch)

A SCANDAL IN BELGRAVIA

Duration: 89 minutes 35 seconds
First broadcast on BBC One 8.30–10.00pm Sunday 1 January 2012
Audience: 10.66 million

Writer....................................STEVEN MOFFAT
Producer ....SUE VERTUE
Director................................PAUL McGUIGAN
Executive Producers ....MARK GATISS,
STEVEN MOFFAT,
BERYL VERTUE
Executive Producer for Masterpiece.................
....REBECCA EATON
Executive Producer for BBC....BETHAN JONES

CAST
Sherlock Holmes... BENEDICT CUMBERBATCH
Dr John Watson..................MARTIN FREEMAN
Mrs Hudson ....UNA STUBBS
DI Lestrade ....RUPERT GRAVES
Mycroft Holmes ....MARK GATISS
Jim Moriarty...........................ANDREW SCOTT
Molly Hooper........................LOUISE BREALEY
DI Carter ....DANNY WEBB
The Equerry ....ANDREW HAVILL
Neilson......................................TODD BOYCE
Jeanette....................................OONA CHAPLIN
Timid Man ....RICHARD CUNNINGHAM
Married Woman.................ROSEMARY SMITH
Businessman............................SIMON THORP
Geeky Young Man ....ANTHONY COZENS
Creepy Guy..........................MUNIR KHAIRDIN
Phil.......................................NATHAN HARMER
Young Policeman..................LUKE NEWBERRY
Plummer ....DARRELL LAS QUEVAS
Kate ....ROSALIND HALSTEAD
Archer ....PETER PEDRERO
Little Girls ....HONOR KNEAFSEY
....ILANA KNEAFSEY
Beautiful Woman ....THOMASIN RAND
and
Irene Adler..................................LARA PULVER

CREW
Line Producer ....CHARLOTTE ASHBY
Editor.....................................CHARLIE PHILLIPS
Production Designer........ARWEL WYN JONES
Director of Photography.......FABIAN WAGNER
Music ....DAVID ARNOLD,
MICHAEL PRICE
Casting Director..
KATE RHODES JAMES CDG
Costume Designer...................SARAH ARTHUR
Make-up and Hair Designer.............................
MEINIR JONES-LEWIS
Sound Recordist ....JOHN MOONEY
1st Assistant Director.........FRANCESCO REIDY
2nd Assistant Director..... JAMES DeHAVILAND
3rd Assistant Director ....
HEDDI-JOY TAYLOR-WELCH

Location Managers ....GARETH SKELDING,
PETER TULLO
Production Accountant.....ELIZABETH WALKER
Script Supervisor..............NON ELERI HUGHES
Production Manager.........................BEN HOLT
Production Co-ordinator........SIÂN WARRILOW
Unit Managers ....RHYS GRIFFITHS,
RICHARD LONERGAN,
GERAINT WILLIAMS
Production Runner............ SANDRA COSFELD
Stunt Co-ordinator..................GARETH MILNE
Stunts......................................MARK ARCHER,
PAUL KULIK
Camera Operator ....MARK MILSOME
Focus Pullers.......................JAMIE PHILLIPS,
LEO HOLBA
Clapper Loaders .... LEIGHTON SPENCE,
SVETLANA MIKO
Camera Trainee ....ED DUNNING
Grip .... DAI HOPKINS
Assistant Grip .... OWEN CHARNLEY
Gaffer..JON BEST
Best Boy...JP JUDGE
Electricians ....STEVE WORSLEY,
STEVE SLOCOMBE,
ED MONAGHAN
Sound Maintenance Engineer ....
STUART McCUTCHEON
Sound Assistant ....ABDUL ABMOUD
Assistant Editor....................BECKY TROTMAN
Supervising Art Director ....DAFYDD SHURMER
Standby Art Director ....
JULIA BRYSON-CHALLIS
Special Effects Supervisor.................................
DANNY HARGREAVES
Production Buyer ....BLAANID MADDRELL
Property Master ....PHILL SHELLARD
Properties ....DEWI THOMAS,
JACKSON POPE
Costume Supervisor ....CERI WALFORD
Costume Assistants ....KELLY WILLIAMS,
DOMINIQUE ARTHUR
Make-up and Hair Artists ....
HANNAH PROVERBS,
LOUISE COLES
Post-Production Supervisor ....SAM LUCAS
Dubbing Mixer..............HOWARD BARGROFF
Sound Effects Editor ....JEREMY CHILD
Supervising Sound Editor ....DOUG SINCLAIR
Colourist ....KEVIN HORSEWOOD
Online Editors...............SCOTT HINCHCLIFFE,
BARRIE PEASE
Plane Graphics.................STEPHEN HOLLAND
VFX Supervisor ....JEAN-CLAUDE DEGUARA
Titles .... PETER ANDERSON STUDIO

ADDITIONAL CREW
Production Trainees .... CHRISTINE WADE,
BRENNIG HAYDEN (via Media Academy Wales)
Casting Assistant .... JASON HALL
2nd Assistant Editor........... STEVEN WALTHAM
Floor Runner ....DANIELLE RICHARDS
Assistant Director Trainee ..... CLARA BENNETT
(via Media Academy Wales)
Assistant Accountant ....SINEAD GOGARTY
Set Decorator ....JOELLE RUMBELOW
Graphic Artists .... LUKE RUMBELOW,
DALE JORDAN JOHNSON
Art Department Assistant ... REBECCA BROWN
Graphic Trainee .... CAMILLA BLAIR
Standby Carpenter ....PAUL JONES
Standby Rigger......................KEITH FREEMAN
Construction Managers ....MARK PAINTER,
SCOTT FISHER
Chargehand Painter................STEVEN FUDGE
Scenic Painter ....JOHN WHALLEY
Carpenter .... CHRISTOPHER DANIELS
Construction Trainees.........JOSEPH PAINTER,
CHRISTOPHER STEVENS
Chargehand............................CHARLIE MALIK
Prop Hands..................................RHYS JONES
Dressing Properties ....PHILLIP JONES
Camera Trainees.....................MEGAN TALBOT,
STEPHEN FIELDING
(via Media Academy Wales)
Make-up and Hair Trainees.............LISA PUGH,
SASKIA BANNISTER
Post-Production ....PRIME FOCUS
Post-Production Sound.....................................
BANG POST PRODUCTION
Location Trainees..........CHANELLE SAMWAYS,
MELODY LOUISE BRAIN
(via Media Academy Wales)
VFX ....THE MILL
BBC Publicity .... GERALDINE JEFFERS
Hartswood Publicity.................ANYA NOAKES
Stills Photographer ....COLIN HUTTON
Unit Drivers ....COLIN KIDDELL,
JULIAN CHAPMAN,
PAUL DAVIES,
GRAHAM HUXTABLE
Minibus Driver ....NIGEL VENABLES
London Transport Captain.......SIMON BARKER
Rushes Runner ....GARETH WEBB
Health and Safety Advisers...............................
ANN GODDARD c/o SAFON,
RHYS BEVAN c/o SAFON,
DAVE SUTCLIFFE
Unit Nurse......................................GLYN EVANS
Facilities....................ANDY DIXON FACILITIES
Caterers .... ABBEY CATERING

THE HOUNDS OF BASKERVILLE

Duration: 88 minutes 22 seconds
First broadcast on BBC One   8.30–10.00pm   Sunday 8 January 2012
Audience: 10.27 million

Writer.. MARK GATISS
Producer .... SUE VERTUE
Director................................. PAUL McGUIGAN
Executive Producers .... MARK GATISS
STEVEN MOFFAT,
BERYL VERTUE,
SUE VERTUE
Executive Producer for Masterpiece.................
REBECCA EATON
Executive Producer for BBC.... BETHAN JONES

CAST
Sherlock Holmes... BENEDICT CUMBERBATCH
Dr John Watson ....MARTIN FREEMAN
Mrs Hudson .... UNA STUBBS
DI Lestrade ....RUPERT GRAVES
Mycroft Holmes .... MARK GATISS
Jim Moriarty...........................ANDREW SCOTT
Henry Knight....................... RUSSELL TOVEY
Dr Stapleton .... AMELIA BULLMORE
Dr Frankland .... CLIVE MANTLE
Major Barrymore.............. SIMON PAISLEY DAY
Dr Mortimer............................... SASHA BEHAR
Corporal Lyons ....WILL SHARPE
Fletcher.................................STEPHEN WIGHT
Gary .... GORDON KENNEDY
Billy .... KEVIN TRAINOR
Grace ....ROSALIND KNIGHT
Young Henry ....SAM JONES
Presenter ....CHIPO CHUNG

CREW
Line Producer ....CHARLOTTE ASHBY
Editor................................... CHARLIE PHILLIPS
Production Designer........ ARWEL WYN JONES
Director of Photography ....FABIAN WAGNER
Music .... DAVID ARNOLD, MICHAEL PRICE
Casting Director... KATE RHODES JAMES CDG
Costume Designer...................SARAH ARTHUR
Make-up and Hair Designer..............................
PAMELA HADDOCK
Sound Recordist ....JOHN MOONEY
1st Assistant Director .... PETER BENNETT
2nd Assistant Director..... JAMES DeHAVILAND
3rd Assistant Director ....
HEDDI-JOY TAYLOR-WELCH
Location Manager..............GARETH SKELDING
Production Accountant.....ELIZABETH WALKER
Script Supervisor..............NON ELERI HUGHES
Production Manager........................BEN HOLT
Production Co-ordinator........SIÂN WARRILOW

Unit Managers ....RHYS GRIFFITHS,
GERAINT WILLIAMS
Production Runner............. SANDRA COSFELD
Stunt Co-ordinators ....LEE SHEWARD,
LÉON ROGERS
Stunts.......................................ROB JARMAN,
MARCUS SHAKESHEFF,
RICHARD BRADSHAW
Camera Operator ....MARK MILSOME
Focus Pullers...... JAMIE PHILLIPS, LEO HOLBA
Clapper Loaders .... LEIGHTON SPENCE,
SVETLANA MIKO
Camera Trainee .... ED DUNNING
Grip .... DAI HOPKINS
Assistant Grip ....OWEN CHARNLEY
Gaffer.. JON BEST
Best Boy................................STEVE McGRAIL
Electricians..JP JUDGE,
STEVE WORSLEY,
STEVE SLOCOMBE
Sound Maintenance Engineer ....
STUART McCUTCHEON
Sound Assistant .... ABDUL ABMOUD
Assistant Editor.................... BECKY TROTMAN
Supervising Art Director ....DAFYDD SHURMER
Standby Art Director.............ALEX MERCHANT
Special Effects Supervisor...............................
DANNY HARGREAVES
Production Buyer ....BLAANID MADDRELL
Property Master ....PHILL SHELLARD
Properties ....DEWI THOMAS,
JACKSON POPE
Costume Supervisor ....CERI WALFORD
Costume Assistants ....KELLY WILLIAMS,
DOMINIQUE ARTHUR
Make-up and Hair Artists ....
HANNAH PROVERBS, LOUISE COLES
Post-Production Supervisor .... SAM LUCAS
Dubbing Mixer...............HOWARD BARGROFF
Sound Effects Editor .... JEREMY CHILD
Supervising Sound Editor ....DOUG SINCLAIR
Colourist ....KEVIN HORSEWOOD
Online Editors...............SCOTT HINCHCLIFFE,
BARRIE PEASE
VFX Supervisor ....JEAN-CLAUDE DEGUARA
Titles .... PETER ANDERSON STUDIO

ADDITIONAL CREW
Production Trainees .... CHRISTINE WADE,
BRENNIG HAYDEN
(via Media Academy Wales)

Casting Assistant .... JASON HALL
2nd Assistant Editor........... STEVEN WALTHAM
Floor Runner...................DANIELLE RICHARDS
Assistant Director Trainee..... CLARA BENNETT
(via Media Academy Wales)
Assistant Accountant ....SINEAD GOGARTY
Set Decorator .... JOELLE RUMBELOW
Graphic Artists .... LUKE RUMBELOW,
DALE JORDAN JOHNSON
Art Department Assistant ... REBECCA BROWN
Graphic Trainee ....CAMILLA BLAIR
Standby Carpenter ....PAUL JONES
Standby Rigger ....KEITH FREEMAN
Construction Managers ....MARK PAINTER,
SCOTT FISHER
Chargehand Painter.................STEVEN FUDGE
Scenic Painter ....JOHN WHALLEY
Carpenter .... CHRISTOPHER DANIELS
Construction Trainees..........JOSEPH PAINTER,
CHRISTOPHER STEVENS
Chargehand............................CHARLIE MALIK
Prop Hands....................................RHYS JONES
Dressing Properties .... PHILLIP JONES
Camera Trainees....................MEGAN TALBOT,
STEPHEN FIELDING
(via Media Academy Wales)
Make-up and Hair Trainees..........LISA PUGH,
SASKIA BANNISTER
Post-Production ....PRIME FOCUS
Post-Production Sound.......................................
BANG POST PRODUCTION
Location Trainees..........CHANELLE SAMWAYS,
MELODY LOUISE BRAIN
(via Media Academy Wales)
VFX ....THE MILL
BBC Publicity .... GERALDINE JEFFERS
Hartswood Publicity.................ANYA NOAKES
Stills Photographer .... COLIN HUTTON
Unit Drivers ....COLIN KIDDELL,
JULIAN CHAPMAN,
PAUL DAVIES,
GRAHAM HUXTABLE
Minibus Driver ....NIGEL VENABLES
Rushes Runner ....GARETH WEBB
Health and Safety Advisers...............................
ANN GODDARD c/o SAFON,
RHYS BEVAN c/o SAFON,
DAVE SUTCLIFFE
Unit Nurse......................................GLYN EVANS
Facilities...................ANDY DIXON FACILITIES
Caterers .... ABBEY CATERING

THE REICHENBACH FALL

Duration: 88 minutes 27 seconds
First broadcast on BBC One   8.30–10.00pm   Sunday 15 January 2012
Audience: 9.78 million

Writer.................................STEVE THOMPSON
Producer ....ELAINE CAMERON
Director......................................TOBY HAYNES
Executive Producers ....MARK GATISS,
STEVEN MOFFAT,
BERYL VERTUE,
SUE VERTUE
Executive Producer for Masterpiece.................
REBECCA EATON
Executive Producer for BBC....BETHAN JONES

CAST

Sherlock Holmes... BENEDICT CUMBERBATCH
Dr John Watson ....MARTIN FREEMAN
Mrs Hudson .... UNA STUBBS
DI Lestrade ....RUPERT GRAVES
Mycroft Holmes ....MARK GATISS
Jim Moriarty...........................ANDREW SCOTT
Molly Hooper........................LOUISE BREALEY
Kitty Riley.............KATHERINE PARKINSON
Sgt Sally Donovan...........VINETTE ROBINSON
Anderson ....JONATHAN ARIS
Ella..TANYA MOODIE
Chief Superintendent ....TONY PITTS
Prosecuting Barrister ....JAYE GRIFFITHS
Defence Barrister.......................IAN HALLARD
Judge .... MALCOLM RENNIE
Claudie Bruhl........................SYDNEY WADE
Max Bruhl ....EDWARD HOLTOM
Bank Director..........................PAUL LEONARD
Prison Governor..........CHRISTOPHER HUNTER
Prison Warder ....TONY WAY
Miss Mackenzie..................LORRAINE HILTON
Reporter 1.........SAMANTHA-HOLLY BENNETT
Reporter 2............................PETER BASHAM
Reporter 3............................REBECCA NOBLE
Gallery Director ....ROBERT BENFIELD
Clerk of the Court.............IFAN HUW DAFYDD
Father ....MICHAEL MUELLER
Assassin ....PANO MASTI
Diogenes Gent ....DOUGLAS WILMER

CREW

Line Producer ....CHARLOTTE ASHBY
Editor.. TIM PORTER
Production Designer........ARWEL WYN JONES
Director of Photography.......FABIAN WAGNER
Music ....DAVID ARNOLD, MICHAEL PRICE
Casting Director... KATE RHODES JAMES CDG
Costume Designer...................SARAH ARTHUR
Make-up and Hair Designer.............................
PAMELA HADDOCK
Sound Recordist ....JOHN MOONEY
1st Assistant Director.............DAN MUMFORD
2nd Assistant Director.....JAMES DeHAVILAND
3rd Assistant Director ....
HEDDI-JOY TAYLOR-WELCH

Location Managers ....GARETH SKELDING,
PETER TULLO
Production Accountant.....ELIZABETH WALKER
Script Supervisor.............NON ELERI HUGHES
Production Manager.........................BEN HOLT
Production Co-ordinator........SIÂN WARRILOW
Unit Managers ....RHYS GRIFFITHS,
RICHARD LONERGAN,
GERAINT WILLIAMS
Production Runner............ SANDRA COSFELD
Stunt Co-ordinator....................LEE SHEWARD
Stunts.......................................RAY DE-HAAN,
ROB JARMAN,
MARCUS SHAKESHEFF,
JORDI CASARES,
SÉON ROGERS,
ANDREAS PETRIDES,
MATTHEW STIRLING,
PAUL HEASMAN,
TOM RODGERS
Camera Operator ....MARK MILSOME
Focus Pullers.........................JAMIE PHILLIPS,
LEO HOLBA
Clapper Loaders ....LEIGHTON SPENCE
....SVETLANA MIKO
Camera Trainee ....ED DUNNING
Grip ....DAI HOPKINS
Assistant Grip ....OWEN CHARNLEY
Gaffer..JON BEST
Best Boy..JP JUDGE
Electricians...........................STEVE WORSLEY,
STEVE SLOCOMBE,
ED MONAGHAN
Sound Maintenance Engineer ....
STUART McCUTCHEON
Sound Assistant ....ABDUL ABMOUD
Assistant Editor...................BECKY TROTMAN
Art Director.......................DAFYDD SHURMER
Standby Art Director....CIARAN THOMPSON
Special Effects Supervisor.................................
DANNY HARGREAVES
Production Buyer........BLAANID MADDRELL
Property Master ....PAUL AITKEN
Properties ....DEWI THOMAS,
JACKSON POPE
Costume Supervisor ....CERI WALFORD
Costume Assistants ....KELLY WILLIAMS,
DOMINIQUE ARTHUR
Make-up and Hair Artists ....
HANNAH PROVERBS, LOUISE COLES
Post-Production Supervisor ....SAM LUCAS
Dubbing Mixer..............HOWARD BARGROFF
Sound Effects Editor.................JEREMY CHILD
Supervising Sound Editor.......DOUG SINCLAIR
Colourist ....KEVIN HORSEWOOD
Online Editors...............SCOTT HINCHCLIFFE,
BARRIE PEASE

VFX Supervisor ....JEAN-CLAUDE DEGUARA
Titles .... PETER ANDERSON STUDIO

ADDITIONAL CREW

Production Trainees .... CHRISTINE WADE,
BRENNIG HAYDEN (via Media Academy Wales)
Casting Assistant .... JASON HALL
2nd Assistant Editor...........STEVEN WALTHAM
Floor Runner....................DANIELLE RICHARDS
Assistant Director Trainee .....CLARA BENNETT
(via Media Academy Wales)
Assistant Accountant ....SINEAD GOGARTY
Set Decorator ....JOELLE RUMBELOW
Graphic Artists ....LUKE RUMBELOW,
DALE JORDAN JOHNSON
Art Department Assistant ...REBECCA BROWN
Graphic Trainee ....CAMILLA BLAIR
Standby Carpenter ....PAUL JONES
Standby Rigger ....KEITH FREEMAN
Construction Managers ....MARK PAINTER,
SCOTT FISHER
Chargehand Painter...............STEVEN FUDGE
Scenic Painter ....JOHN WHALLEY
Carpenter ....CHRISTOPHER DANIELS
Construction Trainees ....JOSEPH PAINTER,
CHRISTOPHER STEVENS
Chargehand..........................CHARLIE MALIK
Prop Hands ....RHYS JONES
Dressing Properties ....PHILLIP JONES
Camera Trainees....................MEGAN TALBOT,
STEPHEN FIELDING
(via Media Academy Wales)
Make-up and Hair Trainees.............LISA PUGH,
SASKIA BANNISTER
Post-Production ....PRIME FOCUS
Post-Production Sound..
BANG POST PRODUCTION
Location Trainees..........CHANELLE SAMWAYS,
MELODY LOUISE BRAIN
(via Media Academy Wales)
VFX ....THE MILL
BBC Publicity ....GERALDINE JEFFERS
Hartswood Publicity.................ANYA NOAKES
Stills Photographer ....COLIN HUTTON
Unit Drivers ....COLIN KIDDELL,
JULIAN CHAPMAN,
PAUL DAVIES,
GRAHAM HUXTABLE
Minibus Driver ....NIGEL VENABLES
Rushes Runner ....GARETH WEBB
Health and Safety Advisers................................
ANN GODDARD c/o SAFON,
RHYS BEVAN c/o SAFON,
DAVE SUTCLIFFE
Unit Nurse....................................GLYN EVANS
Facilities....................ANDY DIXON FACILITIES
Caterers .... ABBEY CATERING

SERIES THREE

Shoot dates: 18 March–23 May & 29 July–1 September 2013

Two years after the devastating events of The Reichenbach Fall, Dr John Watson has got on with his life. New horizons and romance beckon in the shape of the beautiful and smart Mary Morstan. But Sherlock Holmes is about to rise from the grave. And even though it's what his best friend wanted more than anything, for John Watson it might well be a case of 'be careful what you wish for!' In three brand new adventures, Sherlock and John face baffling mystery beneath the streets of London; a wedding that's not quite what it seems – and the arrival of the repellent and terrifying blackmailer Charles Augustus Magnussen. Who is the mysterious disappearing man? How can a Royal Guardsman bleed to death in a locked room? And what is the secret that threatens to blow apart everything the reunited friends hold dear? Sherlock is back, but will things ever be the same again?

SHERLOCK SERIES THREE AWARDS

PRIMETIME EMMY AWARDS
Outstanding Writing for a Miniseries
(Steven Moffat)
Outstanding Lead Actor in a Miniseries
(Benedict Cumberbatch)
Outstanding Supporting Actor in a Miniseries
(Martin Freeman)
Outstanding Cinematography for a Miniseries
(Neville Kidd)
Outstanding Music Composition
(David Arnold and Michael Price)
Outstanding Single-Camera Picture Editing
for a Miniseries (Yan Miles)
Outstanding Sound Editing for a Miniseries,
Movie or Special (Doug Sinclair, Stuart
McCowan, Jon Joyce, Paul McFadden,
William Everett, Sue Harding)

TV CHOICE AWARDS
Best Drama
Best Actor (Benedict Cumberbatch)

SHERLOCK SERIES THREE AWARD NOMINATIONS

CRITICS' CHOICE TELEVISION AWARDS
Best Movie
Best Actor in a Movie or Mini Series
(Benedict Cumberbatch)
Best Supporting Actor in a Movie or Mini Series
(Martin Freeman)
Best Supporting Actress in a Movie
or Mini Series (Amanda Abbington)

FREESAT AWARDS
Best of British: TV Programme or Series
Best TV Drama

MONTE CARLO AWARDS
Best Television Film
Outstanding Actor (Benedict Cumberbatch)
NME AWARDS
Best TV Show

CRIME THRILLER AWARDS
TV Dagger
Best Actor Dagger (Benedict Cumberbatch)
Best Supporting Actor Dagger (Mark Gatiss)
Best Supporting Actress Dagger
(Amanda Abbington)

THE EMPTY HEARSE

Duration: 86 minutes 29 seconds
First broadcast on BBC One   9.00–10.30pm   Wednesday 1 January 2014
Audience: 12.72 million

Writer.. MARK GATISS
Producer .... SUE VERTUE
Director............................JEREMY LOVERING
Executive Producers .... MARK GATISS,
STEVEN MOFFAT,
BERYL VERTUE
Executive Producer for Masterpiece ....
REBECCA EATON
Commissioning Editor for BBC.......................
BETHAN JONES

CAST
Sherlock Holmes... BENEDICT CUMBERBATCH
Dr John Watson ....MARTIN FREEMAN
Mrs Hudson .... UNA STUBBS
DI Lestrade ....RUPERT GRAVES
Mycroft Holmes .... MARK GATISS
Jim Moriarty..........................ANDREW SCOTT
Molly Hooper.......................LOUISE BREALEY
Mary Morstan...............AMANDA ABBINGTON
Anderson ....JONATHAN ARIS
Howard Shilcott ....DAVID FYNN
Laura...................................SHARON ROONEY
Torturer .... TOMI MAY
Bonfire Dad ....RICK WARDEN
Zoe .... TRIXIEBELLE HARROWELL
Reporter 1............................LACE AKPOJARO
Reporter 2.............................. JIM CONWAY
Reporter 3.....................NICOLE ARUMUGAM
Mr Szikora .... DAVID GANT
Mr Harcourt ....ROBIN SEBASTIAN
Tom...ED BIRCH
Anthea ....LISA McALLISTER
Mum ....WANDA VENTHAM
Dad...................................TIMOTHY CARLTON
As himself ....DERREN BROWN

CREW
Line Producer .... DIANA BARTON
Editor.................................. CHARLIE PHILLIPS
Production Designer........ ARWEL WYN JONES
Director of Photography .... STEVE LAWES
Music .... DAVID ARNOLD, MICHAEL PRICE
Casting Director... KATE RHODES JAMES CDG
Costume Designer..................SARAH ARTHUR
Make-up and Hair Designer...........................
CLAIRE PRITCHARD-JONES
Sound Recordist ....JOHN MOONEY
1st Assistant Director .... TONI STAPLES
2nd Assistant Director.............. MARK TURNER

3rd Assistant Director ....DAISY CATON-JONES
Floor Runners .... PATRICK WAGGETT,
CHRIS THOMAS
Location Managers ..BEN MANGHAM (London),
MIDGE FERGUSON
Production Accountant..NUALA ALEN-BUCKLEY
Assistant Accountant ....TIM ORLIK
Script Supervisor................... LINDSAY GRANT
Casting Associate ....DANIEL EDWARDS
Production Manager............. CLAIRE HILDRED
Production Secretary ....ROBERT PRICE
Unit Managers .... DAVID GUNKLE (London),
IESTYN HAMPSON-JONES
Location Assistants ....MATTHEW FRAME,
SANTIAGO PLACER (London)
Production Runner.........................LLIO FFLUR
Stunt Co-ordinator............... NEIL FINNIGHAN
Stunt Performers.............. WILL WILLOUGHBY,
KIM McGARRITY,
GARY HOPTROUGH,
CHRIS NEWTON,
TOM RODGERS
Camera Operator ....MARK MILSOME
Focus Pullers................................. LEO HOLBA,
HARRY BOWERS
Clapper Loaders ....EMMA EDWARDS,
PHOEBE ARNSTEIN
Camera Trainee ....EVELINA NORGREN
Grip .... ROBIN STONE – episode 1
Assistant Grip ....BEN MOSELEY
Gaffer.......................................TONY WILCOCK
Best Boy..LEE MARTIN
Electricians.......................... STEVE WORSLEY,
....WESLEY SMITH
Electrician/Board Operator ... GARETH BROUGH
Boom Operator ....BRADLEY KENDRICK
Sound Assistant ....LEE SHARP
Assistant Editor... CARMEN SANCHEZ ROBERTS
2nd Assistant Editor...............GARETH MABEY
Supervising Art Director ....DAFYDD SHURMER
Set Decorator ....HANNAH NICHOLSON
Standby Art Director.. JULIA BRYSON-CHALLIS
Production Buyer ....BLAANID MADDRELL
Graphic Artist......................SAMANTHA CLIFF
Art Department Assistant ....MAIR JONES
Property Master .... NICK THOMAS
Property Chargehand ....CHARLIE MALIK
Properties ....DEWI THOMAS,
MARK RUNCHMAN,
RHYS JONES

Construction Manager..............MARK PAINTER
Chargehand Painter.................STEVEN FUDGE
Standby Carpenter .... BEN MILTON
Standby Rigger .... KEITH FREEMAN
Special Effects .... REAL SFX
Costume Supervisor ....CERI WALFORD
Costume Assistant ....KELLY WILLIAMS
Make-up and Hair Artists ....
SARAH ASTLEY-HUGHES,
AMY RILEY
Post-Production Supervisor .... SAM LUCAS
Dubbing Mixer............... HOWARD BARGROFF
Supervising Sound Editor DOUGLAS SINCLAIR
Sound Effects Editors ...... STUART McCOWAN,
JON JOYCE
Dialogue Editor .... PAUL McFADDEN
Colourist ....KEVIN HORSEWOOD
Online Editor ....SCOTT HINCHCLIFFE
VFX .... MILK
Titles .... PETER ANDERSON STUDIO

ADDITIONAL CREW
Additional Content Writer .....JOSEPH LIDSTER
Art Department Work Experience ....
JULIA JONES
Construction Apprentice ...... JOSEPH PAINTER
Camera Work Experience ....
VERONICA KESZTHELYI,
HANNAH JONES
Costume Trainee .... HANNAH MONKLEY
Make-up Trainee................... REBECCA AVERY
Post-Production ....PRIME FOCUS
Post-Production Sound......................................
BANG POST PRODUCTION
VFX Supervisors .... ROBIN WILLOTT,
ROBBIE FRASER
BBC Publicity .... RUTH NEUGEBAUER
Hartswood Publicity..................IAN JOHNSON
Stills Photographers........... ROBERT VIGLASKY,
OLLIE UPTON
Unit Drivers ....JULIAN CHAPMAN,
COLIN KIDDELL,
KYLE DAVIES
Minibuses ....HERITAGE TRAVEL
Health and Safety Adviser ...CLEM LENEGHAN
Unit Medics........................... GAVIN HEWSON,
GARRY MARRIOTT,
CERI EBBS
Facilities....................ANDY DIXON FACILITIES
Caterers ....ABADIA

THE SIGN OF THREE

Duration: 86 minutes 6 seconds
First broadcast on BBC One   8.30 –10.00pm   Sunday 5 January 2014
Audience: 10.57 million

Writers ....STEVE THOMPSON, MARK GATISS AND STEVEN MOFFAT
Series Producer............................ SUE VERTUE
Producer ....SUSIE LIGGAT
Director...................................COLM McCARTHY
Executive Producers .... MARK GATISS, STEVEN MOFFAT, BERYL VERTUE
Executive Producer for Masterpiece.................. REBECCA EATON
Commissioning Editor for BBC.......................... BETHAN JONES

CAST

Sherlock Holmes... BENEDICT CUMBERBATCH
Dr John Watson ....MARTIN FREEMAN
Mrs Hudson .... UNA STUBBS
DI Lestrade ....RUPERT GRAVES
Mycroft Holmes .... MARK GATISS
Molly Hooper.........................LOUISE BREALEY
Mary Morstan...............AMANDA ABBINGTON
Sgt Sally Donovan............VINETTE ROBINSON
Irene Adler...................................LARA PULVER
James Sholto .... ALISTAIR PETRIE
Tessa .... ALICE LOWE
Janine .... YASMINE AKRAM
David ....OLIVER LANSLEY
Tom... ED BIRCH
Photographer .... JALAAL HARTLEY
Page Boy .... ADAM GREAVES-NEAL
Mum .... HELEN BRADBURY
Bainbridge ....ALFRED ENOCH
Duty Sergeant...........................TIM CHIPPING
Major Reed ....WILL KEEN
Gail ....RITU ARYA
Charlotte................................GEORGINA RICH
Robyn ....WENDY WASON
Vicky ....DEBBIE CHAZEN
Landlord ....NICHOLAS ASBURY

CREW

Line Producer ....DIANA BARTON
Editor...MARK DAVIS
Production Designer........ ARWEL WYN JONES
Director of Photography.............STEVE LAWES
Music .... DAVID ARNOLD, MICHAEL PRICE
Casting Director... KATE RHODES JAMES CDG
Costume Designer...................SARAH ARTHUR
Make-up and Hair Designer................................ CLAIRE PRITCHARD-JONES
Sound Recordist ....JOHN MOONEY
1st Assistant Director ....MATTHEW HANSON

2nd Assistant Director..........REBECCA CALLAS
3rd Assistant Director .... SARAH LAWRENCE
Floor Runners ....PATRICK WAGGETT, CHRIS THOMAS
Location Managers .... BEN MANGHAM (London), ANDY ELIOT
Production Accountants .... NUALA ALEN-BUCKLEY
Assistant Accountants.......................TIM ORLIK
Script Supervisor....................LINDSAY GRANT
Casting Associates..............DANIEL EDWARDS
Production Manager.............CLAIRE HILDRED
Production Secretary ....ROBERT PRICE
Unit Managers ....DAVID GUNKLE (London) IESTYN HAMPSON-JONES
Location Assistants ....MATTHEW FRAME, HAYLEY KASPERCZYK (London)
Production Runner.........................LLIO FFLUR
Stunt Co-ordinator...................GORDON SEED
Stunt Performers.............. WILL WILLOUGHBY, KIM McGARRITY, GARY HOPTROUGH, CHRIS NEWTON, TOM RODGERS
Camera Operator ....MARK MILSOME
Focus Pullers.................................. LEO HOLBA, HARRY BOWERS
Clapper Loaders ....EMMA EDWARDS, PHOEBE ARNSTEIN
Camera Trainee ....EVELINA NORGREN
Grip ....JIM PHILPOTT
Assistant Grip ....CHARLIE WYLDECK
Gaffer....................................TONY WILCOCK
Best Boy.....................................LEE MARTIN
Electricians.. STEVE WORSLEY, WESLEY SMITH
Electrician/Board Operator .GARETH BROUGH
Boom Operator ....BRADLEY KENDRICK
Sound Assistant ....LEE SHARP
Assistant Editors .... GARETH MABEY, BECKY TROTMAN, SHANE WOODS
Supervising Art Director ....DAFYDD SHURMER
Set Decorator ....HANNAH NICHOLSON
Standby Art Directors ...... NANDIE NARISHKIN
Production Buyer............BLAANID MADDRELL
Graphic Artist...........................SAMUEL DAVIS
Property Master ....NICK THOMAS
Property Chargehand ....CHARLIE MALIK
Properties ....DEWI THOMAS, MARK RUNCHMAN, IFAN RAMAGE
Construction Manager..............MARK PAINTER

Chargehand Painter.................STEVEN FUDGE
Construction Apprentice ...... JOSEPH PAINTER
Standby Carpenters................... BEN MILTON, MARK GOODHALL
Standby Riggers ....BRENDAN FITZGERALD
Special Effects ....REAL SFX
Costume Supervisor ....CERI WALFORD
Costume Assistants ....KELLY WILLIAMS, CLAIRE MITCHELL
Make-up and Hair Artists .... SARAH ASTLEY-HUGHES, AMY RILEY
Post-Production Supervisor ....SAM LUCAS
Dubbing Mixer..............HOWARD BARGROFF
Supervising Sound Editor DOUGLAS SINCLAIR
Sound Effects Editors ......STUART McCOWAN, JON JOYCE
Foley Mixer ....WILL EVERETT
Dialogue Editor ....PAUL McFADDEN
Colourist ....KEVIN HORSEWOOD
Online Editor ....SCOTT HINCHCLIFFE
VFX Supervisors ....ROBIN WILLOTT, ROBBIE FRASER
Titles .... PETER ANDERSON STUDIO

ADDITIONAL CREW

Additional Content Writer .....JOSEPH LIDSTER
Art Department Assistant ....MAIR JONES
Art Department Work Experience JULIA JONES
Camera Work Experience .... VERONICA KESZTHELYI, HANNAH JONES
Costume Trainee ....RUTH PHELAN
Make-up Trainee........................ SOPHIE BEBB
Post-Production ....PRIME FOCUS
Post-Production Sound...................................... BANG POST PRODUCTION
VFX ....MILK
BBC Publicity ....RUTH NEUGEBAUER
Hartswood Publicity.................IAN JOHNSON
Stills Photographers...........ROBERT VIGLASKY, OLLIE UPTON
Unit Drivers ....JULIAN CHAPMAN, COLIN KIDDELL, KYLE DAVIES
Minibuses ....HERITAGE TRAVEL
Health and Safety Adviser ...CLEM LENEGHAN
Unit Medics.......................... GAVIN HEWSON, GARRY MARRIOTT, CERI EBBS
Facilities....................ANDY DIXON FACILITIES
Caterers ....ABADIA

HIS LAST VOW

Duration: 89 minutes 9 seconds
First broadcast on BBC One 8.30 –10.00pm Sunday 12 January 2014
Audience: 11.38 million

Writer......................................STEVEN MOFFAT
Producer .... SUE VERTUE
Director......................................NICK HURRAN
Executive Producers ....MARK GATISS,
STEVEN MOFFAT,
BERYL VERTUE
Executive Producer for Masterpiece..................
REBECCA EATON
Commissioning Editor for BBC........................
BETHAN JONES

CAST
Sherlock Holmes... BENEDICT CUMBERBATCH
Dr John Watson ....MARTIN FREEMAN
Mrs Hudson .... UNA STUBBS
DI Lestrade ....RUPERT GRAVES
Mycroft Holmes .... MARK GATISS
Jim Moriarty..........................ANDREW SCOTT
Molly Hooper........................LOUISE BREALEY
Mary Morstan..............AMANDA ABBINGTON
Anderson ....JONATHAN ARIS
Lady Smallwood ....LINDSAY DUNCAN
Janine .... YASMINE AKRAM
Bill Wiggins...............................TOM BROOKE
Mum ....WANDA VENTHAM
Dad ....TIMOTHY CARLTON
Isaac Whitney...........................CALVIN DEMBA
John Garvie .... TIM WALLERS
Chauffeur...................................GLEN DAVIES
Kate Whitney ....BRIGID ZENGENI
Security Man ....MATTHEW WILSON
Little Sherlock ....LOUIS MOFFAT
Medic....................................DAVID NEWMAN
Sir Edwin....................................SIMON KUNZ
Benji............................KATHERINE JAKEWAYS
Club Waiter........................... WILL ASHCROFT
Security Guard ....GED FORREST
Surgeon ....JAMIE JARVIS
and
Charles Magnussen .... LARS MIKKELSEN

CREW
Line Producer ....DIANA BARTON
Editor...YAN MILES
Production Designer........ ARWEL WYN JONES
Director of Photography.............NEVILLE KIDD
Music ....DAVID ARNOLD, MICHAEL PRICE
Casting Director.....................JULIA DUFF CDG
Costume Designer..................SARAH ARTHUR
Make-up and Hair Designer.............................
CLAIRE PRITCHARD-JONES
Sound Recordist ....JOHN MOONEY
1st Assistant Director .... SARAH DAVIES

2nd Assistant Director.......... HARDEY SPEIGHT
3rd Assistant Directors...........RACHEL STACEY,
CHARLIE CURRAN
Floor Runners ....PATRICK WAGGETT,
CHRIS THOMAS, LUCY ROPER
Location Managers ....
BEN MANGHAM (London), TOBY ELIOT
Production Accountant...............DAVID JONES
Assistant Accountant ....SPENCER PAWSON
Script Supervisor....................LINDSAY GRANT
Casting Associates...........GRACE BROWNING
Production Manager.............CLAIRE HILDRED
Production Secretary ....ROBERT PRICE
Unit Managers ....DAVID GUNKLE (London),
JAKE SAINSBURY
Location Assistants ....MATTHEW RISEBROW,
DARAGH COGHLAN (London)
Production Runner ....LLIO FFLUR
Stunt Co-ordinators ....DEAN FORSTER
Stunt Performers .... WILL WILLOUGHBY,
KIM McGARRITY,
GARY HOPTROUGH,
CHRIS NEWTON,
TOM RODGERS
Camera Operators......................JOE RUSSELL
Focus Pullers................... THOMAS WILLIAMS,
JOHN HARPER
Clapper Loaders .... DAN NIGHTINGALE,
PETER LOWDEN
Camera Trainee ....SAMUEL GRANT
Grip .... GARY NORMAN
Assistant Grip ....OWEN CHARNLEY
Gaffer................................MARK HUTCHINGS
Best Boy.......................STEPHEN SLOCOMBE
Electricians..........................ANDY GARDINER,
BOB MILTON,
GAFIN RILEY,
GARETH SHELDON
Electrician/Board Operator ....GAFIN RILEY
Boom Operators.........STUART McCUTCHEON
Sound Assistant ....LEE SHARP
Assistant Editor.......................GARETH MABEY
Supervising Art Director ....DAFYDD SHURMER
Set Decorator ....HANNAH NICHOLSON
Standby Art Director........ NANDIE NARISHKIN
Production Buyer ....BLAANID MADDRELL
Graphic Artist.........................CHRISTINA TOM
Property Master ....CHARLIE MALIK
Property Chargehand ....MIKE PARKER
Properties ....CHRIS BUTCHER,
NICHOLAS JOHNSTON,
STUART RANKMORE
Construction Manager.............MARK PAINTER

Chargehand Painter.................STEVEN FUDGE
Construction Apprentice ......JOSEPH PAINTER
Standby Carpenter ....MARK GOODHALL
Standby Riggers ....MICK LORD,
DAVID WHEELER
Special Effects .... REAL SFX
Costume Supervisor ....CERI WALFORD
Costume Assistants ....KATHRYN BLIGHT
Make-up and Hair Artists ....
SARAH ASTLEY-HUGHES,
AMY RILEY
Post-Production Supervisor ....SAM LUCAS
Dubbing Mixer..............HOWARD BARGROFF
Supervising Sound Editor DOUGLAS SINCLAIR
Sound Effects Editors ......STUART McCOWAN,
JON JOYCE
Foley Mixer .... WILL EVERETT
Dialogue Editor ....PAUL McFADDEN
Colourist ....KEVIN HORSEWOOD
Online Editor ....SCOTT HINCHCLIFFE
VFX Supervisors ....ROBIN WILLOTT,
ROBBIE FRASER
Titles .... PETER ANDERSON STUDIO

ADDITIONAL CREW
Additional Content Writer .....JOSEPH LIDSTER
Art Department Assistant ....ELIN STONE
Art Department Work Experience ....
JULIA JONES
Camera Work Experience ....
VERONICA KESZTHELYI,
HANNAH JONES
Costume Trainee ....SAMUEL CLARK
Make-up Trainee............DANNY MARIE ELIAS
2nd Assistant Editors ....JOEL SKINNER
Post-Production ....PRIME FOCUS
Post-Production Sound.......................................
BANG POST PRODUCTION
VFX ....MILK
BBC Publicity .... RUTH NEUGEBAUER
Hartswood Publicity ....IAN JOHNSON
Stills Photographers...........ROBERT VIGLASKY,
OLLIE UPTON
Unit Drivers ....JULIAN CHAPMAN,
COLIN KIDDELL,
KYLE DAVIES
Minibuses ....HERITAGE TRAVEL
Health and Safety Adviser ...CLEM LENEGHAN
Unit Medics..........................GAVIN HEWSON,
GARRY MARRIOTT,
CERI EBBS
Facilities....................ANDY DIXON FACILITIES
Caterers ....ABADIA

For Mandy,
for always

ACKNOWLEDGEMENTS

Sherlock is the result of a massive collaboration that began on a train in Cardiff, several years ago, and then spread to include dozens, hundreds of people, before something digging into how they actually did it was even a glint in a publisher's glinting eye. The resulting book is in-depth, it's wide-ranging, it's – I hope – a reflection of the many joys of the show. But it's not comprehensive: there's another six books to be written about this stuff, and that's before we go anywhere near the special that will start filming in January 2015 and the fourth series which will follow that…

The curse – for putting together a book like this – of a phenomenon like *Sherlock* is that all the talent involved in making the series is suddenly in even greater demand, so finding an opportunity to talk to them can be… challenging. Some simply didn't have the time, and I'm immensely grateful to Hartswood Films for making available a vast store of interview footage from the last couple of years. But many of those wonderful creative folk *have* found a few moments to talk about what they've been up to; all at BBC Books, BBC Wales and Hartswood have been hugely helpful as always; and some people on the outer rim of the periphery of the show have had moments of inspiration for how to approach this, and have allowed me to steal liberally from them, or provided much-needed support and help. So my thanks must go, one way or another, to many people, among them:

Amanda Abbington, Guy Adams, Peter Anderson, Jonathan Aris, David Arnold, Sarah Arthur, Louise Brealey, Matt Clinch, Will Cohen, Oliver Crawford, Benedict Cumberbatch, Jeane-Claude Deguara, Albert DePetrillo, Jenny Drew, Kate Fox, Martin Freeman, Lizzy Gaisford, Mark Gatiss, James Goss, Danny Hargreaves, Toby Haynes, Arwel Wyn Jones, Joseph Lidster, Nicola Marchant, Paul McGuigan, Zoe Midford, Lars Mikkelson, Steven Moffat, Charlie Phillips, Michael Price, Claire Pritchard-Jones, Lara Pulver, Andrew Scott, Rachel Stone, Steve Thompson, and Sue Vertue.

Most importantly, Richard Atkinson has done his usual breathtaking design work, turning a bunch of rather clumsy documents into 320 sumptuous pages. It's a privilege to share a title page with him.

Steve Tribe

PICTURE CREDITS

BBC Books would like to thank the following for providing photographs and for permission to reproduce copyright material. While every effort has been made to trace and acknowledge all copyright holders, we would like to apologise should there have been any errors or omissions. All images © BBC, except:

p.11, p.13 (top left), p.14 (top), p.33, p.52 (bottom), p.56, pp.58–9, p.60, pp.62–3, p.65 (centre left, top right, bottom right), p.66 (bottom left), pp.76–7, p.83, p.88 (top right), pp.92–3, p.119 (bottom), pp.110-111 (except *Being Human, Doctor Who, Wind in the Willows*), pp.120–3, p.128 (bottom), pp.132–3, p.150, pp.154–7, p.167, pp.168–9, p.177, p.178 (top, bottom left), p.179, p.191, pp.198–9, pp.202–3, p.207, pp.208–9, pp.210–11, pp.216–17, pp.218–19, pp.220–1, pp.224–5, p.227, p.229, p.231, pp.234–5, pp.236–7, p.249, pp.252–3, pp.254–5, p.257 (top left, bottom left), p.265, pp.268–9, p.271, p.275, p.278, pp.280–1, p.283, pp.292–3, pp.294–5, p.306 © Hartswood Films and courtesy Hartswood Films and Arwel Wyn Jones

p.14 (bottom left), p.15, p.16, p.19 (top left), p.20 (bottom), p.21 (top left, bottom left), p.22 (top), p.28, pp.42–3, pp.48–9 (except *The Office*), p.112, p.138, p.139, p.146 (top), p.149 (except *EastEnders*), p.153 (except *Doctor Who*), p.197, pp.222–3, p296 (except *Sherlock*) © Rex

p.17 (insets), p.18 (top), p.21 (top right, bottom right) © Getty

p.18 (bottom right), p.65, p.109, p.176 (bottom left, bottom right), p.178 (bottom right) © Mark Gatiss

p.146 (*Delicious*) © Zoe Midford

pp.174–5, pp.232–3 © Milk

pp.204–6 © Toby Haynes

p.231 (top left, bottom left) © SecondSync

p.274, p.277 (bottom) © Danny Hargreaves / Real SFX

pp.300 © Peter Anderson Studio

p.315 © Beryl Vertue